W9-AKS-398

*Our Dear Maria,*
*We pray you will read and enjoy this*
*book as you identify yourself as God's*
*beloved daughter.*

1349

# DEFINED

## *Who God Says You Are*

*Love,*
*mom & Dad :)*

## STEPHEN KENDRICK
## & ALEX KENDRICK
### WITH LAWRENCE KIMBROUGH

**B&H**
**PUBLISHING**
**NASHVILLE, TENNESSEE**

Copyright © 2019 by Kendrick Brothers, LLC
All rights reserved.
Printed in the United States of America

978-1-5359-4892-0

Published by B&H Publishing Group
Nashville, Tennessee

Dewey Decimal Classification: 248.84
Subject Heading: GOD-WILL / CHRISTIAN LIFE /
SELF-REALIZATION

Unless otherwise noted, all Scripture quotations are taken from the Christian
Standard Bible®, Copyright © 2017 by Holman Bible Publishers. Used by
permission. Christian Standard Bible® and CSB® are federally registered
trademarks of Holman Bible Publishers.

Also used: New American Standard Bible (NASB), copyright © 1960, 1962,
1963, 1968, 1971, 1972, 1973, 1975, 1977, 1995 by The Lockman Foundation.

Also used: English Standard Version (ESV), ESV® Text Edition: 2016. Copyright
© 2001 by Crossway Bibles, a publishing ministry of Good News Publishers.

Also used: New International Version (NIV), NIV® copyright ©1973,
1978, 1984, 2011 by Biblica, Inc.® Used by permission. All rights reserved
worldwide.

Also used: New Living Translation (NLT), copyright © 1996, 2004, 2015 by
Tyndale House Foundation. Used by permission of Tyndale House Publishers,
Inc., Carol Stream, Illinois 60188. All rights reserved.

Also used: New King James Version (NKJV), copyright © 1982 by Thomas
Nelson. Used by permission. All rights reserved.

1 2 3 4 5 6 7 • 23 22 21 20 19

Dedicated to Our Loving Parents

LARRY and RHONWYN KENDRICK

Dad, you have been a hero to us from the stage,
from the stands, and from the shadows.
Your influence and your legacy run deeper
than you know. Thank you for speaking the truth
in love over us, introducing us to our heavenly Father's
heart, and blessing us with your wholehearted support,
counsel, and prayers. Great is your reward in heaven!

Mom, we thank God for the wonderful mother
that you are. Your love, sacrificial service,
gracious hospitality, and unceasing prayers
have blessed us and so many others for decades
and laid up countless treasures in eternity.
Our identity in Christ was formed early because
of the influence you and Dad had on us.

We love you both so much!

Stephen and Alex

# Contents

# Introduction

STEPHEN KENDRICK

One of the most powerful and life-changing books in existence is the New Testament book of Ephesians. Filled with hope, it is deep, mind-blowing, and very rich. Its six short chapters express God's amazing heart of compassion, how He can meet us where we are, powerfully change us from within, and beautifully redeem our lives for good and for His glory.

For many years when I tried to read Ephesians, my eyes would seemingly glaze over. I would get lost in some of the concepts and skip over sections I didn't understand, not grasping the bigger picture or how to incorporate it into my life. Then a few years ago, something unexpected happened to my family that completely turned the light on for me and unlocked the book in living color.

We adopted a little girl.

Throughout the process of adoption, our new daughter's journey began to surprisingly parallel the concepts in Ephesians. The entire book began to make sense to me for the first time at a deep level. All the truths became more powerful in light of it, and it's now one of my favorite books of all time.

This experience was so profound, in fact, that I've been walking others through Ephesians and showing them how God can use it in their lives. I'm grateful I can now share our adoption story with you and take time to dive into so many incredible truths from Scripture. I'll begin by going back to the defining day when our adoption began.

Early one morning, my wife, Jill, and I were flying to New York to approve the final master of a movie called *Courageous* that my brother and I had produced, before it was released in theaters. While on the plane, I was praying and reading in the Gospel of John, specifically Jesus' words in chapter 10 about how a shepherd will love, protect, and lay down his life for his sheep. I was thinking about my role as a father that morning and how I could better shepherd our four little children at home. In the course of my reading, God suddenly caught me off guard and spoke to my heart very clearly. I turned to Jill, feeling a bit surprised, and said, "I think God wants us to be open to adoption."

My wife smiled and was already ahead of me. I didn't realize she had been quietly praying for years that God would turn my heart toward adoption, but she had not told me because she wanted it to be of God, not of her. I picked up my pen and wrote the word *adoption* next to the key verse God brought to my attention that day, then dated it.

Fast-forward two years. After we'd completed mountains of adoption paperwork, an email popped into my phone with our first referral. I was elated. Staring back at me was the picture of an adorable, eight-month-old girl, along with the question, "Do you want to adopt this child?"

She logically lined up with everything we were asking for, but there was a problem. I don't know how better to explain it than to say a dark, uneasy heaviness came over me. I felt a strong lack of peace that I wrestled with for hours, wondering what was wrong with me. *Am I afraid? What will happen to this girl if I say no?*

I called a friend who is an adoption consultant, asking for help. "This is too big of a decision, Stephen. If it's not a clear *yes*, then it's a *no*." So with a measure of guilt, I sent the agency an awkward email and closed the door. Jill cried.

Over the next few weeks, two more referrals came. Each was a beautiful, precious child. Each was followed by an emotional battle of research, prayer, and indecision. The willingness was there, but no peace. No "*yes.*"

More awkward emails followed.

Our adoption agent said it wasn't uncommon for parents to turn down a referral, maybe even two. I had already struck out three times. The "fear of man" started to kick in. *What will others think if I keep turning away these precious orphans knocking on my door? Didn't we say God wanted us to adopt?*

A fourth referral arrived. But again, no peace.

I turned it down. Jill cried.

It was heart-wrenching. An experience that was supposed to be a joyful journey for us had become a traumatic roller coaster, and I sincerely wanted off. The next month, the agency didn't send us any referrals and, to be quite honest, I was relieved.

Then came March 2013. A fifth referral landed in my in-box.

When I saw it, I dreaded opening it.

She was a two-year-old girl who'd been abandoned in a large city in China, diagnosed with a deadly heart condition. Her physical situation was more severe than any of the other children we'd considered. And yet when we saw her picture, an unexpected peace came over both of us, like Colossians 3:15 talks about. It was as if God was saying, "This is the one you've been waiting for."

After research, we discovered that her birth mother likely couldn't afford her daughter's surgeries and had to face the brutal decision of either keeping her and letting her die or giving her up to save her life. She left her on a street corner wrapped in a red blanket (which in China means "good luck" and "I love you"), along with the papers describing her needed surgeries.

Despite all the potential complications, something seemed very right about making this specific little girl a part of our family. Her file stated her date of birth as February 14, 2011. Jill responded with, "She was born on Valentine's Day with a broken heart." So with peaceful hearts and joyful tears, we sent a welcoming email and locked her in. All was well.

A few weeks later, Jill asked me about that flight where God had spoken to us about adoption. "What day was that?" she wondered. "Do you remember?" I hadn't thought about it and had no idea. I thumbed through my Bible, looking for John 10:16. Opening the page, I found the word *adoption* next to that verse, and the date next to it.

February 14, 2011.

The day this little girl had been born in China was the same day when God had said so clearly to me on the airplane that He wanted us to adopt.

I was overwhelmed and in awe of God. I felt this incredible sense that we were about to be part of something much bigger than we realized. He was undoubtedly in control of this, and we needed to trust Him and move forward.

Things happened quickly after that, with God continuing to affirm His blessing and guidance in everything we were doing. We felt inspired to name her *Mia*, which means "one" in Greek (Eph. 4:5). After we arrived in China, we discovered that the name her birth mother had given to her was the Chinese word for "one" as well.

Finally, after processing Mia's adoption and paying all the fees, the time came for us to bring her home, which led to another interesting plane ride. Our friends had warned us it might be highly difficult. They were correct. During the extremely long flight to New York, our new daughter cried, whined, and screamed loudly for a large portion of the twelve hours. (I have videos.)

Mia, our new China rose, was understandably distraught and very confused about what was going on and who we were. She had no idea that this uncomfortable experience was a necessary and important part of a big, wonderful plan—that we were actually rescuing her from a desperate and hopeless situation.

She didn't know that her future trajectory had been dark. Orphans there get minimal care and often grow up struggling with their identity, sense of value, and purpose. Not knowing the love of a family, not having much help or hope for the future, they frequently end up on the street where they may be trafficked.

But now Mia would have a safe, happy home and a healthy family. She would have two loving parents, four siblings, four grandparents, and more than a dozen cousins ready to welcome her with open arms. At the orphanage, she owned almost nothing. Now she would have a warm bed, clean clothes, and new toys to enjoy. She would also have all the education and medical care she needed. And she would freely receive the same privileges and future inheritance as all her Kendrick siblings. Now she would have hope. Not just wishful thinking, but a bright pathway into the future.

But none of these wonderful changes were happening because of anything she had done or earned or could provide us. They were all set into motion because of one key thing: there had been a change in her identity because of WHO SHE NOW WAS. She was not a hopeless orphan anymore. She was Mia Kendrick: our chosen, wanted, and beloved daughter. And because of this, in rippling effect, everything else in her life would also completely and tangibly change for the better.

If Mia had understood this reality on the plane—who she was, how deeply she was loved by her new family, and how good her life would become—she could have been smiling and cheering instead of weeping in fear. She could have enjoyed the journey and more easily endured the long flight delays. Had she been able to grasp the bigger picture, she could have been celebrating the entire way home.

And so can you . . . because as beautiful as Mia's change of identity sounds, this story directly applies to each of us.

None of us is born knowing who we are or why we're here, any more than Mia did in China. All of us arrive with our own set of issues and genuine needs—not just physical, but emotional and spiritual as well.

We also have heart problems. We battle with selfishness, pride, lust, greed, insecurity, anger, and many more things. Over time we will struggle with fearing the future, as well as wrestling with the pain and dysfunction within our own lives and families. We'll hurt, and *be* hurt, by others. We'll tend to grapple with confusion and question our place in this world.

But the Bible says that God, who is the most loving Father of all, openly expressed His compassionate love for each of us by sending His Son on a rescue mission. Jesus demonstrated a love we did not deserve by laying down His life to save us from a hopeless future. He paid the spiritual fees needed for our redemption, and He offers new life to anyone willing to trust Him by faith.

Think about this. When we place our lives in His hands, God the Father literally adopts us into His family and completely changes our identity. Our spiritual condition, value, and purpose change as well, along with our entire future. God takes ownership over us as His children. He blesses us with new resources, helps us discover how to be more like Him, and explains to us in His Word how to live victoriously as His beloved sons and daughters.

But most people do not understand this—including most followers of Christ, I would argue. When the apostle Paul wrote the book of Ephesians, he was writing to people who knew God but didn't understand their spiritual identity. Paul prayed that God would open their eyes to grasp the depth of *who they were* and *what they had* in Christ because of how it would radically change their entire lives.

That is the purpose of this book.

We have written *Defined* to help you learn who you are. Not at a surface level, but at a much deeper level. We want you to discover more of the amazing truths of Ephesians regarding what God's Word says He's already been doing in your life. We invite you and even dare you to join us, along with countless others, on a journey of discovery through some of the most important passages of the Bible regarding the identity and inheritance God provides for His children.

We'll begin with how God designed us, handles our brokenness, and willingly forgives us. We will study what it means to let go of the past and live out our identity in Him so that it positively affects how we think, speak, and relate in love to those around us. Then we will conclude with how God's Spirit empowers us to handle temptation, criticism, and life's hardest battles more successfully, so that we can walk in victory and still honor God despite our circumstances.

With this purpose in mind, right here at the outset, we would like to challenge you to make a commitment to do three things as you read:

*First,* **READ** *this book a chapter a day.*

We suggest at least five days a week for the next seven weeks, but whatever works for your schedule.

*Second,* **READ** *the Bible each day.*

Let the Word of God teach you who God is and who you are. Consider starting in either Matthew or Ephesians, but we'll also give you specific verses at the end of each chapter that you can look up and study. They should deepen your perspective on what God says about your identity and help you gain the most from this journey.

*Third,* **PRAY** *every day.*

Scripture indicates that prayer is a key component to helping us comprehend and believe truth. Choose a place and time when you can pray alone each day, preferably in the morning (Ps. 5:3). Try to end each chapter by asking God to help you believe and apply whatever He is teaching you. Then take time to pray specifically about any need or difficulty in your life.

We'll end each chapter with a prayer, just as we're doing here in this opening section, extending to you an invitation to approach God with a specific request:

*Heavenly Father, I come in Jesus' name, asking that You would open the eyes of my heart to know You and who You created me to be. Help me daily receive Your love for me, walk in sincere love toward You and others, and live out who I am in You. Bless me and strengthen me to do Your will. Fill me and lead me by Your Holy Spirit, and use my life as a light in this world for Your glory. Amen.*

May we each experience the depth of the love and mercy of God, and may our lives become living examples of His grace and transforming power to bring light and hope to future generations!

# CHAPTER 1

# Identity Matters

*I call to God Most High,*
*to God who fulfills his purpose for me. (Ps. 57:2)*

Jesus Christ inhabited time and space in the first century and is recognized around the world as the most loving, powerful, and influential person ever to have walked the earth. But also this: His entire life is a vivid illustration of the priority of identity.

At thirty years of age, Jesus arrived in Judea to be baptized by the prophet John, who was assigned to prepare the way for the coming Messiah. The Gospels of Matthew, Mark, and Luke all report that at His baptism, Jesus came up out of the Jordan River, and eyewitnesses heard a voice thunder out of the heavens, saying:

"This is my beloved Son, with whom I am well-pleased." (Matt. 3:17)

Now consider the significance of this affirmation at the genesis of Christ's public ministry. God could have said, "Go evangelize the world," or "Do the right thing," or "Fulfill My law," or "When You die, fear not; I will bring You back." But instead of endless other possibilities, Jesus' heavenly Father went straight to the heart and spoke specifically about His Son's identity. This was the priority of heaven.

Identity took precedence over instruction.

Interestingly, God declared this audible blessing of love and acceptance *before* Jesus had preached one sermon, called even one disciple, performed His first miracle, or completed His Father's will. God wanted everyone present—including His Son—to hear exactly who Jesus was and how deeply He was already loved in the eyes of His heavenly Father.

Immediately, the Holy Spirit led Jesus into the wilderness to be tested by Satan for forty days. Both Matthew 4 and Luke 4 state that two of the three recorded temptations that Christ encountered were specific attacks aimed at, of all things, His identity. The tempter kept repeating, "If you are the Son of God . . ." (Matt. 4:3); "If you are the Son of God . . ." (v. 6). That was his allurement, inciting Jesus to compromise in order to *prove* who He was.

Satan knew that Jesus' integrity and desire to live out His identity was a powerful motivator that would strongly influence His decisions. But Jesus consistently responded with the truth of Scripture rather than His own feelings. Despite intense pressure, He trusted what His heavenly Father had already lovingly affirmed.

After this experience, Jesus traveled back to His hometown in Nazareth, walked into the synagogue, and publicly read what the book of Isaiah had prophesied as the job description for the Messiah. Jesus was publicly declaring who He was, acknowledging His calling to "preach good news to the poor" and to "proclaim release to the captives and recovery of sight to the blind, to set free the oppressed" (Luke 4:18–19).

The local citizens did not realize He was their Messiah, so they immediately questioned it. "Isn't this Joseph's son?" (Luke 4:22). Rather than embrace their long-awaited Savior, they were filled with rage and tried to kill Him instead. Jesus' first day of ministry ended in attempted murder. But He knew this was only the beginning, so He walked through the midst of the angry crowd, left Nazareth, and went out to fulfill His mission.

Over the next three years, Jesus founded His entire ministry not on His education, or on the people He knew, or on the miracles He could do, but only on who He was and is. Everything He said and did flowed out of His identity. His teaching was not just brilliant instruction but was modeled by His life.

Regularly, He personified His messages to meet the need of the audience in front of Him. He wanted to specify what some of the various elements of His identity meant. For instance:

His identity guided His *actions*. "I am the good shepherd. The good shepherd lays down his life for the sheep" (John 10:11).

His identity explained His *access*. "I am the way, the truth, and the life. No one comes to the Father except through me" (John 14:6).

His identity clarified His *authority*. "I am the resurrection and the life; he who believes in Me will live even if he dies, and everyone who lives and believes in Me will never die" (John 11:25–26 NASB).

Jesus did not merely declare bold things, but He backed them up with actions and power. After proclaiming, "I am the resurrection and the life," for example, He immediately confirmed it by raising a dead man (Lazarus) from the grave.

His life and ministry demonstrated that (1) knowing our God-given identity is a key priority for each of us, and (2) allowing God to be the One to help us discover it and live it out is foundational to fulfilling our purpose in life.

## What Is an Identity?

The word *identity* describes who you are in totality. It's the real truth about the real you. Since you are not an abstract cloud of nothingness, but rather a definitive, living human being, you already have a specific God-given identity whether you know it, want it, or understand it. It is a cornerstone concept in the comprehension and functionality of human existence.

In *language*, we use the word *when* to reference time, *where* to qualify space, and *who* to refer to a person's identity. The word *identity* is not used in the Bible, but the word *who* is referenced thousands of times . . . to indicate identity.

In *relationships*, it's the interaction of our identities that enables us to know and understand one another. From shaking hands and exchanging basic personal information to eventually sharing and knowing someone's thoughts, feelings, and heart, the health and depth of relationships is greatest when who you are, and who *they* are, can freely open up, understand, and speak the truth in love.

In *Scripture*, anytime God created something, He always marked its identity by *naming* it. The first thing Adam did in the garden was to identify and name the animals under his care (Gen. 2:19). And throughout the generations of history, people all over the world still attach a name to someone when they are born, marking their identity.

In God's Word, a person's name is not only connected to their physical existence but ripples outward to encompass their distinctive character and attributes, their individual significance and value, their relational roles and responsibilities, and can also include their authority, actions, accomplishments, reputation, and personal influence. All of these things that are tied to a name can also be part of your identity as a person.

Welcome to the complicated mystery of you. Hopefully it's clear, as we scratch the surface of it, that your existence, identity, value, and influence are of monumental importance and can be epic in reach. Hopefully you will discover in this book that who you really are matters to God, and discovering what He knows about who you are should matter to you.

Every one of us is on an identity journey. We are born knowing nothing about ourselves before we launch into *real life academy*, where new lessons are to be learned in every season. The full spectrum of what you hear, feel, and assume throughout life can include both good and bad teachers, both weird and wonderful lessons, and will come at you from a wide variety of sources—some trustworthy; some totally unreliable.

Some of your identity lessons are simple and surface: "I have a freckle on my right elbow." Others are major and monumental: "I've never felt loved and understood by my biological father." Over time you discover strengths you never knew you had, as well as weaknesses you long to overcome. Successes you'd like to relive. Shame that you'd like to hide and bury in the past. You accept and adapt to some of these changes; you deny and doubt others. You experience both deep and superficial relationships, and you learn epic lessons of joy and sorrow in the midst of them.

Through it all, the conclusions you make become a lens through which you view yourself, your life, your circumstances, and your relationships.

So, what has real life taught you about yourself? How deeply have you contemplated this issue of your own identity? Do you really know who you are? You may assume you do, which is why you may say you don't think about it that much anymore. But the truth is, your identity is actually a deep, underlying part of your thinking all the time, every day.

Beneath your daily words and ambitions, behind your regular thoughts and emotions, is a pool of hidden beliefs about your own identity and worth that either clarifies or confuses the choices you make in life. It affects almost every area, including how you think and feel at any given time, the way you approach daily opportunities and react to problems, and how you tend to view God and your present circumstances.

Consider the following illustrations inspired by true stories:

Shawn is a sharp, intelligent employee, excellent at solving problems. He loves to share his faith, and he keeps a great attitude—that is, unless he fails or someone criticizes him. Then he panics, explodes in anger, lashes out at others, and withdraws into self-pity for days.

Luann is an amazing mother to her three children. But when her youngest son left for college, she suddenly felt like her life as a mom was over, and she quickly sank into an unexpected depression, including suicidal thoughts.

Colby grew up in church and decided to follow God at a young age. But in his teen years, he developed a dark addiction to pornography that has enslaved him for more than a decade. He desperately wants to be used by God, but he is haunted by shame, and he struggles with ongoing doubts about his own salvation.

Chelsea is a beautiful Christian girl with a bright future. After being sexually assaulted on a date in college, she's been deeply broken emotionally and feels like worthless, damaged goods. Carrying loads of misplaced shame, Chelsea began to drink to medicate her pain and has battled alcoholism for years.

Jerome retired after twenty-five years as a beloved pastor in his community and gladly passed the baton to a young buck, fresh out of seminary. Less than a year later, however, he's frustrated with his empty calendar and has a hard time not being angry at how well the congregation has moved on without him. He fumes with jealousy over the new pastor's success and has grown bitter toward God for taking *his* [Jerome's] church away from him.

If you were to sit down for a meal with each of these people and listen to their heartfelt stories, you might assume that Shawn just has anger issues, Luann's problem is her empty nest, Colby needs an internet filter, Chelsea needs to control her liquor, and Jerome is merely a grumpy old retiree.

But the truth is, in each case, their external behavior is actually flowing out of internal issues deeply rooted in their hearts. Difficult circumstances did not *create* their identity but deeply *tested* it, twisted their understanding of it, and revealed that their identity wasn't anchored where it needed to be. If you dive below the surface, you might find . . .

Shawn doesn't understand how to separate the opinions of others from his worth as a man.

Luann is struggling to believe that her value and purpose are much bigger than even her important role as a mom.

Colby doesn't grasp who he is in Christ or how discovering his identity could help him walk in freedom.

Chelsea doesn't know how to fully accept and walk in the love and acceptance of her heavenly Father.

Jerome doesn't realize, even as a spiritual leader, that he's walking around with identity issues.

Surely, every one of them needs love. They each deserve a listening ear, compassionate understanding, accountable relationships, and encouraging prayer support. But they also need to discover some key truths about their identity and value that could set them free.

The "truth," Jesus said, "will set you free" (John 8:32).

These stories represent only a few of the countless battles people face all around us on a daily basis. Life is extremely complicated, and people clearly struggle with various issues for a wide variety of reasons. It would be overly simplistic to say that an identity adjustment is all anyone needs to solve their problems. We're not saying that. We don't believe that. But we do know identity is a core, foundational issue that greatly affects almost every aspect of our lives. It is deeply misunderstood and often overlooked. And God has so much to say about it that we need to know and understand.

## Do You Know Who You Are?

What about you? If someone placed a giant mirror in front of you today and offered you a million dollars to accurately and honestly define, clarify, and share everything you possibly could about the person looking back at you, what would you say?

After feeling awkward for a minute, you might freely state your name and your driver's license stats of race, gender, height, maybe your home address. Before you shared your weight, financial numbers, or any sensitive personal information, you might ask if this conversation is being recorded. Then you'd likely talk about your family and your relational roles. You'd tell things about your parents and siblings, maybe even some of your extended family. You would state any job titles or positions you hold, as well as some of your day-to-day responsibilities.

You might talk about your nationality, your political and religious affiliations, your educational background. You might smile with modest transparency about your skills and talents, highlighting some of your unique abilities and accomplishments. You would likely open up about what you personally love and hate in life—food and music preferences, sports teams, favorite movies, and personal pet peeves.

At some point, if you felt emotionally safe enough, you'd likely take a deep breath and start sharing personal stories about your greatest memories or even your hardest life experiences, including your deepest regrets that you long to be erased from your past. You might get a little choked up when talking about the people who have loved you the deepest over the years, as well as those who have brought you the greatest pain.

Even still, there might be some areas you'd be hesitant to share. Questions you struggle with. Fears. The deeper layers of your innermost thoughts and secrets. Some of your core beliefs and things you still wonder about. And then, if prompted, you might even share your best guesses at the WHY behind it all, what you think the real purpose and meaning of your life might be.

But after all was said and done, whether it took hours or days to pour out your heart in such unhindered fashion, imagine being asked to look back into that mirror, fix your eyes on your own eyes, and answer as honestly as possible the following challenging questions:

- Do you genuinely like, respect, and care about the person you see?
- What do you truly think about this person?
- Are you grateful to be you, or do you honestly wish you were someone else?
- Are you angry or grateful with what God has done in your life?
- Who do you think influences your view of your own identity the most?
- How loved and affirmed did you feel by your parents growing up?
- Did they make you feel valued and understood?
- How loved do you feel today in your heart and current relationships?
- What do you think God thinks about you?
- Do you believe He really sees, cares, and knows you intimately?
- Do you feel like He accepts you, just tolerates you, or rejects you?
- Do you genuinely believe He loves you?
- How deeply have you been hurt by others?
- Are you still tender and hurting, or have you healed completely?
- When was the last time you were genuinely happy and at peace inside?
- What do you believe is the purpose of your life? Do you have any idea?
- Do you feel empty and hopeless inside, or do you have a hopeful future?
- Do you believe you will go to heaven one day when you die?
- Are you sure? If not, would you like to be sure?
- What is your greatest hope from learning about your identity?

The purpose of this book is not to become self-absorbed or self-centered. Our genuine hope for this experience is that you'll discover so much more about the heart of God as you open up your own heart to the mystery of what He's done and wants to do in and through you.

To know and be known is a powerful thing.

To love and be loved is a beautiful thing.

To know your purpose and fulfill it is a priceless thing.

But to know God and be known and loved by Him is better than life itself.

It is life—"eternal life" (John 17:3).

---

*Heavenly Father, as I begin this journey of discovery, I pray that You will open the eyes of my heart to discover and know the truth about who You are, about who I truly am, and who You created me to be. Give me the grace and strength to trust You with whatever I find. Help me to know Your love and to find and fulfill Your greater purpose for my life. In Jesus' name, Amen.*

---

**TAKE IT DEEPER BY STUDYING**
Matthew 16:13–17 • Mark 9:7–8 • John 5:31–32

---

*Search me, O God, and know my heart! Try me and know my thoughts! And see if there be any grievous way in me, and lead me in the way everlasting! (Ps. 139:23–24 ESV)*

## CHAPTER 2

# *The Confusion of Your Identity*

*Do not be conformed to this age, but be transformed by the renewing of your mind, so that you may discern what is the good, pleasing, and perfect will of God. (Rom. 12:2)*

I dentity confusion is ongoing and everywhere. We live in a digital generation that is being constantly bombarded with random and opposing messages about who we are and what we are. A cloud of ongoing debate swirls around racial and national identity, gender and sexual identity, political identity in government, and even denominational identity in the church. Some of these identifiers are inbred and God-given, while some are matters of belief, values, and choice.

But either way, people we love and care about in our families, friendship circles, and work environments fall on both sides of almost every one of these issues. And we're not talking about marginal, petty disagreements here. We're seeing lives devastated and families torn apart, and nationally we're watching substance abuse and suicide rates on the rise.

Identity is a core issue. What you and I believe about God and about ourselves are two of the most central and foundational beliefs in our hearts. And the further these internal beliefs skew away from truth, the more havoc our distorted interpretations of identity will wreak on our behavior.

To use a sports analogy, a person who doesn't understand his or her true identity is like a football player who doesn't know his position or what team he's on. He can run around on the field chasing the ball and randomly tackling people, but he will function in a fog and frustrate everyone else with his confusing behavior. He might rant, "Quit judging me! I'm trying my best here. This is what I want to do and feel like doing." But his behavior is not the core problem. He doesn't really understand who he is.

Or to use a farming illustration, if a cow begins to think he's a chicken, he will unnecessarily live a life of frustration, depression, and disillusionment, especially when he tries to lay an egg or jump up on a fence post and crow.

People who begin embracing a lie about their identity will constantly struggle with confusion and inconsistencies between their thoughts and emotions on the one hand and the reality of God's Word and everyday life on the other. Jesus warned His listeners that they could easily frame their lives around false assumptions and self-deception (Matt. 7:21–23), and that they needed to be careful and on guard about the people whose teaching they allow to influence their opinions (vv. 15–20).

The apostle Paul warned:

> We are no longer to be children, tossed here and there by waves and carried about by every wind of doctrine, by the trickery of men, by craftiness in deceitful scheming; but speaking the truth in love, we are to grow up in all aspects into Him who is the head, even Christ. (Eph. 4:14–15 NASB)

Regardless of where we've come from and what kinds of identity issues we're dealing with, we need to take these words to heart. Let's not be like gullible children, easily duped by whoever's making the loudest, most impassioned noise at any given moment. And let's not artificially separate walking in love from walking in truth. Both are valuable and necessary, or else we and the people we love will find ourselves building our lives on shifting sands, to tragic results (Matt. 7:24–27)—the following shifting sands of *feelings, desires,* and *other people's opinions.*

## FEELINGS ARE FAULTY

Feelings are powerful communicators but not reliable sources of truth. Your feelings are one of the most shallow and unstable parts of your life. Emotions can swing all over the map, bypassing logic, ignoring reality, and reacting to speculation. Just because something *feels* true does not at all *make* it true. Feelings are basically fickle followers, not dependable leaders. They should be seen as the caboose following the train, not the locomotive that pulls it. The day we quit letting our feelings run our lives and start walking in truth will be a great day of liberation. While feelings can actually help us discover what we *already* believe in our hearts, they're not often a good gauge of what is true—what we *should* believe.

So where do our feelings come from? Different sources. But the Bible gives us a clue about how we can parse out our feelings and trace them back to their point of origin. Each of us is comprised of a body, soul, and spirit, interconnected with one another (1 Thess. 5:23), and all three of them can affect and influence our feelings in distinct ways.

*1. Your body* is a temple, the Bible says (1 Cor. 6:19)—a mobile tabernacle—that needs to stay well fueled and well tuned. Because if not kept under control, it will drive you off a cliff. We're all aware that a lack of sleep, a stomach bug, or the wrong medication can negatively affect how we physically feel. On other days your body may feel great; you almost feel like you could fly or run through a wall. At other times, however, it might feel despondent or demanding and make you think you should overeat, oversleep, or even sleep around.

So it should be led and stewarded well, but not trusted and followed as a moral guide. Your body doesn't care what's right or wrong, and it will betray and enslave you quickly if you let it take the wheel and have its way. That's why the apostle Paul wrote, "I discipline my body and keep it under control, lest . . . I myself should be disqualified" (1 Cor. 9:27 ESV).

2. *Your soul* is commonly believed to be comprised of your mind, will, and emotions, and it can also impact your feelings. Jesus said, the night before His crucifixion, "My soul is deeply grieved, to the point of death" (Matt. 26:38 NASB). His feelings were being informed by His knowledge of what was to come. The thoughts in your head and core beliefs in your heart will directly affect your feelings and emotions. You may be physically and spiritually healthy, but if you mentally allow your thoughts to dwell on evil or believe a lie, you will feel the darkness and bondage of it. Lot, in the Old Testament, "felt his righteous soul tormented" by all the sin he saw in his city of Sodom (2 Pet. 2:8 NASB).

3. *Your spirit* also affects your feelings. Love, joy, and peace are spiritual fruit and can be tangibly felt in our hearts when we walk with God. In contrast, King David felt an agonizing *loss* of joy when he lived in spiritual sin (Ps. 51). God will often guide us with feelings of peace or conviction in our spirits (Col. 3:15), which can be useful in directing our next steps toward obedience. But the filter of His Word must still remain our plumb line of truth (v. 16). Where feelings and His Word do not align, we must trust His Word, which doesn't change, not our feelings, which are always subject to change. First John 3:20 says, "Even if we feel guilty, God is greater than our feelings, and he knows everything" (NLT).

So lock into this. Many people foolishly let their feelings (regardless of the source) determine what they believe to be true about who they are or what is morally right for them. They think: *If I don't feel loved, then I must not be loved. If something feels good, then it must be good. If I feel like I'm right, then I must be right. If I have feelings of attraction for someone, then it must mean God made me this way and it's my destiny to pursue that. If I feel like God hates me, then He must hate me. If I feel like I'm worthless and should hurt myself or someone else, then maybe I should.*

This line of thinking is backward, unreliable, and tragic. A lie will feel true if you choose to believe it. A hypochondriac who mentally assumes he's sick can physically make himself *feel* sick. Worry stirs up fearful feelings as if evil has already happened when nothing real has occurred.

Consequently, painful experiences are powerful teachers. To go through pain so deep that you can hardly breathe or honestly want to die—this is a potent pill to swallow. Emotional experiences are deeply memorable and can leave a scar of poisonous lessons in our hearts. If that message is a lie about our value or identity, and if it is reinforced by so much deep emotion, it's hard for us not to believe it and be deceived by it.

Whether it was verbal, physical, or sexual abuse, if someone rejects you and crushes you, and you start to *believe* that you are worthless or unloved, then you will also start to *feel* that way, even when it's the opposite of the truth. Your feelings will follow your heart's beliefs. Whether it's through the cutting words of a critic or being openly rejected by a former friend, feelings can water the seed of a lie you're considering and help it take root in your heart. Then the lie, when planted, will reinforce itself with more feelings. Angry thoughts lead to angry feelings that lead to more angry thoughts. Depressing thoughts are handcuffed to depressing feelings.

If you are a man who begins to genuinely question, consider, and ultimately start to believe that you are a woman, then be aware that your feelings could naturally follow the thoughts and reinforce those assumptions. We should not believe everything we feel or think. We might say, "I've believed and felt this way for a long time." But God's Word would remind us that believing a lie for a long time doesn't make it true.

We might claim, "Well, I'm just following my heart." But the prophet Jeremiah would warn us that the human heart can be selfish, wicked, deceitful, and deceived (Jer. 17:9). Solomon, after years of learning painful lessons the hard way, warned, "He who trusts in his own heart is a fool, but he who walks wisely will be delivered" (Prov. 28:26 NASB).

So wise discernment of our feelings is vital to maintaining healthy thinking, and thereby maintaining an accurate viewpoint on our identity. Regardless of the source—body, soul, or spirit—we must filter it all through wisdom and truth from God's Word. The Bible instructs us to "destroy arguments and every lofty opinion raised against the knowledge of God, and take every thought captive to obey Christ" (2 Cor. 10:5 ESV).

## DESIRES ARE DECEITFUL

Contrary to what many people believe, your desires do not determine your identity or your destiny. Scripture warns us to follow God-honoring desires but to turn away from sinful ones.

> So I say, let the Holy Spirit guide your lives. Then you won't be doing what your sinful nature craves. The sinful nature wants to do evil, which is just the opposite of what the Spirit wants. And the Spirit gives us desires that are the opposite of what the sinful nature desires. These two forces are constantly fighting each other, so you are not free to carry out your good intentions. But when you are directed by the Spirit, you are not under obligation to the law of Moses.
>
> When you follow the desires of your sinful nature, the results are very clear: sexual immorality, impurity, lustful pleasures, idolatry, sorcery, hostility, quarreling, jealousy, outbursts of anger, selfish ambition, dissension, division, envy, drunkenness, wild parties, and other sins like these. Let me tell you again, as I have before, that anyone living that sort of life will not inherit the Kingdom of God.
>
> But the Holy Spirit produces this kind of fruit in our lives: love, joy, peace, patience, kindness, goodness, faithfulness, gentleness, and self-control. There is no law against these things! (Gal. 5:16–23 NLT)

Regardless of how we feel, Scripture says God never tempts us to sin. Our own sinful desires, not God, are what lure us toward doing something wrong (James 1:13). God is actually the source of every good thing (v. 17). He has our best interest in mind and wants us to enjoy His best desires freely without the heartbreak or the hangover afterward. So the biblical response to wrong desires is to willingly turn from the stumbling blocks in our lives and apply the Word of God instead, to "put away all filthiness and rampant wickedness and receive with meekness the implanted word, which is able to save your souls" (v. 21 ESV).

Remember, God can renew your mind (Rom. 12:1–2), save your soul (James 1:21), restore your soul (Ps. 23:3), fill you with His love (Rom. 5:5), and give you the mind of Christ (1 Cor. 2:16). His best for us is within reach if we are willing to trust Him.

## Other People's Opinions Will Oscillate

The words and opinions of people are varied, contradictory, and can easily change or swing to extremes.

Your mom may glance at your third-grade report card and tell you how smart you are, but later your older brother catches you dripping ketchup on your shirt and informs you that you're a complete idiot. Your football coach gives you a high five and calls you a winner. Your ex-girlfriend posts online that you're the world's biggest loser.

Try releasing a movie and reading the wildly differing reviews.

*"Greatest movie ever made! I've seen it six times!"*

*"Absolute most embarrassing piece of life-sapping garbage ever put on a screen!"*

When it comes to your identity, even if you line up ten people who know you well to tell you who they think you are, they still only know a small fraction of your words, actions, and only a few of your inner thoughts. Who has total omniscience, perfect understanding, and could articulate everything about you flawlessly? Only God, not them.

Jesus did not base or alter His own sense of identity on what other people thought or said about Him. Some people listened and followed Him, while others questioned and angrily opposed everything He did. The night Peter was vowing to die for Christ, Judas was simultaneously betraying Him behind the scenes. Even when people were believing in Him, Jesus "would not entrust himself to them, since he knew them all and because he did not need anyone to testify about man; for he himself knew what was in man" (John 2:24–25). He understood "it is better to take refuge in the LORD than to trust in man" (Ps. 118:8 NASB).

Throughout our lives, we will each hear a wide variety of helpful and hurtful things said about us. Some loving; some hateful. Some completely true; some totally wrong.

Words can be so powerful. "Death and life are in the power of the tongue" (Prov. 18:21). Sometimes what people say about us can feel like a curse. Their words cut deep, go to the heart, and feel true. Then we can replay them hundreds of times in our minds. We may reject them, believe them, or wonder if they *might* be true. Then when anything happens that reinforces them, we can overreact out of fear and struggle to prove them wrong. Whether it's the fear of looking stupid; fear of failure; fear of being overlooked or replaced; or the fear of being rejected, unloved, or abandoned, all of these can be horrible tormentors to someone's thinking if that person is not grounded in the solid truth of what God says about them. We must remember:

The fear of mankind is a snare, but the one who trusts in the LORD is protected. (Prov. 29:25)

For God has not given us a spirit of fear, but of power and of love and of a sound mind. (2 Tim. 1:7 NKJV)

In conclusion, be careful about grounding your identity in fluctuating things that will set you up for failure and disappointment. You should be defined by God, not by your changing feelings, fickle desires, Facebook likes and reviews, or others' assessments of you. We all have issues and should continue to walk in humility and love, being willing to learn and grow. But as we will discover in future chapters, to discover who you really are, as told by the One who truly knows you, can be a life-changing breakthrough that unlocks how best to live. The best is yet to come.

*Heavenly Father, give me wisdom and discernment to filter all the messages that are coming at me, and help me build my life and thinking on truth. Change my heart, O God, and cleanse me of any sinful or hurtful way that is in me. Renew my mind and habits by Your grace. Help me speak the truth in love and not be swayed by my feelings or desires that are leading me away from loving You and obeying Your will. In Jesus' name, amen.*

TAKE IT DEEPER BY STUDYING
John 8:30–36 • 2 Corinthians 10:4–5 • James 1:19–25

*O send out Your light and Your truth, let them lead me. (Ps. 43:3 NASB)*

CHAPTER 3

# The Source of Your Identity

*"He is actually not far from each one of us, for in him we live and move and have our being." (Acts 17:27–28 ESV)*

Moses was a man who struggled with identity issues. Born to Hebrew parents, he was given an Egyptian name and then raised by Pharaoh's daughter as her adopted son. After secretly murdering a man in defense of his own people, Moses was questioned by his Hebrew brethren: "Who made you a prince or a judge over us?" (Exod. 2:14 NASB). Fearful for his life, he fled Egypt while Pharaoh tried to kill him for what he had done. Now a fugitive alien in the foreign land of Midian, he embraced the low-key life of a wandering shepherd for forty years.

Then one day, God Himself unexpectedly appeared to Moses through a burning bush on Mount Sinai, coming down to meet him and speak directly to him.

The conversation terrified Moses. God called him by name, spoke his language, was fully aware of his past ancestors and his present siblings, and informed Moses that He had created him and was calling him to go back as His ambassador to rescue God's people from Egypt. God also knew and referenced details of Moses' future (Exod. 3:12).

It was crystal clear God already knew everything about Moses, but Moses didn't know much about God or grasp his own identity and purpose.

Insecure and confused, Moses said, "Who am I that I should go to Pharaoh and that I should bring the Israelites out of Egypt?" (v. 11). He saw himself merely as an immigrant shepherd, ineloquent speaker, and unqualified leader. After repeatedly questioning God's calling, Moses kept making excuses and asking Him to send someone else instead.

But God knew exactly what He was doing and also every intimate detail about Moses' true identity, abilities, and human limitations. God also knew He would powerfully enable Moses to accomplish this world-changing task that would miraculously humiliate all the gods of Egypt, mightily rescue an entire nation from slavery, and establish a covenant people whose descendants would usher in the incarnate Christ and bring salvation to the world.

From an earthly perspective, Moses was an eighty-year-old migrant worker who'd settled into his routine for the rest of his life. His earthly track record and identity appeared cowardly, convoluted, and checkered. His thoughts about himself were not really positive or confident. His feelings and desires persuaded him completely against this whole idea. And if Moses had asked his wife, brother, or anyone in Egypt what they thought about this mission or his qualifications, they would probably have laughed at him as someone completely out of his mind.

But the great "I AM" (Exod. 3:14) speaking powerfully to him through the fire had systematically and sovereignly been developing Moses his entire life to be the ideal man for this job. He was the right person to travel the same road back to the country where he was born and raised, armed with a shepherd's staff he knew so well, able to communicate with the Pharaoh in a language Moses understood, deliver his own Hebrew people from the slavery his family had lived under, and then shepherd more than two million people back across the desert to Mount Sinai, where Moses had already been working for forty years.

Who knew Moses' true identity? Moses or God?

Now let's shift gears and apply this story to you. Who knows your true identity? You or God? If God were to speak to you and tell you He knows your name, has been watching you all your life, and is asking you to trust Him regarding what He says about you and what He's calling you to do, would you trust Him or want to run away?

What are you honestly trusting right now as the most reliable source to help you understand your life? Yourself? Your family? Your experiences from the past? Or the God of the universe, who made you in His image, who cannot lie, who is giving you every next breath, and who holds your eternity in the palm of His hand?

You should consider a few things about His qualifications.

*1. God has perfect knowledge of you,* including every single detail of your entire life. God's Word reveals that He has searched you completely and knows you intimately (Ps. 139:1–6). He is more accurately conscious of where you are than anyone on the earth, including the location tracking software on the phone in your pocket. God can hear your heart beating, see what your eyes are seeing, and knows when you sit down and stand up, when you take a step or take a breath.

He is well acquainted with every tear you've cried (Ps. 56:8) and why you cried them. He could tell you the exact number of hairs on your head, even if you are bald (Matt. 10:30). Especially if you are bald. He has no problem counting to zero—or to infinity for that matter (Ps. 90:2).

But even more incredible is the fact that God knows your thoughts before you think them and your words before you speak them. He is well versed on your total past, your schedule today, and all your tomorrows. He knows every question, loving thought, and secret sin rooted in your heart (Jer. 17:10). God knows the names of all your ancestors, is aware of your greatest hopes and darkest fears, and can tell you where you will be in a thousand years (2 Pet. 3:8). He's heard every word, seen every text and internet post you've created, and remains the reigning, resident expert on all things you-related (Ps. 33:15).

Who do you really believe understands you the best in all the universe? Your mother? Your brother? Your lover?

No, God alone. Hands down. No one else is even close.

*2. God has complete ownership of you.* He doesn't just know you; He owns you. First, He created you (Ps. 100:3). Second, He redeemed and purchased you through Christ (Isa. 43:1; 1 Cor. 6:19–20). From a satellite view, God owns it all anyway. "The earth is the LORD's, and all it contains, the world, and those who dwell in it" (Ps. 24:1 NASB). In a generation that claims "*my* body," "*my* rights," and "*my* choice," anytime they want to justify something, God reminds us that these conclusions are based upon a complete lie about our own ownership.

To be honest, those times when the two of us have argued with God in our minds, wrestling with something we think He might want us to do or not do, we've each had moments when we've heard His voice in our hearts reminding us, "I own you." And this one phrase, coming to us individually, has calmed us down and helped us trust Him. As Owner of our lives, God has the right to claim us, name us, lead us, and tell us who He wants us to be.

*3. God has ultimate authority over you.* No one has a higher authority than God. "The LORD has established his throne in heaven, and his kingdom rules over all" (Ps. 103:19). Speaking of Christ, God the Father "subjected everything under his feet and appointed him as head over everything" (Eph. 1:22). Or as Jesus said Himself, "All authority has been given to me in heaven and on earth" (Matt. 28:18). And the one who has the most authority gets to make the final call.

To illustrate this, let me (Alex) share a personal illustration:

After my ninth-grade daughter Joy tried out for high school basketball, her coach informed her that she would be in the starting varsity lineup for the season. She couldn't believe it and was thrilled. As a freshman, she expected to begin each game on the bench.

But then she came to me concerned. What would the older girls think about this? What would parents in the stands say when their daughter might not play as much as this newbie ninth grader?

Fortunately in Joy's case, everyone was happy for her and believed in what she brought to the team. But what if they didn't? What if the older girls told her she didn't belong on the starting five? What if other parents had complained, called the school, and written angry letters of concern? Or what if Joy herself didn't feel like a starter or deserving to be one? None of that really mattered.

Because the only thing that counted is what the one with the authority over the team had decided. The coach. It was his call. He was responsible for deciding Joy's and every other girl's position on his team. And no matter what other people wanted or said—people who had no authority—it wasn't going to change things.

Likewise, as we've said before, the Creator gets to define His creation. He has the authority to define YOU. But it doesn't mean there won't be lots of other loud, clamoring, non-authoritative voices trying to insert themselves into the conversation and act like they get to help God make the call.

The culture will seek to define you. Other people in your life—at home, at work, at church, in your community—will try to weigh in on who you are. Even an official intelligence test, or an emotional quotient quiz, or a certified psychological test may seem as though some expert has the right to define you.

*Not so, Moses.*

Only your God, the One who made you—and only Christ, the One who redeemed you—has the perfect knowledge, full ownership, and absolute authority to define who you are and what He's created you to become. You are who He says you are. Period. And the sooner you can discover that and find out what He says, the better off you will be.

## THE KEY TO THE IDENTITY OF EVERYTHING

Two of the most important questions in life that Moses was trying to answer, and which we need to answer clearly as well, are, "Who is God?" and "Who am I?" What we may not realize, however, is that the answers to both of these questions are intimately connected together. An apple and the apple tree it came from can reveal a lot about one another. All of creation ultimately finds its true meaning and identity in God, its Creator.

Since everything God says and does flows out of who He is, and since He is true to Himself and functions with perfect integrity, He will not say or do anything contrary to His nature. Hence, the identity of every individual thing He created is permanently linked to the nature and attributes of God Himself.

> For since the creation of the world His invisible attributes, His eternal power and divine nature, have been clearly seen, being understood through what has been made. (Rom. 1:20 NASB)

The word *creation* in this verse is an identity word presupposing our Creator. But this is also true of everything else God says we are. Being created, sustained, known, loved, or forgiven also requires a Creator, Sustainer, Knower, Lover, and Forgiver.

Our identity and *being* can only be understood within His.

"In him we live and move and have our being" (Acts 17:28).

Ironically, even evil and sin find their identity only in how they relate to the nature of God. Sin is described as being *un*godliness or *un*righteousness (Rom. 1:18)—in other words, *unlike* who God is. Things that are *un*holy and *un*loving are the opposite of God's specific attributes of holiness and love.

Just as darkness is the absence of light, and cold is the absence of heat, so also lying is the absence of truth (Rom. 1:25), hatred is the absence of love, and death is the absence of life (1 John 3:13–16). So if you want to better understand evil, then you don't study evil; you study God. What is hidden in the darkness is revealed by turning on the light, not by dwelling in darkness.

Knowledge, understanding, and wisdom flow out of God—the ability to discern between right and wrong, between truth and error, between what is godly and what is sinful. To dwell on sin and darkness is to *lose* discernment about what is and isn't wrong in your life and in this world. But the same thing that's true about how we better understand our sin is also true of how we understand everything else in creation. Knowing God—who He is—turns on the light for us to see and understand more about all of life. He is the Light of the world! So the greater the knowledge a person has of God's character and attributes, the greater their foundational knowledge and understanding will be of the rest of the world He's created and the wisdom for knowing how to live rightly as a result.

It's what helped some of history's greatest scientists and inventors better understand how the world is designed and put together. Galileo (the telescope); Robert Boyle (chemistry, the scientific method); Sir Isaac Newton (calculus, gravity); Johannes Gutenberg (the printing press); George Washington Carver (cooking oil, printer's ink); and Guglielmo Marconi (the radio) all had a deep respect for, faith in, and growing knowledge of God.

"The fear of the LORD is the beginning of knowledge" (Prov. 1:7). It is also "the beginning of wisdom, and the knowledge of the Holy One is understanding" (Prov. 9:10). "For the LORD gives wisdom; from his mouth come knowledge and understanding" (Prov. 2:6). "No wisdom, no understanding, and no counsel will prevail against the LORD" (Prov. 21:30). "In [Christ] are hidden all the treasures of wisdom and knowledge" (Col. 2:3).

If you were to ask God to help you understand and grasp who you truly are, He would not only honor that request, but part of His answer would be an invitation for you to focus on Him and get to know Him much better.

With this in mind, let's go back to the moment when Moses asked God His name.

God responded: "I AM WHO I AM" (Exod. 3:14)—based on the root words for "to be" or "to exist." Initially, to our ears, "I AM WHO I AM" sounds like a non-answer, or something so obvious as to not be helpful. But if you keep thinking deeply on what God said about who He is and the implications of it, its meaning explodes with epic ramifications.

You might be able to come up with more, but here are fifteen attributes of God that come from this single revelation . . . as a starter list.

## "I AM WHO I AM"

| Implications | God is . . . | In the Word |
|---|---|---|
| He is, not "He isn't" | Existent | Heb. 11:6 |
| He exists alone ("I") and whole ("Am") | One | Deut. 4:4 |
| He exists as He currently is | Present | Ps. 46:1 |
| He exists by His own ability | Powerful | Rev. 19:1 |
| He is not unlike Himself | Pure | Ps. 18:26 |
| He is as He is, not anything false | True | 1 John 5:20 |
| He is revealing what is unseen | Light | John 1:9 |
| He exists ever-presently and alive | Life | John 1:4 |
| He exists as Himself consistently | Faithful | 1 John 1:9 |
| He is separate from everything else | Transcendent | John 1:3 |
| He is as He is without changing | Eternal | Rev. 4:8 |
| He is eternal and transcendent | Uncreated | Ps. 90:2 |
| He is communicating coherently | Intelligent | Col. 2:3 |
| He is communicating in a known way | Knowable | John 17:3 |
| He is revealing all this about Himself | Intimate | John 17:3 |

Your identity will become the clearest to you, most reflective of reality and clarifying in terms of your future, as you grow in your understanding of God. And since Jesus is the fullness of God expressed in human, bodily form (Col. 2:9; Heb.1:3), your growing knowledge of Christ will also give you a growing knowledge of God, and then of yourself. With this in mind, drink deeply from this verse: "For God who said, 'Let light shine out of darkness,' has shone in our hearts to give the light of the knowledge of God's glory in the face of Jesus Christ" (2 Cor. 4:6). To know Him is to also know you.

*Heavenly Father, I thank You that You are a God who knows us intimately and makes Yourself known. Help me to comprehend and honor Your ownership and authority over my life. I pray that You would shine the light of Your truth and the knowledge of You into my heart, through Your Spirit and through Your Word, so that I may know You better, love You more, discover who I am, and align my life with who You are. I pray this in Jesus' name, amen.*

**TAKE IT DEEPER BY STUDYING**
Exodus 3:1–15 • Psalm 89:11–18 • Romans 14:8–9

*We know that the Son of God has come and has given us understanding. (1 John 5:20)*

# PART I

# INTENTIONALITY
*How Your Story Begins*

CHAPTER 4

# You Are Created with Purpose: Uniquely Designed

*I will give thanks to You, for I am fearfully
and wonderfully made; wonderful are Your works,
and my soul knows it very well. (Ps. 139:14 NASB)*

Not only did God personally create you; He made you amazingly unique.

Of the intercontinental billions of people breathing right now, no known duplicates exist . . . or have *ever* existed. That's mind-blowing if you think about it. You are a never-before-seen, one-of-a-kind, original masterpiece.

Your personalized fingers, for instance, are leaving your signature prints on this book. Your beautifully detailed iris patterns have been entrusted to you alone; the design in your right eye reading this sentence is even different from your left. Your teeth are also a bit unique to you. Your taste buds, sweetly distinct. Your gait walks alone and your voice sings a solo tone. Your heart beats a signature rhythm and your face has a special recognition. Even identical twins are distinct in the details.

Coiled within your cells are *billions* of miles of DNA, programmed and coded to you. Every biometric marker is like a written signature, focusing the spotlight of the universe back on how special you really are.

All of this is by God's intention, prerogative, and completely unlimited ability. He does it because He can. He does it because—why wouldn't He?

Expecting God to make two people exactly the same would be like asking Mozart to rewrite the same symphony, line for line, note for note. Why would he do that? That work has already been done. Only something refreshingly new will do. Your distinctive design, your wonderful uniqueness, your *irreplaceability*, makes you incredibly valuable . . . a walking miracle.

Because think about it. On the dawn of your conception, you beat the odds among 300 million rivals, racing to become you. And you won. Then billions of miracles at the cellular level successfully occurred over months, enabling you to develop and stay alive. In your mother's womb, God was interweaving and interconnecting a wide variety of complex systems so that they could not only function properly and communicate to your brain quickly but ultimately unite into the tapestry of your life. That's why human conception and birth has been called life's greatest miracle.

Then, for you to take your first breath, your mental headquarters, pulsing heart, expanding lungs, and newly formed muscles needed to unite and harmonize like a symphony orchestra. You are not an accident.

You are the opposite of an accident.

At this moment, in fact, in order for you to read *these very letters*, your body is hard at work allowing your eyes to receive light, for your oxygenated brain to process them into a language you understand, and for your nutrient-rich neurons to rationalize abstract thoughts.

It's just vividly clear that you are brilliantly designed, magnificently complex, functionally wired, and holistically connected. To claim you're the result of mere time and chance is laughable and ludicrous. It's like believing that the most complex computer in the world could accidentally design itself, wire its own circuitry board by chance, plug itself in, haphazardly create a coherent digital language that enables it to communicate, then write all the code for its own operating system, and unintentionally survive and reproduce itself successfully for thousands of generations. *Not a chance.*

As the Bible emphatically says, we did not make ourselves (Ps. 100:3). A brilliantly creative, lovingly intentional, powerfully capable God designed and crafted each one of us (Ps. 139:13). That's why your identity is excellent and not a walking accident.

God is the One who made your heart to beat and your brain to think. He is the One who lovingly chose your race and your gender, connected your bones together, and networked every one of your organs as precious gifts to you. He chose your height, textured your hair, and timed your birth. He is the One who seasoned your face with expressions and your personality with your own palette of emotions.

So with all of this in mind, pause for a moment and ask yourself: How have you responded to God's design of you? Have you thanked Him? Have you trusted Him, or have you resisted Him?

Are you grateful for His choices, or are you angry about the way He made you? Have you embraced and appreciated His handiwork, or have you resented it? Think deeply about this. Is it not true that when someone pours their heart, mind, and effort into a gift that they want to give someone they love, they're hoping the person will joyfully receive it and genuinely appreciate it?

This is also God's desire from you. Look at this passage from Romans 1, some of which we presented in the previous chapter, and follow the progression as to what happens when people choose to be resistant and ungrateful for God's goodness in their lives.

Since the creation of the world His invisible attributes, His eternal power and divine nature, have been clearly seen, being understood through what has been made, so that they are without excuse. For even though they knew God, they did not honor Him as God or give thanks, but they became futile in their speculations, and their foolish heart was darkened. Professing to be wise, they became fools. (Rom. 1:20–22 NASB)

When people recognize God and appreciate His design, they grow wiser and more understanding in regard to His character and attributes. But when they reject Him and refuse to be grateful, their hearts become futile and darkened, prideful and foolish.

This is our arrogant human tendency—to see the worst and complain, to view ourselves as a victim and argue with our Creator, to judge Him instead of trust Him as the One giving us every breath. We tend to compare our weaknesses to someone else's strengths, our moments of pain to their moments of pleasure. Then we jump to false conclusions, thinking we're somehow inferior or less valuable than others, and that God is somehow less caring or concerned about us.

But let's be honest. Doesn't God have the right to do whatever He wants? And does He really owe any of us an explanation for any of His decisions? Since clay is not wiser than the potter (Isa. 29:16), we are actually quite unqualified to argue with our Maker. As Romans 9:20 says, "Who are you, a mere man, to talk back to God? Will what is formed say to the one who formed it, 'Why did you make me like this?'"

What about *your birth*? What if your parents were not planning on having a child when they had you? This could be anyone's story. But it really doesn't matter. Regardless of the situations and circumstances surrounding your birth, you are not an accident or insignificant. Even if you weren't man-planned, you were still God-planned—which is far greater. If you keep thinking God made a mistake when He made you, then you'll keep beating yourself down and have a hard time grasping your value and trusting Him in other important areas.

What about *handicaps*? We tend to view special needs as mistakes. But even in these situations, God's conclusions are kind. "This came about," Jesus said regarding a man born blind, "so that God's works might be displayed in him" (John 9:3). Moses was insecure because of a speech impediment and tried to use it as an excuse not to obey God or lead Israel out of slavery. But God asked Moses, "Who has made man's mouth? Or who makes him mute or deaf, or seeing or blind? Is it not I, the LORD? Now then go, and I, even I, will be with your mouth, and teach you what you are to say" (Exod. 4:11–12 NASB).

Would God intentionally make someone deaf or blind or mute? According to this passage, yes. He as Creator may willingly and wisely do this. As in the case of Mia's heart condition, we see now that those special needs are a special part of His special plan. God said He designed Moses' speaking handicap for a good purpose. And His plan obviously worked because Moses not only learned to rely on God rather than himself when he confronted Pharaoh, but he became the most humble man "on the face of the earth" (Num. 12:3). It set him up to be very close to God and mightily used by Him.

Do you have an imperfection or limitation? A learning disability? An abnormality? Could it make you more dependent on God? More humble? More compassionate, kind, and loving? Will you dare to thank and glorify God with it instead of pridefully misjudging His long-term intentions?

What about *your family*? Have you accepted the people He gave you as parents and siblings? Are you honoring God for the family He placed you inside?

This is a common struggle for many of us. We all have imperfect families. In Scripture, Cain resented his amazing brother so much that he killed him and suffered for it (Gen. 4:3–16). David's older brothers ignored, belittled, and devalued him. Still, God made him the victorious underdog in one of the greatest stories in history. We still talk about "David and Goliath" encounters today.

Many people grow up harboring a great deal of anger toward their family after having endured painful events beyond their control. Others decry being born to a single mother, or raised through a painful divorce, or brought up as an adoptive child, feeling passed over by their biological parents. Yes, all families have issues, and maybe yours seems to take imperfection to a new level of low. And maybe you've struggled with how a good God could have allowed all that's happened to you.

But God's Word has stated all along that we are broken people living in a broken world, and that God is interested in shining His light into our darkness, meeting us in our mess, then redeeming our situation in magnificent ways. He always sees the bigger picture and is a Master at bringing really good things out of really bad things.

Consider Joseph, whose brothers hated him and betrayed him (Gen. 37:23–28). Then he was falsely accused and thrown in prison. Tough cards to be dealt. But God met him there. And when Joseph was later promoted in Egypt, he was a humble and unselfish man who used his position to save millions of lives. He recognized God's good plan for allowing him to go through all the abuse and pain he endured. He later said to his brothers, "You planned evil against me; God planned it for good to bring about the present result—the survival of many people" (Gen. 50:20).

What about you? Feeling rejected and betrayed? Feeling imprisoned in your own family, in your own body, or in your marriage? It's time to invite God into your tough situation, be courageous enough to thank Him in the midst of it, and then choose to glorify Him as His light in a dark place.

---

Let's take this to the next level. Do you know why you were born the year you were born? Or in the country where you were born? God's Word says He predetermines *where* we will live and *when* we will live there. For a reason.

> From one man he has made every nationality to live over the whole earth and has determined their appointed times and the boundaries of where they live. He did this so that they might seek God, and perhaps they might reach out and find him, though he is not far from each one of us. (Acts 17:26–27)

Notice why He put us in a place at a specific time. To seek Him and find Him. Have you been seeking Him? Have you found Him yet? God uses His creation to reveal to us that He is alive and well and cares for us.

Think about this. God could easily have made you differently, positioned your life in the 1800s, and caused you to be born in another country. He could've made your skin another color, given you a different gender, your personality a different temperament, and your background a different family. But He didn't. Perfectly seeing the bigger picture, He didn't. He wanted to make you, *you*. Not as a curse but as a blessing. And not to bless just you alone but the world. His design for you is both excellent and purposeful. You can trust that He knows exactly what He is doing.

Let this truth sink into your heart!—because being assured of it can positively change you forever. But the choice is yours. You can spend the rest of your life stuck on first base, rejecting His design, or you can trust God and worship Him for all He has done for you, then move forward with confidence and assurance. This is exactly what David wrote about in Psalm 139. Remember he was the runt of the litter and the belittled brother. Read carefully the following prayer he prayed. Notice what he'd discovered about himself and also how he was responding to God as a result.

You made all the delicate, inner parts of my body and knit me together in my mother's womb. Thank you for making me so wonderfully complex! Your workmanship is marvelous—how well I know it.

You watched me as I was being formed in utter seclusion, as I was woven together in the dark of the womb. You saw me before I was born. Every day of my life was recorded in your book. Every moment was laid out before a single day had passed.

How precious are your thoughts about me, O God. They cannot be numbered! I can't even count them; they outnumber the grains of sand! (Ps. 139:13–18 NLT)

This is where we need to land. Not in a prideful place but a joyfully grateful place. God's Word says we are "wonderfully complex" and His design of us is "marvelous." His thoughts toward us are countless and "precious." Our lives and days are not random but planned.

Our hearts should bloom with trust and honor toward God instead of doubting Him and hating ourselves. We need to stop resisting and start rejoicing and thanking.

So without any egotistical pride, but rather with humble gratitude, would you be willing to end this chapter by lifting a prayer of thanks to your Creator? Would you choose to quit resisting His design of your life, and dare even to *thank Him* for whatever aspect of your body, your family, or your circumstances you've had the hardest time receiving? Would you pray that God meets you where you are, in your difficulty, in your pain, and redeems your past, your weaknesses, and your life for good, for the good of the world, and for His glory?

*Dear God, I believe that You created me. Thank You for making me unique and wonderfully complex. Forgive me for times when I've assumed the worst, when I've resisted You and Your design of my body and family. You see my life from beginning to end, and You understand the bigger picture. I choose today to trust You and thank You instead. Help me seek You and know You better and trust that Your plans are for my good and Your glory. Redeem my life and my future, and help me be a light in this world for You. In Jesus' name, amen.*

### TAKE IT DEEPER BY STUDYING
Psalm 95:6–7 • Isaiah 43:1–7 • John 1:1–4

*He is our God, and we are the people of his pasture,*
*the sheep under his care. (Ps. 95:7)*

# CHAPTER 5

# You Are Extremely Valuable: Made in God's Image

*Then God said, "Let us make man in our image,*
*according to our likeness." . . . So God created man in his own*
*image; he created him in the image of God. (Gen. 1:26–27)*

The wonder of your design is intricate, specialized, and fascinating. But the fact is, many aspects of your physical body and how it operates so brilliantly and efficiently could be also said of the masterful design of a hummingbird, mountain lion, or river beaver. Animals, too, have unique brains and bones and blood supplies, which God has orchestrated and given. The DNA code embedded in a pit bull is unique from every other pit bull. This does not take away from *your* incredible value, but it highlights the fingerprints of the same glorious God whose consistent character is reflected in all of His creation.

But something additionally colossal happened at creation that we need to note. God chose to do something expansive in human beings that flies to the heart of your identity. The Bible says that unlike the plants or animals, you have been made "in the image of God" (Gen. 1:27), recognized by the Latin phrase, *imago Dei* (ih-MAH-go DAY).

It's like finding out your motorcycle has been upgraded to a luxury jet. This blueprint advancement substantially increases your capabilities, relational potential, and eternal value. In Genesis 1, after God powerfully created light and sky, land and sea, plants and trees, and the sun, moon, and stars, He then shifted gears to make a teeming, world-class assortment of flying, swimming, and crawling animal life. After He declared them all to be "good" (Gen. 1:25), He paused for an important conversation within the Godhead before forming the crowning finale of His creation. God said:

> "Let Us make man in Our image, according to Our likeness; and let them rule over the fish of the sea and over the birds of the sky and over the cattle and over all the earth, and over every creeping thing that creeps on the earth." God created man in His own image, in the image of God He created him; male and female He created them. (Gen. 1:26–27 NASB)

So on the last day of Creation, God made the most advanced, intelligent, governing, and relational being of all on Earth. He made human beings in His image. And what an incredible honor for each of us to be made in God's image!

The Hebrew word for *image* here can mean "resemblance," like how a statue resembles the shape and form of a person or animal it was carved to look like (Rom. 1:23). But your status as someone made in the image of God goes far beyond physical resemblance.

The Hebrew word for *likeness* is also used in other passages to describe *looking* like (Ezek. 8:2), *sounding* like (Isa. 13:4), or *being* like something else (Ps. 58:4). So you are able, because of how God made you, not merely to *resemble* Him, but in some ways to *be* like Him. We know from the rest of Scripture that He fully intended for us to *reflect* His attributes and glory, *represent* Him with authority in this world, and *relate* to Him and others directly in an intelligent, intimate, glorifying way.

The full list of features included in the *imago Dei* is a mystery. Some interpret it to mean man's potential *physical* resemblance to God (Ezek. 1:26–28)—that we actually look like Him—while others claim it's more about similarities in mental aptitude, moral character, or relational capacity.

But let's not debate things here that are impossible to be sure about, or presume that we know God's complete thinking at Creation beyond what He's undeniably stated for us in His Word. We can rest assured, however, that being made "in God's image and likeness" means we are much more *like* Him than anything else on Earth, all lions in Judah and lilies of the valley included.

We could say that being made in God's image is either *inclusive of,* or at least *accompanied by,* multiple amazing things that are distinctively human, things that should each cause us to be filled with gratitude and praise toward God for His goodness in our lives.

The psalmist wrote:

What is man that you are mindful of him, and the son of man that you care for him? Yet you have made him a little lower than the heavenly beings and crowned him with glory and honor. You have given him dominion over the works of your hands; you have put all things under his feet. (Ps. 8:4–6 ESV)

So we certainly know this much: God thinks of us, cares about us, has made us *lower* than Himself and the angels (Heb. 2:5–9), but also *superior* and *over* the earth, plants, and animals. He also gave us ruling authority and dominion over the works of His hands (Ps. 8:6).

What else do we know, from what we've been told in Scripture, that may tell us how human beings are like God?

We know people, made in God's image, have been given . . .

*1. Rich value* (Gen. 9:6). Scripture communicates that even after the sinful fall of man, we still maintain the image of God (1 Cor. 11:7) and are "crowned with glory" (Heb. 2:9). That's why cursing people is said to be so wrong—because those people are "made in God's likeness" (James 3:9). God specifically says that murder is forbidden and worthy of capital punishment because the people killed have been made in His image.

"Whoever sheds human blood, by humans his blood will be shed, for God made humans in his image" (Gen. 9:6).

What would happen if we began viewing ourselves, our spouses, our families, and every person we meet, not as evolved animals or random accidents of nature, but in the way that God intended them: uniquely prized creations made in His image, worthy of love, respect, honor, and protection? This would solve countless problems and positively change our lives, our churches, and this world forever.

*2. Ruling capacity and dominion over the earth* (Ps. 8:4–6). Companies, churches, governments, and sports teams all try to find the strongest, wisest, most competent leaders to oversee and lead their organizations. After God created the earth and all the animals, He specifically created people with the capacities, abilities, and responsibilities to govern, steward, and rule over His creation.

Animals do not have this responsibility but are stuck in self-preservation mode without the. mental capacity to even have one coherent conversation about solving the world's problems. As humans, though, we're obviously capable of involving ourselves in understanding and managing things like electricity, nuclear energy, biochemistry, space travel, satellite technology, blood transfusions, and the internet. God has given us the ability to farm land, build cities, advantage technologies, stop disease, leverage resources, recycle waste, communicate globally, and solve international conflict. He wants us to take advantage of and fully enjoy the good resources He's provided (1 Tim. 6:17; Isa. 65:21), while also balancing them with a sense of stewardship and preservation of the world that He owns and has entrusted to us (Ps. 24:1). Adam, for example, was not to trash the garden but to oversee it, work it, organize it, enjoy it, and keep it (Gen. 2:15; Eccles. 2:24–25).

*3. Resemblance to the human form that Jesus took on.* Whether Adam and Eve looked like God or not, we do know that God the Father sent Jesus to the earth through Mary's womb, and that He took on human form as a man made in the image of God (Phil. 2:6–7). He did not show up on Earth as a bear, fly down as an angel, or swim in as an aquatic creature. Even when He was resurrected and appeared to people in a glorified body, He still retained a *human* body, walking, eating, and interacting as a man.

"Put your finger here and look at my hands," He said to doubting Thomas. "Reach out your hand and put it into my side" (John 20:27). The image of God in the resurrected body of Christ still looked like . . . you! At least more like you than an animal in the zoo or an angel with wings.

Jesus came to save sinners who were made in God's image, not animals. And He offered human blood on the cross as a worthy sacrifice for sin. It was "not by the blood of goats and calves, but by his own blood" that He entered the holy place, once for all, "having obtained eternal redemption" (Heb. 9:12). Wouldn't it be sad if we humans remained the ones condemned in our sins because Jesus had come in the form of a tiger, and His death could only redeem tigers, who have no knowledge of sin?

Thank God that He intercedes for us as a Man who can fully relate to us (Heb. 4:15). He could only bridge the gap between God and man as our Mediator if He was equal to both parties. *And He is.* "For there is one God and one mediator between God and humanity, the man Christ Jesus" (1 Tim. 2:5).

When John wrote down his revelation, he described the appearance of Jesus in heaven as being "like the Son of Man, dressed in a robe" (Rev. 1:13–14). He had feet, eyes, and hair like a man, and could be seen walking around. He spoke in a human voice, had hands, and had a face that shone "like the sun at full strength" (v. 16).

Was He stunning? Yes. The Scripture says John "fell at his feet like a dead man" (v. 17). It was more than he could absorb. But it wasn't the fear of a monster or an otherworldly beast. John was purely, without filter, seeing in the person of Jesus—who was still in the form of a man—God in flesh, representing the glory of God in human form.

*4. Relational depth for intimacy with God and others.* God said, "Let Us make man in Our image." The perfect unity within the Trinity is modeled here. Adam and Eve's uniqueness within their unified oneness is reflective of the oneness of God (Gen. 2:18, 24). It's clear that Eve was uniquely designed to be able to relate to and rule with Adam at a highly intelligent, emotionally deep, and spiritually intimate, God-honoring level. The qualities he needed in a helper obviously could not have been met by an animal, only by another human who was like himself.

Likewise, according to Ephesians 5:22–33, all men and women, made in the image of God, possess the capacity for representing the relationship of Christ (our spiritual Bridegroom) with His body and bride (the church). But this is only because we, more than anything else on Earth, are able to relate to, love, and rule with Jesus. He repeatedly prayed that we would be One, both with Him and with each other, even as He and the Father are One (John 17:21).

We have the ability to worship God, to love Him and one another, something that animals are incapable of doing. Dogs, cats, and monkeys may be intelligent, affectionate, and make enjoyable pets, but they are not made in the image of God. Nowhere in Scripture does God refer to Himself as their Father, or to them as His children. Jesus repeatedly referred to Himself as the "Son of *Man*." Animals will not stand at the judgment and be rewarded for their righteous deeds or condemned for their sins.

So the "trees of the field" may "clap their hands" (Isa. 55:12), but they have no mental idea they're doing it. The mysterious ways of an animal—like "the way of an eagle in the sky" (Prov. 30:19)—may be beautiful, but only someone saved by the grace of God and filled with His Spirit can worship God. Our calling to love Him with all we are, and to love our neighbor as ourselves, takes on new meaning in light of the fact that we were made in the image of a loving God, who Himself is love (1 John 4:16).

*5. Representative glory.* Many of God's awesome attributes are unique to Him alone, such as *omniscience*—His limitless knowledge and wisdom; *omnipresence*—His ability to be everywhere at once. Even so, He has chosen to place within you a number of traits that *are* similar to His and are glorifying to Him. It's why you're able to know and be known. To love and be loved. To experience intimacy with Him, to worship Him. To connect with Him and with others in real, genuine relationships.

Together these inborn components of your identity make you much more than just a unique, physical wonder.

He desires for His character and attributes as a relational and loving God to be present inside you—inside the uniqueness of who you are—so that He can make Himself known through your life and story in a way that's unlike how anyone else can do it. You have eternal value, based on this purpose alone.

This is why He's wired you to worship Him. It's why He's awakened your sensitivity toward others' needs. It's why He's given you the ability to think of people outside of yourself, so that you're able to reach out to them, meet them at their point of need, communicate God's truth to them, and show them His love. It's why He's tailored you for signature tasks, which He's "prepared ahead of time" for you to do (Eph. 2:10). It's why He's positioned you in a specific time and place, like He did with Esther, "for such a time as this" (Esther 4:14).

Being made in God's image is simply so much more than just a passing statement we recognize from reading Genesis.

So in seeking to personalize this—which we know is a big, outsized concept—we ask you to realize that you've been given an enormous treasure by being created in the image of God. It's an enormous trust, an enormous privilege, an enormous value and responsibility. He made you superior in rank to all other beings and natural creations on the earth, no matter how grand or majestic, no matter how adorable or appealing. He gave you, unlike the animals, a conscience, which Jesus shed human blood to make clean (Heb. 9:13–14). God created you to be a representation of Himself (2 Cor. 5:20), able to be seen and recognized by others, able to point them to the One who made them. Knowing Him, making Him known, and bringing Him glory is the reason you exist! (John 17:3–4).

Do not disregard both the treasure and opportunity of this gift. It is massive.

You are physically, emotionally, and experientially unique. *And* you are made in the image of God with all the things we've talked about here: rich value, ruling capacity, human resemblance to Jesus, relational depth, and representative glory to point people to God. You are a wonder of His power and love.

What do you think your Creator would want this truth to communicate to you on those days and in those moments when you feel worthless, unseen, and unimportant?

> *Dear God, I'm amazed at what You've chosen to invest in me. You didn't make me a plant or an animal, but a living soul made in Your image. Thank You for creating me with purpose and responsibility. Help me to truly know You, to sincerely worship You, and to intimately draw close to You. I bow before You today in awe and praise, asking You to take me further inside Your purposes for me than I've ever sought to go before. Do what You want to do through me, in Jesus' name, amen.*

**TAKE IT DEEPER BY STUDYING**
Genesis 1:25–31 • 1 Corinthians 15:47–49 • Colossians 1:15–17

*Just as we have borne the image of the man of dust, we will also bear the image of the man of heaven. (1 Cor. 15:49)*

# CHAPTER 6

## *Once upon a Design: The Parable of Fred*

*A person's own foolishness leads him astray,
yet his heart rages against the LORD. (Prov. 19:3)*

Once there was a young man named Fred, whose parents loved him very much and gave him a new car for his graduation. His dad instructed him that he needed to learn the road rules, read the car manual, and follow the law, but Fred assumed his dad was trying to be difficult, limit his freedom, and take away his fun, so Fred ignored him.

Fred didn't want to pay for gas, so he put cooking oil in the gas tank instead. Naturally, Fred's car wouldn't start. So he had to ride his bicycle to work for a week while it was being repaired. Fred got very angry with God for allowing his new car to stop working and for making him ride his bike in the heat of the day. *How could God truly be loving and allow this to happen to me?* he thought.

After Fred traded in his broken new car for a working used car, he ignored the irritating warning lights on the dashboard and never changed the oil. One day, Fred's car overheated, blew up, and the engine was permanently damaged. Fred got very, very angry with God for allowing his car to blow up and for now making him ride his little brother's bike to work for two months during the summer while he searched for a cheaper car.

Fred finally found an old used car that he could afford. It had broken headlights, a cracked windshield, and smelled like dog hair. But the taillights worked, so Fred decided to drive his car backwards using his rearview mirror to see. Everyone, including Fred, was extremely stressed out on the road as he swerved back and forth to work. They honked their horns to warn him, but Fred shouted out the window for them to leave him alone.

The next day, Fred caused a gigantic wreck. Many people were hurt, and Fred's car was featured on the news, lying upside down in a ditch. Fred got very, very, *very* angry with God for allowing him to get into a wreck and letting the police take away his license. He was also mad that God made him spend a week in the hospital, six months in jail, and permit Fred's boss to fire him for not showing up to work. *How could God be good and allow all these bad things to happen to him?* he thought.

The entire next year, Fred had to ride his little sister's bike around town while he worked at a lesser paying job. One day, Fred's dad came and told him that he would help him get another used car if Fred would agree to read the car manual, put only gas in the gas tank, not drive it without changing the oil, not drive it backwards, and follow the road laws.

Fred got very angry and told his dad to stop judging him and trying to control him. He said he needed more freedom, not more rules. So he packed up his belongings and hitchhiked to another city. With a prison record and no transportation, Fred ended up as a homeless man, begging on the streets, and got very, very, *very*, VERY angry with God for making him sit out in the heat, sometimes miss meals, and sleep in a cardboard box. *How could God be merciful and allow all this to happen to him?* he thought.

One morning, while eating pork rinds out of a trash dumpster, Fred found a car manual and decided to read it. That afternoon, Fred had a life-changing revelation. He realized for the first time how cars were designed to work. He was surprised to discover that the instructions showing him how to operate a car were not intended to hurt him or take away his fun but to help him be as safe and as free as possible. The book even had clear warnings about using the right kind of gas and regularly changing the oil.

Fred also discovered many wonderful features designed in cars, like seat belts, radios, and air conditioners. He had heard about these things but never understood how to operate them until now. As he finished reading the last page of the car manual, Fred began to cry. He realized in his heart that his father had loved him all along, and so did God. That night, Fred decided to go home, ask for his father's forgiveness, and then listen to him in the future.

One year later, Fred smiled as he turned on the air conditioner and radio in his car, fastened his seat belt, and drove safely to his job where he worked with his dad, the most successful car lot owner in the country, and also Fred's new best friend. *The End.*

*"I know the plans that I have for you," declares the* Lord, *"plans for welfare and not for calamity to give you a future and a hope." (Jer. 29:11 NASB)*

# CHAPTER 7

## *You Are Broken and Imperfect*

*Just as sin entered the world through one man,
and death through sin, in this way death spread
to all people, because all sinned. (Rom. 5:12)*

This might be the hardest chapter for you to get through. Be strong and hang on! It's a little like going to the doctor to hear the results of an unwanted blood test. But it's good in the long run to discover the truth so you can know exactly what you can and should do. Don't worry, it only gets better and better from here!

God not only masterfully designed our bodies and made us in His image, but He also designed how all of life works. He is the ultimate Architect. His Word shows us how to handle and honor Him with our responsibilities and relationships, our marriages and money, our love and sexuality, our families and freedoms, and many other key aspects of life.

His ways are much higher and better than ours. He built the blueprints and created the copyrights on life. We should trust Him! Then as we follow Him, we'll discover that by honoring His nature, His character, and His design, we'll consistently see things function in a healthier, wiser, less stressful, and more fruitful way.

His ways lead to a happier home. A healthier family. More fulfilling relationships. A healthier body. More meaningful work. A more positive impact on the world. Each different type of instruction that God gives us leads to a desirable reward. Consider Psalm 19:7–11 and the benefits of following God's Word:

> The law of the LORD is perfect, restoring the soul; the testimony of the LORD is sure, making wise the simple. The precepts of the LORD are right, rejoicing the heart; the commandment of the LORD is pure, enlightening the eyes. The fear of the LORD is clean, enduring forever; the judgments of the LORD are true; they are righteous altogether. They are more desirable than gold, yes, than much fine gold; sweeter also than honey and the drippings of the honeycomb. Moreover, by them Your servant is warned; in keeping them there is great reward. (NASB)

As demonstrated in the story of Fred, when people ignore God's laws and design, then their lives, relationships, and reputation, as well as their physical, mental, and emotional health eventually end up in a ditch. Though God created us with care and made us in His image, He has known all along about a problem and tendency we all have. We want to go our own way.

The Bible calls it sin—things that fall short of our purpose to reflect and glorify Him. It's actually the opposite of loving God and honoring Him. Sin is fun for a little while, but then it ultimately leads to death (Rom. 6:23).

It's also the greatest impediment to enjoying all of God's blessings and walking closely with Him, and is the cause of so many unnecessary problems and painful heartaches that poison our lives. This includes the sin in our own hearts, the sin in others' hearts, the sin in this world—the sin we apparently want more than we want God's pleasure and blessings.

We simply tend to think we know better than Him, and so we want our way instead. We feel as though we can ignore His Word and create our own versions of how our lives should go. Sometimes we actually believe we *need* to sin in order to be happy, that we're missing out on real living if we confine ourselves to living the way our own Creator has lovingly designed us to operate. He wants us to live in truth and sincerity, love and unselfishness, honor and humility, purity in heart and mind, and we don't always want that.

It's not just you; it's all of us. Everyone in the world is imperfect and broken by sin. From God's omniscient perspective, "There is no one righteous, not even one. There is no one who understands; there is no one who seeks God" (Rom. 3:10–11). "For all have sinned and fall short of the glory of God" (Rom. 3:23). All of us. None of us is immune from this dark and twisted disease of the heart.

And to be clear, according to Scripture, we are born this way. There's nothing we could've done to avoid starting off in this situation. David said, "Indeed, I was guilty when I was born; I was sinful when my mother conceived me" (Ps. 51:5). We inherited this sin as the biological children of a sinful family tree. Paul explained it this way: "By the one man's trespass [the sin of Adam], death reigned through that one man" (Rom. 5:17). We didn't come into life a clean slate, always wanting to do what's right and to walk in selfless love and truth. We came already bent toward selfishness and deceit. Preconditioned to resist and rebel. Pridefully thinking we know better and are more important than others. "Dead" in our "trespasses and sins" (Eph. 2:1).

Sin is a worldwide, universal problem. Every person is *born* this way.

God's Word says we've been born into a world that is morally and spiritually broken. All we need to do is watch the news to know it's absolutely true. You don't see God's attributes pouring across your screens, filled with love, unity, honesty, purity, humility, and integrity. You see the opposite in every layer and corner of society.

Ungodliness. Unrighteousness. Unkindness.

Untruthfulness. Unfaithfulness. Ungratefulness.

Please don't confuse this with the truth of your good design. What God did with you in your mother's womb is beautiful and wonderful. You are not a mistake or an accident. God wired your physical body in love, with intention, with forethought. But the way you began, the starter ingredients that your mom and dad included, were not only physical

DNA but their spiritual DNA as well. People are morally broken by inherent sin which comes standard on every human model.

So do not feel singled out by this. God's Word is simply telling us the God's honest truth. We are sinners at heart, by nature. Our lives are naturally, spiritually disconnected from God. Not mindful of Him. Not following Him. Not all that aware of Him.

That's why as children we didn't need to be taught and lectured on how to lie or whine or steal or judge or rebel. All of these things, and many others like them, came quite naturally to us. The apostle Paul wrote, "I am of the flesh, sold as a slave to sin. For I do not understand what I am doing, because I do not practice what I want to do, but I do what I hate" (Rom. 7:14–15). Can you relate to his words?

Welcome to the harsh reality of our humanity.

Have you noticed that you don't know any perfect people at all? Anytime you meet new people, they can look very impressive and seem to have it all together . . . until you actually get to know them and see the brokenness. Hidden issues. Selfishness. Self-centeredness. Self-absorption. Woundedness. Anger. Pride. This includes everybody:

• *Your parents*, as wonderful as they may be, are still sinners. And when their individual issues leak over into failing you, you can feel the pain of it.

• *Your spouse* has surely been a disappointment to you sometimes. (Your spouse would say the same thing about you, by the way.) They can be uncaring, unsupportive, unavailable, unreliable, insensitive, and overbearing in their attitudes, words, and actions. They obviously need your ongoing patience and love with these errors, just as you need theirs. But the point is, as much as you love them, your spouse is also a sinner.

• *All your friends*, all your coworkers, all your neighbors, even the strangers you come across in life—have you noticed they're all sinners? Just like you're a sinner? And while you'll surely experience many blessings from the encounters you share together, every one of these people, same as you, is broken by this common disease of the heart. They will fail you in various ways. We never need to be shocked or derailed by this.

The Bible is painfully clear on this subject: "The heart is more deceitful than anything else, and incurable—who can understand it?" (Jer. 17:9). "We are all like an unclean thing, and all our righteousnesses are like filthy rags" (Isa. 64:6 NKJV). "If we say, 'We have no sin,' we are deceiving ourselves, and the truth is not in us" (1 John 1:8). Or as Nehemiah said to the Lord in his monumental Old Testament prayer, "You are righteous concerning all that has happened to us, because you have acted faithfully, while we have acted wickedly" (Neh. 9:33).

Sin is historically consistent and personally pervasive. It clouds and darkens. It burdens us and beats us down. It enslaves us to ruthless things that we feel desperate to overcome yet frustratingly incapable of conquering.

But the world's *general* sin translates into each of our lives as *specific* sin. While the root is the same for all of us, the individual fruit grows up and can look unique.

Everyone deals with the main trunk lines of sin—"the lust of the flesh, the lust of the eyes, and the pride of life" (1 John 2:16 NKJV). But where one person's "lust" may lead them toward adultery or pornography, another person's lust may lead them toward financial greed or various forms of cheating or stealing. One person's "pride" may lead them toward superiority, self-righteousness, and being overly judgmental, while another person's pride may lead them toward feelings of self-absorbed inferiority, maybe as jealousy or gossip, thinking they need to pull others down in order to get ahead. But the stench of it all is flowing from the same exhaust pipe.

That's why we don't need to judge people just because they sin differently than we do. Romans 2 admonishes us for condemning others when we're actually guilty of the same things ourselves. We think we're not. But the root cause is the same, even if it may look differently on the outside.

Same catalog; different package. Same contents; different wrapping. Jesus said it this way:

"For from within, out of people's hearts, come evil thoughts, sexual immoralities, thefts, murders, adulteries, greed, evil actions, deceit, self-indulgence, envy, slander, pride, and foolishness. All these things come from within and defile a person." (Mark 7:21–23)

That's a pretty long list He identified. Reading through it, perhaps you spot the one that comes to mind when you think of your greatest battle. You may also, because of the human tendency to compare and categorize, give each of them a grade, and rank them on your own artificial scale. That's how we become more tolerant of our own issues and less tolerant of others.

But this, too, is our "pride of life" at work in our hearts. Because it's *all* actually bad and un-God-like. We've *all* broken God's law and stand guilty before Him. No one is clean and flawless compared to God. We all have enough grounds for a guilty verdict. Even if someone could keep "the entire law," James said, but only fail to be obedient "at one point," they are still guilty before God. "For he who said, 'Do not commit adultery,' also said, 'Do not murder.' So if you do not commit adultery, but you murder, you are a lawbreaker" (James 2:11).

So our personal sin, even when sugarcoated and renamed and dressed up a bit, is still sin. It's still a rejection of God's character and control, and His Word says it disqualifies us from being welcomed into His holy presence. Sin puts each of us on a collision course with God's judgment. "Your iniquities are separating you from your God," the Bible says, "and your sins have hidden his face from you" (Isa. 59:2).

Sin kills. We see it kill trust, intimacy, joy, hearts, marriages, and families. It also brings death to businesses, governments, and even nations (Prov. 14:34). Therefore, as the prophet Isaiah lamented:

The earth mourns and withers; the world wastes away and withers; the exalted people of the earth waste away. The earth is polluted by its inhabitants, for they have transgressed teachings, overstepped decrees, and broken the permanent covenant.

Therefore a curse has consumed the earth, and its inhabitants have become guilty. (Isa. 24:4–6)

We can blame our sin on our family background, the tragic and painful experiences of our past, the injustices in the world, or our presumption that God has not been good to us. We can justify any sin in our lives. But ultimately, we must take responsibility for what we—made in the image of God—have done with the intelligence, freedoms, resources, and choices we've been given. When we take the steering wheel and drive our lives the way we want, we often end up in perpetual and habitual sin. It can make us feel lost.

Do you sometimes feel like you'd do anything to get out of this pattern of sin? Out from under all this guilt and shame? To be forgiven and free?

*You can!* God is not worried about the darkness of your situation, as if it's too much for Him to handle or know what to do with. He is fully aware of what's going on and knows exactly how to reach out and help each one of us individually. We'll soon be discussing how we can invite Him to meet us right where we are and get us out of any ditch we've found ourselves in.

Because though we honestly deserve His wrath, He invites us to turn to Him for mercy. To come humbly by faith. He can powerfully turn our guilt into forgiveness, our emptiness into hope, our restlessness into peace, and bring mercy and healing to every wounded corner in our weary hearts. He is not asleep or uncaring.

He has a brilliant master plan in place and has already dealt radically and mercifully with our sin situation through Jesus. He is always ready to offer us real, lasting solutions. As Jesus said:

"Come to me, all of you who are weary and burdened, and I will give you rest. Take up my yoke and learn from me, because I am lowly and humble in heart, and you will find rest for your souls. For my yoke is easy and my burden is light." (Matt. 11:28–30)

This is a beautiful, loving, and powerful invitation. We just need to humble ourselves and be honest with Him about where we are and reach out to Him in faith.

Later, we'll explore how your unique places of brokenness are actually destined to demonstrate the beauty and grace of God's forgiveness and power in an amazing way, and how they can become part of your own unique mission in this world. Stay tuned!

---

*Lord, I'm humbled today, thinking about the extent of my sin. It is so wide and so deep. I despair to look on it. And yet You, Lord—who can see the true color of its wickedness through a much clearer eye than mine—continue to give life and breath to me, countless kindnesses I don't deserve. I should receive only Your wrath, not Your mercy. Bring me to the end of myself until I'm looking only to You and nowhere else for my satisfaction. In Jesus' name, amen.*

---

**TAKE IT DEEPER BY STUDYING**
Jeremiah 2:21–28 • Romans 3:10–18 • Romans 6:16–18

---

*For the wages of sin is death, but the gift of God is eternal life in Christ Jesus our Lord. (Rom. 6:23)*

To help prepare for the next chapter, we strongly encourage you to take the Heart Check on the following pages.

# HEART CHECK

Human tendency is to justify ourselves and look down on others but avoid self-examination. We dare you to work through the following Heart Check and be honest with yourself and God about where you truly are. This is not someone accusing you of anything. And you don't have to share your answers with anyone. It's just you being willing to let God's standards shine on your life and your conscience and be honest about the current state of your heart. Ask yourself the simple questions below, based upon the Ten Commandments (Exod. 20:3–17 NASB).

**COMMANDMENT #1: "You shall have no other gods before Me."**
**Questions:** Is there anything that God would say I'm putting before Him right now? Are there others in my life and heart who are a greater priority than Him? Am I consistently choosing other things over Him? Do I honor Him in my schedule? Do I argue with God and resist His Word? Does He have full control over my life? Do I love Him and quickly obey Him, or ignore Him and turn away?

**COMMANDMENT #2: "You shall not make for yourself an idol. . . . You shall not worship them or serve them."**
**Questions:** Do I have any idols? Are there worldly things I love more than I love God? Do I love money or my pleasures more than Him? Do I have any addictions in my life? What is consuming my money, thoughts, time, and heart? Am I idolizing certain people and orbiting my life around my obsession with them?

**COMMANDMENT #3: "You shall not take the name of the Lord your God in vain."**
**Questions:** Do I honor God with my mouth? Do I thank Him and praise Him in my circumstances, or do I grumble and complain? Do I have a foul mouth? Do I use God's name as a curse word? Am I allowing filthy things to come out of my mouth, rather than gratefulness, encouragement, and respect?

## COMMANDMENT #4: "Remember the sabbath day, to keep it holy."

**Questions:** Am I a workaholic? Am I a slave to my work, or do I honor God with a day of worship and rest every week? Is God the priority of my week, or is something else? Do I make church a priority for my family and me each week, or do I make excuses not to go?

## COMMANDMENT #5: "Honor your father and your mother."

**Questions:** Do I honor the parents that God gave me by how I listen to them, speak to them, and talk about them to others? Is their reputation safe on my lips? Am I making sure they're being taken care of as they age? Am I treating them the same way I would want to be treated if I were in their shoes?

## COMMANDMENT #6: "You shall not murder."

**Questions:** Do I demonstrate an honor and value for all human life? Is there anyone I wish I could kill? Is there anyone I hate? Do I show love and respect for my friends only, or also for my enemies? Is there anyone against whom I hold a grudge, bitterness, anger, or jealousy?

## COMMANDMENT #7: "You shall not commit adultery."

**Questions:** Do I walk in sexual purity, or have I been embracing immorality? Am I pure in my thoughts, or am I filled with lust and perversion in my thinking? Am I looking at pornography or flirting with sexual sin? Am I committing any sexual sin outside of God's design for marriage? Am I honoring my marriage vows?

## COMMANDMENT #8: "You shall not steal."

**Questions:** Have I been stealing from anyone in any way? Have I stolen intellectual property through illegal downloads and piracy? Am I lazy at work and not doing a day's work for a day's wage? Am I slow to pay my debts? Do I have unreturned items? Do I have unpaid taxes?

**COMMANDMENT #9: "You shall not bear false witness against your neighbor."**
**Questions:** Have I been lying to others in any way? Do I exaggerate when I report the facts? Am I completely trustworthy? Have I broken any of my vows and promises? Do I manipulate or deceive others in any way? Am I a gossip? Are the reputations of others safe on my lips? Do I share confidential information given in trust?

**COMMANDMENT #10: "You shall not covet . . . anything that belongs to your neighbor."**
**Questions:** Am I content and grateful for what God has provided, or am I always wanting more? Do I secretly covet and long for someone else's job or possessions? Someone's spouse? Or house? Do I long to get rich? Is there anyone I'm really envious of and jealous of? Is there something I'm coveting in my heart?

CHAPTER 8

# You Are Sought by God: Lost and Found

*"The Son of Man has come to seek and to save
that which was lost." (Luke 19:10 NASB)*

Even in just the few chapters we've spent together so far, we've covered a lot of significant ground. These are huge, epic questions and statements we've been discussing about your heart, life, and identity. Universal in scope. And not only do they literally apply to everyone, they are *foundational* to everyone. There's nothing incidental here, truths like . . .

- Why your identity matters. In everything.
- Why the Creator alone is authorized to define His creation.
- How you've been made *exactly, uniquely* the way you are.

Then, of course, the most sobering reality of all: the indwelling evidence of sin, present in every human heart. Different only by detail and degree, but still with daily and eternal consequence. It is the dead end of all dead ends.

But God is not afraid of our sin. His life is stronger than our death. His love is bigger than our unloveliness. His grace is bigger than our spiritual debt. He knows how to step in and provide a way—a perfect way—the only way we ever need if we're willing to humble ourselves, trust Him, and receive it.

The question is, are you certain already of where your relationship stands with God?

Please don't rush through this chapter without taking time to contemplate (or to recognize again) the persistent, impassioned love of God for every person He's made . . . His seeking love. God hasn't given up on us.

The proof of it is found in one of the most beloved, epic, life-changing verses in the Bible. It summarizes so much of the depth of all sixty-six books in one short sentence. And it reminds us of what God has done in light of our fractured spiritual condition.

"For God so loved the world, that He gave His only begotten Son, that whoever believes in Him shall not perish, but have eternal life." (John 3:16 NASB)

Have you understood this verse in the past? If so, how have you honestly responded to it? And how are you responding to it today? What if you knew your life and identity actually depends upon it?

We've seen how God uniquely created you as a prized and treasured human being. This is *one* expression of His devotion and kindness toward you. But there's much more to the story of your life than just your life itself. To clarify tons of confusion that people tend to have about themselves and God, Jesus taught a parable to summarize our human spiritual condition and God's heart for us. He summarized one epic story, told in three acts.

---

## Act One: The Lost Sheep

A certain man owned a flock of a hundred sheep, which he lovingly cared and provided for. But one of them, as sheep tend to do, wandered off from the main herd. Nowhere to be found. Still, it was only one sheep. The man still had ninety-nine others that had stayed where they belonged. What would you expect the shepherd's next move to be, if he's a really good shepherd?

## Act Two: The Lost Coin

A woman was the proud owner of ten silver coins, highly valuable. She kept them close, protected them, and always knew their where-abouts. But one night, when checking the place where she kept her trea-sure, the woman noticed that one of the coins was missing. What would she do—what would she *not* do and overturn—in order to get it quickly back in her possession?

## Act Three: The Lost Son

A father had two sons, one of whom brazenly declared—long before he was responsible and ready for independence—that he wanted to get his father's inheritance early, abandon his faith and family, and leave home. So he struck out on his own, flush with a full suitcase and a full wallet he'd done nothing to earn. Then after diving into debauchery and squandering his father's investment on prostitutes, drunken parties, and who knows what else, he soon collapsed under the weight of his stupid, selfish, and sinful choices. What do you think the father would do with a child who said he wanted his distance?

You've probably read or heard about these parables of Jesus, in their much longer forms from Luke 15. They've been used for years to bless all kinds of people in a wide variety of situations. But they speak so pro-foundly as well about the vital importance of identity.

*Your* identity. *Our* identity. Most importantly, *God's* identity . . . how the One who created us understands, far better than we do, just how far away we really are, because of the condition of our hearts. And He knows what can truly become of us if He never intervened and our identity were never to be changed from sinner to forgiven. From lost to found.

So notice what Jesus is saying about us and about God. Consider what's true about the identity of all three of these—the lost sheep, the lost coin, and the lost son.

*All three had an owner,* just as we have an Owner. As we've previously discussed, the One who made us, owns us. "You are not your own" (1 Cor. 6:20). None of us would be here if not for what God has done to put us on this earth.

*All three lost items were highly treasured,* as we are "remarkably and wondrously made" (Ps. 139:14). Each of us is extremely valuable to Him, even with the tarnish of sin on our hearts. Jesus, in crafting these parables, made sure each lost article was something His audience would instantly recognize as being of tremendous value. They weren't the first-century equivalents of a hamster, a penny, or a person we hardly know. They were so much more.

The lost sheep represented a shepherd's life, love, and livelihood. The coin represented this woman's greatest treasure and security. The son—how much more valuable could anything be to a parent than their relationship with and the well-being of their own child? And you, too, the entire package of you, are of priceless worth to God. Every person— *every single person*—is enormously valuable. Not because of what we've done to earn or deserve it, but because of what God has done in us and for us.

But despite any person's value or that of a prized animal or earthly possession, they are capable of becoming lost. And we, through our ungodliness, have become lost in God's eyes. No matter how loved, no matter how uniquely and purposefully made, we are like that lost sheep, lost coin, and lost son. Valuable, but out of place.

*Lost.* We are actually described as being "dead" in our trespasses and sins (Eph. 2:1). Like a man walking in the dark, we are "blinded" to the truth of our condition (2 Cor. 4:4). Like a criminal found guilty before a judge, we are "condemned" through our unbelief in Christ (John 3:18).

Like a hard-hearted atheist living in meaninglessness, we are "without hope and without God in the world" (Eph. 2:12). Like a person inflicted with a deadly disease, we are spiritually "perishing" (1 Cor. 1:18).

*We are lost.*

People tend to falsely assume they're actually okay, that God will overlook all of the sins they've committed throughout their lives, all the lies they've told, the foul words they've spoken, the immoral thoughts and decisions they've made, the people they've wronged and hated, and will still welcome them into His holy presence to enjoy the rewards of heaven for eternity.

But what would you think of a judge who sets the guilty free or condemns the innocent? Total injustice. "He who justifies the wicked and he who condemns the righteous, both of them alike are an abomination to the LORD" (Prov. 17:15 NASB).

God is not an unjust judge, and He won't commit an abomination. Though He created us with value, our sins disqualify us from being welcome into His holy presence. And we would honestly have to agree with this. Holiness requires purity and separation from sin.

Look at it this way. How much disease do you want in your body? How much poison do you want in your tea? How many rattlesnakes do you want in your bed? How many criminals do you want breaking into your home? Likewise, God allows no sin into heaven.

And yet each of us is sinful.

A coin doesn't know it's lost. That's where some of us are. The sheep wandered into lostness, just like we've done as well. "All we like sheep have gone astray; we have turned, every one, to his own way" (Isa. 53:6 NKJV). Some sins are planned and intentional; some are random and impulsive. The father's wayward son *ran* into sin. We've done that too. We've wanted it. We've run after it. We've sought it out and believed it held what we most desired from life, more than we desired the love, protection, provision, and intimacy of the One who made us.

And the longer something stays lost—as we all know from experience—the lesser the likelihood that it will ever be found. As a result, we *waste* the precious lives we've been given by the One who gave us life. This is what the word "prodigal" actually means: waste.

*All three lost items became a waste.* The lost sheep could provide no fleece for the shepherd's warmth or his business, no meat to feed his family or to sell at market. The lost coin couldn't be used for life savings, for investing, for helping others, or for making any purchase. And the lost son, when he left, took along with him the joy of his father's heart, the honor of his family name, the hope of future generations, the potential his father had made possible for him in life, not to mention the loss of his own satisfaction, relationships, and contentment as well.

It was gone. All of it gone. All of it a waste. All of it lost.

The Bible tells us to consider ourselves *lost*.

But with this being true, how can we stare into these amazing hands that God made for us . . . how can we look into a mirror, ignoring the value of the uniquely priceless person looking back at us . . . knowing we have the *imago Dei*, that we are made in His image . . . knowing we have a distinctiveness to our nature that makes us capable of knowing God intimately, walking with Him relationally, honoring Him gratefully . . . knowing of our own need for His forgiveness and peace and hope and love . . .

How can we recognize all of that, and choose to stay lost? To not cry out to be saved?

We do it because the hook of our sin and the resistance of our pride is that deeply rooted. We do it because the hardness of our hearts is that unfeeling. We do it because we think we somehow need to get our lives in order first, that we must clean ourselves up before we can earn the right to be forgiven by the One we've sinned against, the One whose blessings we've wasted and squandered in many ways.

We do it because we don't understand God's heart for the lost.

But the story doesn't end there. All three owners of all three lost properties—notice this—*all three owners deeply wanted back what they lost and pursued it,* just as your Owner wants you back, too, enough to passionately pursue you. That's the epic message to be learned from these three-act parables. Look at what each owner did:

"What man among you, who has a hundred sheep and loses one of them, does not leave the ninety-nine in the open field and go after the lost one until he finds it? When he has found it, he joyfully puts it on his shoulders, and coming home, he calls his friends and neighbors together saying to them, 'Rejoice with me, because I have found my lost sheep!'" (Luke 15:3–6)

"Or what woman who has ten silver coins, if she loses one coin, does not light a lamp, sweep the house, and search carefully until she finds it? When she finds it, she calls her friends and neighbors together, saying, 'Rejoice with me, because I have found the silver coin I lost!'" (vv. 8–9)

"But while the son was still a long way off, his father saw him and was filled with compassion. He ran, threw his arms around his neck, and kissed him. The son said to him, 'Father, I have sinned against heaven and in your sight. I'm no longer worthy to be called your son.' But the father told his servants . . . 'Let's celebrate with a feast, because this son of mine was dead and is alive again; he was lost and is found!'" (vv. 20–24)

Sought and found.

And "I tell you," Jesus said, there is that kind of "joy in heaven over one sinner who repents" (v. 7)—"joy in the presence of God's angels" (v. 10)—every time the lost is found. Your God "wants everyone to be saved and to come to the knowledge of the truth" (1 Tim. 2:4). He wants "all to come to repentance" (2 Pet. 3:9).

If you are lost in any capacity, God wants you to be found in every capacity.

From wherever you're lost.

Your story—your multi-act story, with all its hidden twists and turns and scenes of pain; with all its confusion, woundedness, sin, and rebellion; even with all its heartbreaking events of hopelessness, loss, and rejection—can still be rescued by the powerful reality of another story

. . . the true story where Jesus Christ, the man, came to this earth, was born of a virgin, and lived a sinless life. He willingly died the death that you and I deserved, intentionally paid the overwhelming price we could never afford to pay, and then "erased the certificate of debt, with its obligations, that was against us and opposed to us" and took it all away from us "by nailing it to the cross" (Col. 2:14). He paid our impossibly high fine so that we could walk out of the courtroom of condemnation and go free.

Therefore, in light of all this, Scripture cuts to the heart and strongly appeals to us: "'Come back to God!' For God made Christ, who never sinned, to be the offering for our sin, so that we could be made right with God through Christ" (2 Cor. 5:20–21 NLT).

The story Jesus told of the lost coin, sheep, and son is our story.

But it's also His. Jesus is the name of the Great Shepherd who came after us, the lost sheep, to save us from perishing after we ran away from Him. God is the owner of the treasured investment of our life. God is also the loving Father who knows exactly how we've squandered the blessings He's given and entrusted to us, yet sees us in our need and runs toward us to embrace us and welcome us home with open arms, if we will come to Him.

No, God doesn't allow sin into His presence, but He knows His Son died and rose again to pay for every one of our sins so that we could be completely forgiven and washed clean. This happens when we humble ourselves and turn to "our great God and Savior, Christ Jesus, who gave Himself for us to redeem us from every lawless deed, and to purify for Himself a people for His own possession" (Titus 2:13–14 NASB).

From death to life, from lost to found, from condemned to forgiven, from worthless to priceless. This is the best news ever.

So today, before we go any further into this book and the rich identity and inheritance that God wants for you, first be honest about where you are with Him.

A path-changing, identity-changing choice stands before you. You might have taken the Heart Check and realized you're actually in a good place, that you've given your life to Jesus and He has changed you and is leading you, that you are following Him and enjoying Him every day.

But perhaps you're realizing that you've been kind of running from your Owner all your life, not once having your eyes opened wide enough to see that you're only getting yourself further and further lost. Or perhaps you can attest to many times throughout your life when He's found you, when He's rescued you from the wasteful places where you've ended up. But you've kept running off, forgetting the way home, and you realize now—like never before—you don't want your life to be wasted any more, separated from the closeness that You know He wants you to experience with Him.

Sin has surely broken you. It breaks all of us. And you might be swimming in it right now. But Jesus, the perfect Son of God, gave His own body to be fully broken so that you could experience the total forgiveness and spiritual healing and freedom that you need, so that you could experience the joy of being found in Him.

God makes it easy for us. He knows we can't save ourselves or clean ourselves up or change our own hearts. We're like a lost sheep in the dark who realizes all we can really do is cry out for Him to come and save us. And He faithfully will. "Everyone who calls on the name of the Lord will be saved" (Rom. 10:13).

We don't need to die on a cross to pay for our own sins. He's handled it already and tells us to receive it by faith. Therefore, "if you confess with your mouth, 'Jesus is Lord,' and believe in your heart that God raised him from the dead, you will be saved" (Rom. 10:9).

If you've never received Him in this way, by repenting of your sin— admitting it, truly desiring to turn away from it—and by believing in Christ and His death for you, which the Father accepts as full payment on what you owe Him, then let today be the day of salvation. Let this be the moment in your life when you tell God you are lost, and you are ready now to be found.

*Dear God, I know I've done wrong things and sinned against You, and I need Your forgiveness. I'm calling on You now to help me and save me. I humbly bow before You, believing You care about me and that You proved it by sending Your Son. I believe Jesus died for me on the cross, and I confess Him as the Lord and boss of my life. I lay my life before You and ask You to take control. Cleanse me, change me, fill me and help me to be the person You created me to be. Use my life for Your glory now and help me never be ashamed of You. I pray in Jesus' name, amen.*

**TAKE IT DEEPER BY STUDYING**
Ezekiel 34:10–16 • John 10:11–15 • 1 Peter 2:24–25

*You were like sheep going astray, but you have now returned to the Shepherd and Overseer of your souls. (1 Pet. 2:25)*

# CHAPTER 9

# *You Are Able to Test Your Faith*

*Do you yourselves not recognize that Jesus Christ is in you?—unless you fail the test. (2 Cor. 13:5)*

C an a person really know for sure if they're a believer and have eternal life? Can they be certain that God has saved them, that the promises He's given to those in Christ are true for them individually as well?

The answer is yes. You can know. God wants you to know.

The apostle John, writing to a first-century church, said he was writing his letter to those "who believe in the name of the Son of God so that you may know you have eternal life" (1 John 5:13). Being truly assured of your salvation is a fundamental key to discovering, embracing, and walking out your identity in Christ. If you *don't* know Christ, then you don't have a new identity in Him. If you truly *do* know Him, then you need to anchor yourself in the assurance of it.

Satan will try any strategy against a believer's heart to get them to doubt their salvation and keep them from living out their spiritual identity (Rev. 12:10). As long as they're doubting it and questioning God's faithfulness to them, he knows they won't be experiencing real joy and victory each day. They won't realize that God's promises for believers also apply to them. They won't be praying with confidence from within an intimate relationship with the Father or sharing their faith with others. It's a big, brutal win for the enemy.

But he works the other angle as well. He's equally deceptive at trying to convince *unsaved* people that they're doing just fine, and that they have no real need to go overboard with religion or trust what the Bible says they should do or believe. As long as they're comfortable in their sin, and are self-assured with their safe measure of religious belief or ceremony, he wants them to feel good about where they *aren't* with God.

*Everything should be okay in the end,* he argues. *If there's a God, then His goodness will let you into heaven regardless of what you've done or believe. You're a fairly good person, doing your best, right?*

It's not a hard argument for the devil to make because salvation, God says, is a "gift" from Him—"not from works, so that no one can boast" (Eph. 2:8–9). It's easy to assume that salvation is something God just wants us to have, something He'll provide us regardless of what we do or how we live.

But that's not reality. God does ascribe salvation to us as a free gift (Rom. 6:23; Eph. 2:8–9), but it's not automatic. Our relationship with God is always on His terms, not ours. We don't choose how we prefer to be saved or how we'll relate to Him. He promises salvation to those who repent and trust His Son (Acts 2:39; 1 John 5:12).

We're talking about eternity here. This is serious. Forever is way too long for us to be wrong about where we stand with God and our eternal destination.

Jesus repeatedly told people who thought they were spiritually in a good place that, if they thought salvation was a birthright or were putting all their confidence in themselves, they were far away from God and would be going to hell when they died (Matt. 23:13; Mark 10:21; John 3:5; 5:39–40).

In His first recorded sermon, Jesus did not hold back but strictly warned people:

> "Not everyone who says to me, 'Lord, Lord,' will enter the king-
> dom of heaven, but only the one who does the will of my Father

in heaven. On that day many will say to me, 'Lord, Lord, didn't we prophesy in your name, drive out demons in your name, and do many miracles in your name?' Then I will announce to them, 'I never knew you. Depart from me, you lawbreakers!'" (Matt. 7:21–23)

You may doubt that God would judge people with hell. But if He already allows us to face consequences for what we do with our lives on Earth, even currently—which He does (Rom. 1:18; Gal. 6:7)—would He not also allow lasting consequences in eternity for those who reject Him and the sacrifice of His Son? Especially if He's repeatedly promised it's what He's going to do? (Heb. 10:29–31). "The one who believes in the Son has eternal life, but the one who rejects the Son will not see life; instead, the wrath of God remains on him" (John 3:36).

That's why Jesus didn't waste His time on Earth. Like a soldier who jumps on a grenade to save his beloved friends, the sinless Son of God offered up His life to the harsh reality of death by Roman crucifixion. It wasn't just a good man's death; it was the death of God's perfect Son (Rom. 5:6–8), paying the full price of our sins.

Again, we didn't earn or deserve this. Salvation is an amazing gift from the Lord. You never need to help Jesus pay for your sins by proving you're even a candidate for heaven. That's the opposite of what grace and the gospel means.

But God, who does all the saving of you, intends for His salvation to change *all* of you—to take away not only the penalty you owe for your sin but to free you from its ongoing, enslaving, everyday power. He wants the world to see in you the extent of what His grace can do. He wants your life to show how He can transform a spiritually dead person into a spiritually alive person—someone whose transformation cannot be explained in any other way except for the life-altering power and presence of God. People can see the proof and evidence of it.

And *this* is something we can actually test for. The fruit of our lives is something we're instructed to evaluate. Scripture clearly challenges us . . .

Test yourselves to see if you are in the faith. (2 Cor. 13:5)

Let a person examine himself. (1 Cor. 11:28)

Let each person examine his own work. (Gal. 6:4)

That's because salvation, which begins with an event, is proven to be real by a genuine life change and a lifestyle of genuine faith. God isn't interested in playing games with us. Trusting Him is like a marriage— true vows backed up by years of faithfulness. It's definitely much more of a long-term covenant than a one-day event or religious ceremony.

Salvation is immediate, yes, and real. It requires nothing but faith in Christ alone. But the following weeks, months, and years will disclose the real story. Did it remain? Is there a living root that was planted and is still bearing live fruit?

God really *wants* you to find out and know.

Now you may be someone who's been following Christ for many years. Or you may be someone who prayed to receive Christ at the end of the last chapter of this book and have just now begun experiencing this relationship. That's incredible! Or you may be someone who's still walking in a state of doubt or skepticism, still not sure about who Jesus is, not feeling ready or convinced of what you want or need to do.

But this new, soul-anchoring identity that we're ramping up to explore is only yours if you are in Christ. Paul, in writing to one of the early churches, spoke of what salvation entailed: "He has reconciled you by his physical body through his death, to present you holy, fault-less, and blameless before him" (Col. 1:22). This is your true identity as a believer. *If.*

. . . if indeed you remain grounded and steadfast in the faith and are not shifted away from the hope of the gospel that you heard. (v. 23)

Paul knew that a short-lived, quickly abandoned faith is not real faith at all. He knew that people are fickle and can be like Judas, a big religious fake. So he was looking for lasting changes and lasting works. "Show me your faith without works," James said, "and I will show you faith by my works" (James 2:18).

There's no way that God the Father can adopt you into His family, and that Jesus Christ can take over and become your Lord, and that the Holy Spirit can invade your heart, and you not change at all. That's like thinking you can swim in the ocean and not get wet, or detonate a stick of dynamite in your living room and not influence your decor.

This line of thinking may sound harsh to you. Judgmental and restrictive. *Nobody else's business.* But that's not the heart in which the Bible teaches it, and it's not our heart in repeating it here for emphasis. The material in this chapter comes from merely looking with humility to the Lord and His Word, and deferring everything we may assume or feel to what He states is true. It comes from not wanting anyone— ourselves or *anyone else*—to miss out on what God has done for His people and not experience to the fullest what our identity in Christ truly means.

With this in mind, here are seven things that are specifically mentioned in God's Word as follow-through indicators, or fruits, that show up and reveal true salvation. Ask yourself these questions, and see if the output of your daily life lines up with the identifying marks of a sincere Christian.

## 1: How do you respond to GOD'S COMMANDS?

"This is how we know that we know him: if we keep his commands" (1 John 2:3). The first evidence of true faith is a growing lifestyle of obedience toward God. Before we come to Christ, we are bent toward sin.

But repentance and faith in Him means a turning from sin and a turning to God in submission. Basically stated, a nonbeliever will not seek out or obey God's commands, but a true believer will. Though Christians still retain their fleshly propensity for sin, and will continue to make mistakes in life (1 John 1:8–10), the overall pattern of a truly saved heart becomes one of increasing submission to and obedience to Christ, feeling more and more compelled to cooperate with the Holy Spirit. They're not faking it to make it. Their real faith is producing real faithfulness.

Is that you? Have you seen an increasing obedience toward God over time? Is it not only the desire of your heart but the growing testimony of your feet? "The one who says, 'I have come to know him,' and yet doesn't keep His commands, is a liar, and the truth is not in him. But whoever keeps his word, truly in him the love of God is made complete. This is how we know we are in him: The one who says he remains in him should walk just as he walked" (1 John 2:4–6). The way you respond to Christ's commands is a key test in helping you know if you truly know Him or not.

## 2: Who do you BELIEVE and SAY that JESUS CHRIST is?

"Who is the liar, if not the one who denies that Jesus is the Christ?" (1 John 2:22). Believers confess and don't deny that Jesus is the Son of God. He has revealed it to them, and they just know in their hearts it's true (Matt. 16:17). People who are agnostic or follow other religions may concede that Jesus was a good example, a good teacher, a respected prophet, even a messenger from God. But God's Word says Jesus is the Christ, the sinless Son of God, the Lord of all—God in flesh (John 1:14). And "no one who denies the Son has the Father." Only "he who confesses the Son has the Father as well" (1 John 2:23). So test yourself. Who is Jesus to you? A good man, a good teacher and example, maybe even a good prophet? Or is He God the Son? Divinity and humanity? If so, that's a sign of true salvation.

## 3: How do YOU RESPOND to the SIN IN YOUR LIFE?

Jesus said, "Unless you repent, you will all perish" (Luke 13:3). The way a believer and nonbeliever respond to their own sin is markedly different. Though each of us will "stumble in many ways" (James 3:2), and though we should remain humbled at all times by our susceptibility to sin, true believers won't be able to swim in it and freely walk in sin without eventually turning from it. Nonbelievers don't deal with it. They have little to no desire to repent of it. But believers, despite having an ongoing battle with it, will continually return back to a place of confession and repentance after they've found themselves in sin (Prov. 24:16).

"No one who is born of God will continue to sin, because God's seed remains in them; they cannot go on sinning, because they have been born of God" (1 John 3:9 NIV). How long are you typically able to keep trailing along in a sinful attitude or behavior before you're on your knees asking Him to change you? How do you respond to sin?

## 4: How does GOD RESPOND to YOUR SIN?

This may sound odd. But whenever you sin, you should *want* to see God convicting and disciplining you. "For what son is there that a father does not discipline?" the Bible says. "If you are without discipline . . . then you are illegitimate children and not sons" (Heb. 12:7–8). The discipline of God in the life of believer is not a sign that He's done with you; it's a sign that you're dear to Him.

Believers have the Holy Spirit in their hearts, and He will be turning on the light of God's truth, convicting you of things that displease Him. Having no conviction is not a good sign. But if the Holy Spirit just keeps bringing it up and pouring it on, that's living proof of God's love within you.

It's evidence that you can consider yourself as one of "God's children" (1 John 3:1). He will not let His children walk in rebellion uncontested. He loves you, and so He'll allow things in your life to wake you up. Warning shots over the bow. Humbling circumstances that feel like a wake-up call. If there's still no repentance, then He will turn up the heat some more, to crush through your hard heart and cause you to turn back to Him.

A good earthly father is faithful to discipline his children when they get out of line—not to hurt them but to help them, because he loves them so much (Prov. 13:24). So we, too, should expect our heavenly Father's discipline when needed. Have you experienced the Father's clear discipline in your life when you've been in sin?

## 5: How do you treat OTHER BELIEVERS?

"Whoever does not do what is right is not of God, especially the one who does not love his brother or sister" (1 John 3:10). *Especially* them. When you're tempted to doubt your salvation, note this indicator as clear evidence of a believing heart. "We know that we have passed out of death into life because we love our brothers and sisters. The one who does not love remains in death" (1 John 3:14). "God is love," the Bible says (1 John 4:16). Not merely as a verb *(God loves)*, but as a noun. Love is who He is. And so naturally, in salvation, God's love is "poured out in our hearts through the Holy Spirit who was given to us" (Rom. 5:5). In fact, the Scripture takes it to the extreme: "Everyone who hates his brother or sister is a murderer, and you know that no murderer has eternal life residing in him" (1 John 3:15).

Therefore, this is a good diagnostic test for salvation: Do you have a deep, genuine love for other believers? It's amazing to meet brothers and sisters in other countries and immediately sense a love for them, even though you know little to nothing about them. Jesus said the world will know we are Christians by our love for one another (John 13:35)—but *WE* will know we're Christians by this same love too!

## 6: Does your life give EVIDENCE of the HOLY SPIRIT within you?

"This is how we know that He lives in us: We know it by the Spirit he gave us" (1 John 3:24 NIV). True believers can be convinced of their relationship and standing with the Father because "the Spirit himself testifies together with our spirit that we are God's children" (Rom. 8:16). And that's not all. The Holy Spirit inside us actively convicts us of sin (John 16:8); reveals what God's Word is saying as we read it (John 14:26); and stimulates the bearing of His fruit in our lives—things like love, joy, peace, patience, kindness, and all the rest (Gal. 5:22). Have you been experiencing these evidences of the Holy Spirit's indwelling presence? "For all who are being led by the Spirit of God, these are sons of God" (Rom. 8:14 NASB).

## 7: What are you TRUSTING for your SALVATION?

"The one who has the Son has life. The one who does not have the Son of God does not have life" (1 John 5:12). It's that simple, the Bible says, and yet that hard on human pride. Paul wrote that he was giving up his spiritual résumé and his personal religious pedigree and embracing Jesus alone as His source of salvation. He said he was not depending on a "righteousness of my own from the law, but one that is through faith in Christ—the righteousness from God based on faith" (Phil. 3:9). Are you trusting in anyone or anything else for your salvation besides Christ alone?

Paul also strictly warned the Galatian church that if they were placing their faith in their own religious deeds or performance, then they were estranged from Christ and not true believers. Do you consider your church or your upbringing or any other person—including yourself—as being the "basis" of your faith? Or are you trusting in Jesus alone and what He did on the cross as full payment for your salvation?

---

These seven indicators are signs of a changed life. Think of them as litmus tests revealing whether you've truly trusted God to transform you into a new creation, or whether you're still clinging to something else as your hope of salvation.

None of these things comes naturally to us. They're impossible to fake long-term. So if you're feeling guilty at not seeing them evident in your life, it's not reason for shame but for surrender.

God is not against you. The world, the flesh, and the devil—*that's* what is against you, pushing you in the opposite direction from embracing your new identity. God is *for* you, eager for you to receive His grace and live out the full privileges of your identity.

So with complete honesty, in fearless introspection, or through the accountability of someone who knows you well and will shoot you straight, consider carefully the following questions.

In the last few months, looking at yourself big-picture from a thirty-thousand-foot view:

- Do you exhibit a patterned lifestyle of obedience to God?
- Do you readily confess Jesus Christ as the Son of God?
- Do you freely and sincerely repent of your own sins?
- Do you experience God's Fatherly discipline for sin?
- Do you possess a genuine love for other believers?
- Do you exhibit the presence of the Holy Spirit?
- Do you trust Jesus Christ alone for salvation?

*Lord, thank You for the reality of Your love for me, Your love for lost sinners. Thank You for reaching out in love to save me. But, Lord, while I know from Your Word that I can rest in Christ's sacrifice for me, help me never treat it lightly. Help me not be satisfied simply letting Your salvation make minor improvements in me or, worse, leave me trusting more than ever in myself. I ask You to completely renew and transform me, for Your glory alone, in Jesus' name.*

**TAKE IT DEEPER BY STUDYING**
Ezekiel 18:21–32 • Matthew 7:13–23 • Titus 2:11–14

*We know that the Son of God has come and has given us understanding so that we may know the true one. (1 John 5:20)*

# CHAPTER 10

# You Are Part of God's Epic Plan

*We have also obtained access through him by faith
into this grace in which we stand, and we rejoice
in the hope of the glory of God. (Rom. 5:2)*

Why would God be so kind to us when we don't deserve it? We
could never repay Him in a million years for any of it—for creat-
ing us, sending His Son to save us, forgiving us, giving us salvation as a
free gift, and willingly preparing a home for us in heaven . . . along with
countless other things!

Our typical worldly mind-set is so transactional, so justice focused,
that our unworthiness makes all this extravagance feel almost wrong. It's
hard to fully comprehend. We are so bent toward performance-based
religion, so used to trying to work to earn. Even after embracing Christ
and His gospel, we still may tend to view and approach the Christian life
as if God just wants us to get busy trying to repay the great debt we owe
Him. And so we sweat it out each day, hoping to please Him, working
harder, yet still failing Him too often and getting discouraged.

But Christianity, true Christianity, is so much more than just a daily
battle and grind. We're to live by the awesome and amazing riches of
God's grace through Jesus (Eph. 2:7; 3:8), even though it's often the
opposite of what we tend to do.

In order to understand why we walk through life wired for justice, not grace, we need to look in the rearview mirror at the law.

When Moses came down from Mount Sinai in the book of Exodus, he brought God's law (the Ten Commandments) to the children of Israel to help them govern themselves wisely. This amazing short list provided a universal value system and peaceful working structure to help citizens of any society function without destroying themselves and imploding. The Ten Commandments teach human beings to prioritize God, honor their parents, protect their marriages, avoid burnout, live honestly, value personal property, respect the sanctity of every human life, and avoid jealousy and discontentment.

Interestingly, people all over the world, regardless of nationality or religious background, intuitively know these laws are correct. That's why they get angry and feel a strong sense of injustice in their hearts when their children dishonor them, or when someone lies to them, or steals from them, or kills someone they know, or commits adultery with their spouse. How is it possible that God's law is so intuitively known around the world?

It's possible because God has wired His law into the human heart, whether a person is ever taught His law in their culture or not. This has been true for thousands of years. Paul said long ago:

Even Gentiles, who do not have God's written law, show that they know his law when they instinctively obey it, even without having heard it. They demonstrate that God's law is written in their hearts, for their own conscience and thoughts either accuse them or tell them they are doing right. (Rom. 2:14–15 NLT)

That's why we all tend to view our world and relationships through a lens of justice.

But justice requires a lot of scorekeeping. If you're likable, then I will like you. If you're nice to me, then I will be nice to you. If you steal a dollar, then you owe me a dollar. Eye for an eye. Tooth for a tooth. People treat others according to who they are and what they've done.

But when Jesus stepped onto the scene, He revealed another aspect to the nature and heart of God and a higher level to live by.

It's called *grace*.

This was a radical shift in thinking and a major upgrade to our human operating system. In this new way of living, injustice is still subject to being punished by legal governments, yes, but not in your personal dealings. From now on, because of grace, you don't treat people based upon who *they* are or what *they've* done anymore. Instead you treat them based upon who *you* are in Christ and what God has done for *you*. Decisions are to be based on the identity, heart, and character of the *giver*, and are no longer dependent at all on the performance or worthiness of the *receiver*.

Consider this: the sun doesn't shine on us because we are so deserving of its light; the sun shines on us because its nature is to shine. And it will continue to shine whether we request it, want it, or deserve it.

God wants us to live this way in all of our relationships. *The way of grace*. Since God is love, and since we are loved in Him, He wants us to be loving at all times in all places toward all people, even as the sun shines all the time by its nature.

Many of Jesus' seemingly unrealistic commands suddenly now make sense in "light" of this.

"You have heard that it was said, Love your neighbor and hate your enemy. But I tell you, love your enemies and pray for those who persecute you, so that you may be children of your Father in heaven. For he causes his sun to rise on the evil and the good, and sends rain on the righteous and the unrighteous. For if you love those who love you, what reward will you have? Don't even the tax collectors do the same? And if you greet only your brothers and sisters, what are you doing out of the ordinary? Don't even the Gentiles do the same? Be perfect, therefore, as your heavenly Father is perfect." (Matt. 5:43–48)

Jesus is telling us to disconnect from performance-based thinking and living, and shift to a dynamic of living by grace—because of *who we are* and *who God is*.

The epic book of Ephesians cannot be truly understood without first getting a handle on this secret key to the whole book. *Grace!*

Grace is mentioned twelve times throughout Ephesians and touches us at almost every level. Grace is the fuel behind why our salvation is given freely as a gift (Eph. 2:4–9). Grace is what ushered Paul into the ministry and daily gave him the strength to live out his calling (Eph. 3:7–8). Grace is how God gives us spiritual gifts (Eph. 4:7) and is described as one of the big-picture reasons why God has adopted us spiritually and given us so much so freely (Eph. 1:6–7).

We've sung or heard "Amazing Grace" countless times, but what exactly is grace?

Let us answer that question with a story.

In 2 Samuel 9, King David was enjoying so much success and wealth, and felt so overwhelmingly blessed by God, and his heart was so full of joy and gratefulness, that he began to overflow with a desire to bless others. So he searched for any living relatives of his best friend Jonathan (who had died) so that he could show "the kindness of God" (v. 3) to someone from Jonathan's family.

When he discovered that Jonathan had a living son, named Mephibosheth, who was lame in both feet, David summoned him and told him he wanted to give him all the former property of his grandfather, King Saul. This gift included great land, many servants, and a welcome seat to eat at the king's table daily.

Mephibosheth no doubt felt overwhelmed and unworthy. *Could this even be real?* Yes, it was completely real. In an instant, a forgotten crippled man who was likely unable to work became one of the richest men in the country. This blessing had nothing to do with Mephibosheth's good deeds, impressiveness, or character as a citizen. It had everything to do with the heart of a loving and generous king who was looking for someone he could bless.

It's called grace.

A gift revealing "the kindness of God."

Grace is an unearned, undeserved gift that is freely and generously poured out on a chosen recipient. It might meet a great need in their lives or simply be a blessing intended to bring joy to their hearts. Either way, grace is amazing!

Grace is not purchased, earned, or deserved, or else it wouldn't be grace. It wouldn't be the gift that it is intended to be (Rom. 11:6). Grace is never bought; it's bestowed. It flows out of the lovingkindness and goodwill in the heart of a benevolent giver.

Just like children are not asked to pay for their own gifts at Christmas, and a spouse would never be given a bill to cover their anniversary gift, grace is never to be paid back. It is love being poured out. It's actually the *opposite* of a debt. The goal of grace is to cause gladness and well-being in the life of another, which produces joy and rich thanksgiving in the heart of the giver as well. Jesus said, "It is more blessed to give than to receive" (Acts 20:35). And God, who is more gracious than anyone and more generous than anyone, is also more blessed than anyone as He pours out His grace upon us.

---

When you think of God's grace, you should think of a river.

It's not a potful, a puddle, or a swimming pool that could run dry. It's an endless supply. Unlimited capacity. Constantly flowing from a faithful source.

A river on Earth doesn't flow downstream simply because all the fish, beavers, and water spiders who depend on it have been praying three times a day for it or are getting good grades in their schools. A river continues to flow because of the nature of the source, not the worthiness of the destination.

So when this river of God's grace pours out truth on us, it's not because we've earned the right to be trusted; it's because God is always completely truthful. He doesn't forgive us because we are so cuddly and forgivable, but because He is so merciful and forgiving. He doesn't love us because we are so lovable, but because He is so loving. The word *lovingkindness* is one of the core ingredients of grace!

Think about this. The imagery of a "river" runs throughout the Bible from Genesis to Revelation. Beginning at the dawn of Creation, we learn that "a river went out from Eden," continually watering this beautiful garden (Gen. 2:10). David later wrote, in the first psalm, how the righteous are "like a tree planted by the rivers of water," so that whatever they do will "prosper" (Ps. 1:3 NKJV).

Later, God gave the prophet Ezekiel a picturesque vision of a river flowing out from underneath the temple of God (Ezek. 47). The depth of the river progressively rose from being ankle-deep, to knee-deep, to waist-deep, until "it was a river that I could not cross on foot," the prophet said. "For the water had risen; it was deep enough to swim in" (v. 5). It gushed onward and outward into the world, into the future, a tributary of life and health and vibrant refreshment everywhere its waters reached.

By the time of Jesus' arrival, He was telling people (like the woman at the well) that He was capable of giving them "living water" (John 4:10). No longer did their lives need to be confined to cups and buckets that quickly ran out, or to the tiring routine of constantly returning to the same well thirsty. "Whoever drinks from the water that I will give him will never get thirsty again," Jesus said. "In fact, the water I will give him will become a well of water springing up in him for eternal life" (John 4:14).

The river flows on, unending.

Then in the last chapter of Revelation, the last book of the Bible, we discover something amazing going on in heaven. It is an introduction to "the river of the water of life, clear as crystal, flowing down from the throne of God and the Lamb" (Rev. 22:1). This heavenly river is flowing out of God's throne and sustaining life, producing bountiful fruit, even making the leaves on the trees capable of "healing the nations" (v. 2b). It's not a cup of water to be passed around the room. It's not a trickle to be pooled and stored. It's a mighty, flowing, everlasting stream of life, enriching and refreshing everything in its path.

God's people throughout history have been buoyed by the river of God's love, His truth, His wisdom, His comfort. Representing the unlimited resources of God, this river has cascaded across time, carrying us along on the current of His goodness and His covenant.

As we gaze now into the book of Ephesians, we see grace being poured out like a river on us from God. There we see ourselves as former slaves who previously lived under the control of "our fleshly desires, carrying out the inclinations of our flesh and thoughts," people who were "by nature children under wrath" (Eph. 2:3). But God, "who is rich in mercy, because of His great love that He had for us" (v. 4) has funneled us into His river by grace.

And not just because God saw our need and felt deep compassion for us. Not just because we had no hope otherwise.

God did it "so that in the coming ages he might display the immeasurable riches of his grace through his kindness to us in Christ Jesus" (Eph. 2:7). He did it "so that God's multi-faceted wisdom may now be made known through the church [that's us] to the rulers and authorities in the heavens" (Eph. 3:10). Paul adds, "This is according to his eternal purpose accomplished in Christ Jesus our Lord" (v. 11).

So God has had an epic plan all along. He's been planning for our lives, our salvation, our forgiveness, and our new identity in Him to be a public, cascading display of the loving grace of God. The story of your redeemed life is sort of an in-your-face to the devil and his demons (who are the "rulers and authorities" that Paul was talking about in Ephesians 3:10). Even as Job, by God's grace, succeeded in staying true to the Lord despite the all-out war Satan had waged against him, the grace that God gives you to overcome your sin, your past, and your brokenness is all part of how He says to His enemies: "I win!"

God's grace is His weapon to help us "win" the battle over death and hell and the devil. For "where sin multiplied"—as it surely has done in all of us—"grace multiplied even more" (Rom. 5:20). So even if the enemy were to persist every day in trying to accuse you and belittle you for the worst things you've ever done, he cannot succeed in condemning you because "just as sin reigned in death, so also grace will reign through righteousness, resulting in eternal life through Jesus Christ our Lord" (v. 21).

What was God's purpose in saving you? To show the world—to show every living being in every dimension of existence—that He and His grace are absolutely amazing and should be praised. You, in your new identity, are living proof of that.

The Christian life is not about what *you* have done but what *God* has done. It's not about trying harder, being more committed, working harder, and being better by your own willpower. It's about diving into that *river*—the river of His grace—and letting Him carry you through everything that comprises your life so that it sings out "to the praise of his glorious grace" (Eph. 1:6).

That's the phrase you see repeated in Ephesians 1 as Paul is spelling out the details of who you are, and what you have, and why the Lord has done all this. He's done it "to the praise of his glorious grace that he lavished on us in the Beloved One" (v. 6). He's done it "so that we who had already put our hope in Christ might bring praise to his glory" (v. 12). He gives us His Holy Spirit as both the proof of His promise and the power we need for living until we're finally home with Him, "until the redemption of the possession, to the praise of his glory" (v. 14).

It's all in praise of His grace.

---

God will receive glory regardless of what people do. The question is, what kind of glory?

He will be praised and given glory for both His judgment and His mercy. In the Revelation, when you see His overdue wrath justifiably poured out on the world's wickedness and sin, the hosts of heaven react in joyful worship. Not in glee at seeing people swept away by God's righteous fury, but in awe of Him who will have the final word and bring total justice to all the injustices in the world.

"His judgments are true and righteous" (Rev. 19:2), they say. What else *can* be said when those who rebelled against Him, scoffed at His authority, denied His Word, revolted against His commands, and then refused to bend their knees to His Son pay the price for their sin?

Only one other thing can be said . . . that we, too, deserved God's wrath, in the same deadly fire and destruction. And yet God, "to the praise of his glorious grace"—

We almost can't write it without taking a deep breath of gratitude. We should be so humbled by what God has done for us and given us. We should be so grateful for receiving such abundant mercy that is entirely, unfathomably undeserved. All we deserve is God's wrath for our sin, for our thoughts and our words and our regrets. And instead we've been given . . . *grace*?

Yes. Our judgment has been placed on God's Son. And don't you know He'll be praised for that grace in heaven? And don't you know it's being seen and noticed and scoffed at right now by the evil one and those in the spiritual realms?

Can you think of anything else we ought to be doing today, no matter what else of importance we're doing, than praising Him for pouring out grace like a river on someone so undeserving as us? We are Mephibosheth being blessed. We are the woman at the well being valued. We are the one caught in adultery being pardoned. We are Peter, being restored after denying Him so many times. We are the recipients of the riches of His grace. Praise the Lord!

Now, one of the things we guarantee the enemy will do as you work through the next two parts of this book on your *identity* and your *inheritance* in Christ—he will whisper to you, *Hey, you know you don't deserve that.* And he'll be correct, even in being condemning.

"But where sin multiplied"—remember? Romans 5?—"grace multiplied even more." As the father said to the prodigal, "Bring out the best robe and put it on him; put a ring on his finger and sandals on his feet. Then bring the fattened calf, and let's celebrate with a feast, because this son of mine was dead and is alive again; he was lost and is found!" (Luke 15:22–24).

"We have all received grace upon grace from his fullness," the Bible says, "for the law was given through Moses; grace and truth came through

Jesus Christ" (John 1:16–17). In God's kindness to us in Christ, He has invited us into salvation and has poured out the riches of His grace on us. The river is flowing—around us, behind us, on every possible side of us, even pouring out through us and from us in grace toward others.

We don't deserve any of it, yet He's given us an ocean of it.

Your job is to walk in grace—receiving it, sharing it—so that everyone sees what "the kindness of God" has done for you.

*Father in heaven, what a wonder Your grace is to me. How often I misunderstand Your intentions, what You expect of me, why You love me. I've wasted so much time trying to earn Your grace, when it is freely given because of who You are. Lord, help me know and walk in the greatness of Your love and grace. Thank You that I am saved by grace, called by grace, empowered by grace, and my life is for the praise of the glory of Your grace. Help me live this out! Make my life a gigantic THANK YOU back to You! In Jesus' name, amen.*

TAKE IT DEEPER BY STUDYING
Psalm 25:5–7 • Ezekiel 47:1–12 • 2 Corinthians 4:14–18

*Everything is for your benefit so that, as grace extends through more and more people, it may cause thanksgiving to increase to the glory of God. (2 Cor. 4:15)*

## CHAPTER 11

# *Once upon a Divide:*
# *A Parable of Twins*

*So now, little children, remain in him so that when*
*he appears we may have confidence and not be*
*ashamed before him at his coming. (1 John 2:28)*

There once was a married couple who had twin sons. They named them Luke and Blake. After going through a painful divorce, the wife took young Luke with her to the West Coast, and the husband kept Blake with him on the East Coast. The couple never spoke to one another again.

Over the years, both boys grew to excel in sports and in academics, and both graduated from college. Both got married, had children, and eventually owned their own profitable businesses. Sadly, after both became wealthy, they would each die of cancer. But Luke and Blake, though they looked, walked, and sounded similar to one another, lived completely different lives.

Blake was told as a young man in school that he was an accident of random chance. Empty stardust. He got an A on that test, but walked away from it feeling like his life was kind of meaningless.

On the West Coast, Luke's mother began taking him to church in middle school. At a church camp, he learned that God had created him with a purpose, loved him, and had a specific plan for his life. Luke gave his life to Christ that summer and began to get deeply involved in his youth ministry at church. His youth pastor became a close friend, like a father figure to him.

Back east, Blake learned that he only got attention from his distant, workaholic father if he made all A's or performed well in sports. So he did everything he could do to win his father's approval and earn the praise of his teachers and coaches. Blake began to live for applause and awards and slowly grounded his identity in winning at all costs, which was his only sense of feeling loved. He also realized that if he failed, he would be ignored by his dad and benched by his coaches. So winning became everything to him. Blake became the quarterback on his high school football team. He always felt a high level of anxiety during games, but tried to use it to motivate himself to play harder. After the cheers and high fives had quickly faded, Blake was already thinking about where he could find his next big win.

Luke also excelled in sports and became a wide receiver on his team, catching many touchdown passes. Luke became a leader in FCA on his high school campus and led Bible studies for his teammates, encouraging them to give God their best. His mother always told him that she was proud of him. Before every game, she would text him the same message: "I love you, no matter what." Though he was always disappointed with a loss, he didn't let it devastate him. In fact, some of his closest friendships came out of his ability to comfort and encourage his friends after a hard loss.

His brother Blake almost never lost at anything. The thought of losing disgusted him, and he avoided it at all costs, willing to sacrifice his integrity and his friendships if that's what it took. But internally, he struggled with a fear of failure and depression over never feeling truly loved. He harshly drove every team and teammate he played with, becoming angry and combative with anyone who didn't respond to his motivation or if he was criticized or failed in any way. When his team lost the state championship in football during his junior year, Blake yelled at the refs, cursed out two of his friends, and didn't talk to his father for a week.

The next year, he came back with a vengeance. He even worked tirelessly at his academics, striving to beat the other students and make sure he was valedictorian. At his graduation, he made a speech about how everyone should reach for the stars and do whatever it takes to come out on top. After all, "Life has no time for losers."

Out west, Luke got very sick his senior year after going on a mission trip to Peru. He spent three weeks in the hospital, but he shared a strong Christian witness to the nurses and staff, and sparked a lifelong friendship with his doctor, who was beginning medical mission work in Uganda. Luke graduated as salutatorian of his class and made a speech about the difference between living a life of success versus significance. He thanked his teachers, his coaches, and his youth pastor for investing in his life. He then thanked his mom publicly for teaching him about unconditional love. He even admitted he'd asked God for a wife one day who possessed the same strength and character his mother had. Everyone cheered as she cried.

In college, on a football and academic scholarship, Blake continued to push himself tirelessly to succeed. But none of the stickers on his helmet or trophies in his dorm ever seemed to fill the void he felt inside. No success was ever enough. As he jumped from one short-term relationship to another, Blake began struggling with alcohol and porn addiction. Saturday nights were for bars; Sundays were for hangovers. Then he was back in the gym and at practice on Monday mornings, chasing the next win or cramming for the next test. Always stressed, easily angered, Blake constantly felt like he needed to keep proving his worth, again and again.

During one big game, Blake exploded after a wide receiver missed a pass that cost them the victory. Later that night, he got drunk, drove his car into a tree, and spent the weekend in jail for a DUI. He was put on team suspension and had to watch the remaining games from the bench. He was devastated and never forgave his teammate for dropping the ball or his coach for not letting him play.

What he didn't know was that his brother Luke also made the football team in college, but saw even less playing time than Blake did. Though he was disappointed, Luke didn't lose even one night of sleep over it. He decided to become the team chaplain and was renamed "Chappie" by his teammates. He started leading Bible studies, assisting in workouts, and helping his teammates stay in class during the week and out of jail on the weekends. Though he saw limited playing time, his coach loved having him around and gave him a "Most Valuable Preacher" trophy to a standing ovation on senior awards night. More than half the players shared how he had personally impacted their life, how he'd taught them the difference between earthly rewards and heavenly ones.

After college, both brothers joined the workforce. Blake married a beautiful girl from his graduating class, then became a top salesman and a workaholic at his company. As he moved up the ladder at work, he tore down his wife at home with unrealistic expectations and his legalistic perfectionism. Their marriage lasted two years before she left him. Despite his inner demons, Blake was a master at making himself look good in public. He was promoted to a management position and quickly drove his employees to do whatever it took to come out on top. Extra hours. Cutting corners. Lying about the competition. Everything was focused on the next big win. His second wife and two children watched him from a distance, and learned that their value was always connected to their appearance and performance.

Also in management now, Luke was considered the most generous and caring boss that his employees had ever known. They worked hard for him. Although profitable, he demonstrated that the bottom line numbers were never as important as the people under his care. He greeted them by name, encouraged them, and would generously give them time off if a family or personal need arose.

Luke married a dynamic Christian girl at his church that his pastor called "the best catch in the county." They had two sets of twins within the first seven years, and his wife helped him start a citywide fellowship of local business owners to help municipal leaders work in unity.

Because he had never seen a successful marriage or a strong fatherly example growing up, Luke regularly met with older men from his church for breakfast. Every time Luke and his wife would argue, he would call them for counsel. They taught him how to live out his identity in Christ at home and to love his wife unconditionally no matter what. As a result, their kids grew up in a home that was marked by forgiveness, love, and laughter.

Over time, Blake became increasingly hard and bitter, while Luke became more gracious and tenderhearted. Blake's business meetings were stressful. His employees couldn't be transparent about problems because he couldn't handle criticism. Luke, however, encouraged honesty, and it paid off in faster learning and more positive working relationships.

Over the decades, Blake's leadership left a wake of ulcers, depression, broken relationships and health issues wherever he went. Luke left blessings, truth, and kindness behind him.

In their mid-sixties, both brothers received cancer reports from their doctors. Blake immediately came unglued and began taking anxiety medication. He fought with his company's leadership team to maintain control during his treatments. He eventually was isolated to a useless figurehead position and continued to drown his grief in alcohol. With a failing liver from years of abuse, Blake went downhill fast and died in the hospital. He was buried in an expensive casket at a small funeral.

After his burial, his two kids launched into a bitter fight over his inheritance and control of his company. In large display cases at his house were dozens of dusty sports awards and business trophies. Each one represented thousands of hours of his life, but all of them were thrown into a dumpster the day his house was sold.

When Luke got his cancer report, he held his wife as they cried and prayed together in the parking lot outside the doctor's office. The next week they shared the news with their kids, their business team, and their church family. They asked their friends and family for prayer support and that God would help them finish well and glorify Him regardless of what happened.

With rallied encouragement, a network of great doctors, a diet change, and ongoing prayers, Luke and his family graciously walked through a year of surgery and treatment. His wife and kids cheered the day he rang a bell at the hospital after completing his treatments and being given a clean bill of health. Luke was so grateful for how God had used the entire experience to draw him closer to Christ, to his family, and to help him assess how to make the most of the remaining years of his life. Over the next ten years, Luke retired from his job and became more involved in service to his community and his church. He went on multiple mission trips with his grandkids and invested lots of quality time into his family.

After the cancer returned in his late seventies, Luke and his family took the news in stride. He knew he was ready to finish well.

There was standing room only at the church on the day of Luke's funeral. So much love and so many good stories were told. His wife, four children, sixteen grandchildren, and four great-grandchildren wept as multiple church members, pastors, friends, and former employees shared their stories about Luke's legacy. Videos were shown from pastors in Haiti and Africa who honored Luke's company for significantly funding medical missions and orphanages in their countries.

The legacy of his life had reached across his family, his church, his community, his nation, and internationally on the mission field. He had left an impact on countless thousands of lives.

Everyone at Luke's funeral was deeply blessed and inspired by the service. They sang praise to God for how His grace had been so deeply at work in a life well lived. They knew the greatest treasures of Luke's life were lasting and eternal, and many in attendance were inspired to follow his example as they looked forward to enjoying their own rich rewards and eternal inheritance with God one day in eternity.

---

*I have fought the good fight, I have finished the race, I have kept the faith. (2 Tim. 4:7)*

# PART II

# IDENTITY
*Who You Are in Christ*

# CHAPTER 12

# *You Are Defined at Your Core*

*Set your hearts on things above, where Christ is,*
*seated at the right hand of God. (Col. 3:1 NIV)*

The greatest tests of your identity often come when a major storm hits your life. It could be an unwanted doctor's report; a pink slip terminating your job; marital separation or divorce papers; a phone call informing you of tragic news. It could be suffering a physical injury, being arrested, or losing a relationship or role that you've always cherished. But in these tumultuous moments, not only are you forced to wrestle through the hard reality of unwanted change. You also begin to see where your identity is actually grounded. You begin to question internally who you are, your purpose, and your value in light of it all.

In Genesis 37, when Joseph was betrayed by his brothers and sold into slavery, he immediately lost all his relationships, his home, and his possessions. All of his freedoms and dreams were crushed. The favored son of Jacob was now a trafficked slave in a foreign land.

Years later, another tragic storm hit his life. After being falsely accused, he was stripped of all he'd earned and then unjustly imprisoned. His reputation as a trusted servant and all of his privileged roles and responsibilities were immediately gone. Who was he now? Not even a slave. He was an unwanted prisoner with a tarnished reputation in an

Egyptian cell. He no doubt battled with his identity and value in those dark moments. All he had left now, it seemed, were his beating heart and his faith in God.

In the book of Ruth, an elderly woman named Naomi also experienced great trauma. In the process of her family trying to survive a famine, her husband and both of her sons died, leaving her in a foreign land without support. No longer an active wife or mother, Naomi was left in poverty with no direction and no sense of her own purpose and value. When people greeted her by name, she contested them: "Do not call me Naomi [meaning *pleasant*]; call me Mara [*bitter*], for the Almighty has dealt very bitterly with me. I went away full, and the LORD has brought me back empty" (Ruth 1:20–21 ESV). In the midst of deep grief, Naomi was also reeling in her own identity crisis.

In the book of Job, after this highly respected man had suffered the losses of his children, servants, and possessions, he clung to God in his devastation. But Job struggled with his own meaning in the midst of his suffering. He went on to curse the day of his birth, wishing he'd just died in his mother's womb (Job. 3:11).

Life can have a brutal way of stretching and fiercely testing who we are. We've all likely seen these kinds of things happen to people we know. Someone loses not only their job or a precious relationship, but also loses their reason for getting out of bed in the morning. We hear the tragic news of an attempted suicide after a significant loss or a failure that took away a person's public respectability. When cherished seasons end and our positions on the team or the job are lost, we can unexpectedly spiral into a season of grief and begin looking in the mirror questioning who we are now, sincerely wondering if we have any real purpose or value left.

We've seen singers and actors lose their top billing and fall into drugs and depression when they're replaced by the newer sound or fresher face. We've watched someone who's strong and active grow older, angry, and bitter when forced to realize that their get-up-and-go apparently got up and went. We see widows never finding hope again after their husbands pass. We witness church members who stumble into sin and never rise above their own self-induced shame.

But what about you? How have you responded to tragedy and loss in the past? How have you responded to harsh criticism or false accusation? Have you been betrayed by a friend or passed over for a position or an honor that you thought you deserved? Have you lost jobs, relationships, or loved ones? How did you sincerely respond? Were you disappointed but still trusted God in the midst of the grief? Or were you devastated and fell apart in a storm of confusion, deeply questioning God's goodness and your own sense of value and purpose?

When our foundation is not strong, we will likely not stand firm when the toughest storms beat down on us. If we've been basing our lives and the perception of our identity on changing things, then we've been setting a trap for our own feet.

We must each come back to the truth that Jesus taught, how we must anchor ourselves on an unshakable foundation—"on the rock" (Matt. 7:24–25)—knowing that at some point, everything we hold dear in this short life will eventually be tested, altered, or taken away at some level. As the stories of Joseph, Naomi, and Job inform us, we need to lock in our core identity and anchor it in God and His unchanging Word.

## THE CORE OF YOUR IDENTITY

When Job lost everything, he shaved his head, fell to the ground and said, "Naked I came from my mother's womb, and naked I shall return there. The LORD gave and the LORD has taken away. Blessed be the name of the LORD" (Job 1:21–22 NASB). He had gotten down to the core of who He was, and had nothing to hang onto but God.

God's greatest commandment has always been for you to love Him with your entire self, the totality of your identity. But His command to "love the Lord your God" specifically starts with "your heart," before it can ripple out to include loving Him also with your soul, mind, and strength (Mark 12:30). And so we get to the heart of your identity— your heart—which is what the word *heart* actually means. Your spiritual heart is described in Scripture as the innermost part of your being that guides and influences everything else in your life (Prov. 4:23), just as your physical heart pumps life-giving blood to every living cell in your body.

Your heart is the central headquarters where all of your true beliefs (Rom. 10:10), innermost thoughts (Heb. 4:12), deepest values (Matt. 6:21), greatest desires (Ps. 37:4), future plans (Prov. 16:3), and root decisions (2 Cor. 9:7) originate and reside. Both love and hatred start in the heart (1 John 3:14–22). Joy and sorrow spring from there. Bitterness and forgiveness can reside there (Matt. 18:35; Eph. 4:31–32). And both truth and lies can be spoken and rooted there. As Jesus explained, "The mouth speaks from the overflow of the heart" (Matt. 12:34). Our entire lives are affected by the condition of our hearts.

Follow the succession. From inward to outward. The core beliefs in our hearts lead to the thoughts we think in our minds, which guide the words we speak with our lips, which leads to the ways we live out our lives, the daily deeds we do, and the resulting fruit of our impact on the world. You see this sequence in Scripture: "I, the LORD, search the heart, I test the mind, even to give to each man according to his ways, according to the results of his deeds" (Jer. 17:10 NASB).

So the condition of your heart is vitally important. Which is why the Bible warns us, "Watch over your heart with all diligence, for from it flow the springs of life" (Prov. 4:23 NASB), because you can lie to yourself and deceive your own heart (James 1:26). That's why God wants us to discover His truth and then speak and believe it in our hearts (Ps. 15:2)—first, the truth about *Him*; then the truth about *ourselves*.

But how is this going to happen?

By finally being different—truly different—in our hearts.

Scripture communicates that we need to be changed at the heart level, at the core of who we are, because of how it affects everything else. We need God to transform our hearts, not just to make a bad heart good, but to make a dead heart alive. We like to tweak little things about our lives rather than pursue any major or uncomfortable changes in what we think or do. But changing your external behavior is merely changing the packaging without changing the product inside. Jesus warned people not merely to change their outward appearances: "Either make the tree good and its fruit will be good, or make the tree bad and its fruit will be bad; for a tree is known by its fruit" (Matt. 12:33).

If we're looking to our self-help efforts as being our path to growth—trying harder, being more disciplined, being more committed—we won't change at the heart level and will only be modifying the fruit, not fixing the root. We'll keep fighting the same battles, over and over again, and not see any long-term, genuine transformation.

God alone can truly change a person's heart from within and also change their core identity. This is one of the greatest benefits of true salvation—how when He heals what's actually wrong with our heart, our new identity then filters outward to renew our minds, clean up our mouths, fix our habits and relationships, and bless and use us for His good, perfect, and eternal purposes.

## Two Identities

When Job was suffering and cursing the day of his birth, something else was happening behind the scenes, something he didn't realize was going on.

Job actually had two identities: one on Earth, and one in heaven.

His identity on Earth was that of an extremely successful man in every way. He was a faithful husband, a loving father to ten children, and a respected, wealthy landowner with thousands of livestock and a great number of servants. He was considered "the greatest man among all the people of the east" (Job 1:1–4).

But what Job didn't know was that he also had an identity and reputation in heaven. God called him "My servant Job," and said, "There is no one like him on the earth, a blameless and upright man, fearing God and turning away from evil" (v. 8 NASB).

One man; two identities.

When tragedy struck, Job's identity on Earth was rocked, stolen away, and crushed to powder. Satan left him as a depressed, impoverished man with ten dead children, with his flocks and crops either stolen or destroyed, and with a broken body covered in boils. But despite everything that happened to him, God noted that Job's identity in heaven had never changed. He was equally as loved and respected by God, and he still had the same identity, purpose, and value.

So we ask you: which of the two was Job's real identity? The one on Earth, or the one in heaven? His earthly identity changed back and forth multiple times. It would be true for a season, and then be changed or taken away. But which identity was more important? Clearly the one from God. The eternal one. The person identified as Job in heaven's eyes was by far his most important and lasting identity.

Wasn't the same thing true of Joseph? As he sat in prison, he surely felt worthless and despondent. But God's faithful love for him had not faltered. From heaven's perspective, Joseph was a blessed, loved, wise, and rich man. God was about to promote him to second in command in Egypt, use him to help rescue the world from starvation, and also establish a new nation through the preservation of his brothers and family. His identity in heaven was Joseph's true identity all along.

And Naomi? Same thing. When her circumstances were harsh, she didn't understand that God's love, His genuine concern, and His good purposes for her had never changed. She didn't know where her next meal was coming from, but God knew she would be instrumental in bringing the future King David's great-grandparents together, in helping raise David's grandfather, and in glorifying God through her part in His epic plan of redemption for the nations (Matt. 1:5).

Likewise, if you want to understand your true identity—your monumentally more important identity; your lasting identity—then you need to take your eyes off your present circumstances. How you feel, what people say, and any titles or roles attached to your name will eventually blow away with the wind. But God sees you and knows your future. And His Word teaches that you can discover, believe, and set your heart on your true identity—your identity in heaven.

The real you. The one at the very heart of you.

So if you have been raised with Christ, seek the things above, where Christ is, seated at the right hand of God. Set your minds on things above, not on earthly things. For you died, and your life is hidden with Christ in God. When Christ, who is your life, appears, then you also will appear with him in glory. (Col. 3:1–4)

## THE BOOK OF EPHESIANS AND YOUR HEAVENLY IDENTITY

In light of this, we encourage you to relook at the book of Ephesians. We discussed in the introduction how Ephesians presents a deep explanation of our true, eternal identity and walks us through how we can discover it, how we can let God incorporate it into our lives today, and then live a victorious life in light of it. The first three chapters talk about a believer's heavenly identity in God's eyes—who God says you are! Much of what you'll be reading in this section comes from what God says in this vibrant book of the Bible.

But before we turn the page, be aware of a few key things about how Ephesians is laid out. The first half (chapters 1–3) doesn't tell you to *DO* much of anything. It's filled with tons of foundational truths about your identity in heaven that you need to discover and understand before anything else. These *indicatives*, or truths to believe, are a little like explaining the bigger picture, what team you are on, and your position on the field before sending you out into life.

Then the last half of Ephesians (chapters 4–6) is filled with powerful *imperatives*. These are specific commands and instructions to live out your true, heavenly identity in your daily life on Earth. So the *indicatives* turn on the lights and explain who you are, your purpose and value; then the *imperatives* help you align your life—your thoughts, words, relationships, and mission—in such a way that they match up with your identity in Christ.

Since most people tend to prefer practical, easy-to-follow instructions, there's a tendency for Bible readers and pulpit preachers to jump over the deeper first half of Ephesians and dive into the practical "now what?" applications near the end. But that's like trying to build a house without looking at the blueprint, or fly a plane without first learning how. Daily applications will be very difficult—impossible, really—to contextualize and implement without the foundations of doctrinal truth that the first three chapters of Ephesians provide.

You can try as hard as you want, living the Christian life on your own energy, but you will likely wear yourself out and inevitably fail at trying to follow God's instructions if you don't first grasp the bigger picture of who you are, who He is, what He has done for you, and what resources are available to help you. That's why we hope this book will be, and has already been, a huge blessing to you.

As we close this chapter, note also how the writer of Ephesians, the apostle Paul, prayed for his readers. Two different prayers appear in the first half of the book (Eph. 1:15–19; 3:14–19) that we highly recommend you read. In both of them, Paul did *not* pray for their health, jobs, families, or financial issues (though there's nothing wrong with that). He also did *not* pray for them to clean up their behavior and relationships and start acting like godly people (though there's nothing wrong with that either).

In both prayers, he went straight to the heart and prayed that God's Spirit would reveal truth deep in their hearts, giving them understanding to know *who they are* in Christ, *what they have* in Christ, and *how much God loves them* through their relationship with Christ. Paul knew that discovering these things in our hearts will change us at the core of our being, where it can then ripple out to positively influence every other layer of our identity and life.

These prayers are a great inspiration for us as we continue this journey. It would be highly appropriate to pause and pray the same thing for yourself . . .

*Heavenly Father, thank You for what You have done and continue to do in my life. I pray that Your Spirit would give me wisdom and revelation in the knowledge of who You are. I ask that You would open the eyes of my heart so that I will know the bigger picture of Your calling and plan on my life. Show me who I am in Christ, the rich inheritance I have in Christ, and Your great power at work in and through me, through all of us who believe. Open my eyes to know the width, length, depth, and height of Your love for me. Help me believe and receive these things by faith. Fill me with Your Spirit today, and use me in this world for Your glory. In Jesus' name, amen.*

## TAKE IT DEEPER BY STUDYING
Romans 10:6–10 • Ephesians 1:15–19 • Ephesians 3:14–21

*. . . to know Christ's love that surpasses knowledge, so that you may be filled with all the fullness of God. (Eph. 3:19)*

# CHAPTER 13

## *You Are Beloved as God's Adopted Child*

*I pray that you, being rooted and firmly established in love, may be able to comprehend with all the saints what is the length and width, height and depth of God's love. (Eph. 3:17–18)*

The length, the width, the height, the depth—*it's so long, it's so wide, it's so high, and it's so deep.* The love of God. If only we could grasp and understand it even more. God is unlimited and eternal. So His love is the length of eternity, higher than the stars, wider than the universe, and deeper than any ocean. It flows out of the identity and heart of God (1 John 4:16).

Everyone who has encountered the truth of the gospel and believed in Jesus Christ and His death and resurrection—everyone who is trusting Him as Lord and Savior—has a new identity in Christ and in heaven's eyes. And that identity is as a chosen, adopted, beloved child of God.

This river of the Father's love has not just been placed near you or around you; it is even now being "poured out" on you—"poured out in our hearts through the Holy Spirit who was given to us" (Rom. 5:5).

And you probably don't believe it . . . because you probably don't fully realize it and always feel it . . . because unconditional love has probably not been faithfully modeled in your past experiences and relationships in life.

But the Word of God is the Word of God for a reason. The ways of God are not the ways of man (Isa. 55:8). And as we enter into this section, exploring the new identity that God says is true of you in Christ, it is time for the "eyes of your heart" to be "enlightened," as Paul prayed, "so that you may know" (Eph. 1:18)—so that you may know who you really, truly are—so that you may know what all has been done for you, and is being done for you, to live inside this actual reality, every single moment.

In Christ, you are loved. Let's just start there. You are *unconditionally* loved. This is who He says you are in Him. You are God's beloved child, chosen "before the foundation of the world . . . to be adopted as sons through Jesus Christ for himself, according to the good pleasure of his will" (Eph. 1:4–5). You aren't just given *love*; you are given the title "beloved." It is now your identity and is rooted in the Greek word *agape*, which is God's unconditional, 1 Corinthians 13, all-encompassing, all-enduring love. *Beloved* basically means, "one who is unconditionally loved by God."

Stephen speaking here: Do you remember Mia's story from the beginning of this book? She did nothing to earn our love. In fact, unlike how God already knows us—how He knows us while we're still in our mother's womb (Ps. 139:15–16)—Mia was a total stranger. We didn't even know she existed on the planet until her referral showed up in our inbox. But we set our hearts on her. We chose her. In our "good pleasure," we freely, willingly, eagerly, excitedly reached out to love her. And today she is our beloved, adopted daughter. Mia is in a permanent relationship with us. (I even hugged her earlier this morning, told her I loved her, and looked into her smiling face. She has been recovering so well from her heart surgery!)

But there was a time, of course, when she *wasn't* ours or in a relationship with us—just as there was a time when *you* weren't in permanent, loving relationship with the Father.

"You were dead in your trespasses and sins in which you previously lived according to the ways of this world" (Eph. 2:1). But those ways— those earthly, human, conditional ways of striving to be loved, of trying to earn acceptance and hoping to clean ourselves up and become worthy of loving approval—they are not the ways of God. His way is grace!

And so when you walk around feeling unloved as His child, it's because the "ways of this world" are speaking more loudly in your heart than God's loving ways. If you feel unloved, it is not because you're not loved; it's because you are not believing by faith and receiving from Him the love that He is *pouring out* on you even now.

If you are always feeling unloved, even though know you are God's child, it might be because of bitterness or unconfessed sin in your heart that is blinding your eyes and clogging your spiritual ears from seeing and hearing what God's Spirit is saying to you about who you are (1 John 3:13–24). But He is love and loving whether we're in tune to His voice or not.

"God, who is rich in mercy, because of his great love that he had for us, made us alive with Christ even though we were dead in trespasses" (Eph. 2:4–5). "God proves his own love for us in that while we were still sinners, Christ died for us" (Rom 5:8). "Those who were not my people," He said, "I will call 'my people,' and her who was not beloved I will call 'beloved'" (Rom. 9:25 ESV).

Right *there* is the Word and the heart of your Father toward you. *There's* the One who wants you to "know" the deep, wide, immeasurable love of God for you, and to be "rooted and firmly established" in it, anchored and secured inside it forever.

This word *know* from Ephesians 1:18 speaks of an intimate, experiential knowing—a knowing that is deeply realized though not fully comprehended. You don't have to understand air to breathe it in, or understand light to see it, or understand the molecular structure of water to be able to drink it and be refreshed by it. Just because you can't see or explain God's love for you or even feel it sometimes, you can still "know" it is there.

God simply chooses to graciously give it to us as His children.

God chooses.

He chose Israel, the Bible says, to be His special people, to be known around the ancient world by His name. "He loved your fathers," Moses told them—Abraham, Isaac, Jacob, Joseph—and "he chose their descendants after them and brought you out of Egypt by his presence and great power" (Deut. 4:7).

He didn't require them to earn this distinction, any more than He demands *you* to prove yourself worthy of His love. In fact, of these forefathers that God said He loved, each one could be exasperating. Abraham had a bad habit of lying to get himself out of uncomfortable situations; Isaac seemingly failed to be an unbiased spiritual leader in his home; Jacob tricked and connived his way through life; Joseph bragged to his brothers as the favored son in their family. These men that God loved had many unlovable sides to them—as did their offspring, the children of Israel, who moaned and groaned over anything they didn't find satisfactory about living in *freedom*—yes, the daily freedom that He'd sprung upon them as He rescued them from brutal, merciless Egyptian slavery.

Israel was not choice material for being chosen. The Lord said, for example, He did not choose them on the basis of their being "more numerous than all peoples," because actually they were "the fewest of all peoples" (Deut. 7:37). He chose them, at least in part, because they didn't fit the profile of what a mighty, conquering nation was supposed to look like—which appears to be His pattern and purpose even now, even with us.

> Brothers and sisters, consider your calling: Not many were wise from a human perspective, not many powerful, not many of noble birth. Instead, God has chosen what is foolish in the world to shame the wise, and God has chosen what is weak in the world to shame the strong. God has chosen what is insignificant and despised in the world—what is viewed as nothing—to bring to nothing what is viewed as something. (1 Cor. 1:26–28)

The point being: His heart of love and His willing desire to be gracious to us is the only thing that makes any sense as to why He's chosen us. Again, God doesn't love us because we're so lovable; He loves us because He is so loving.

Do you realize the richness of that? Do you *know* this to be true in your heart?

If you don't, it's understandable. Our tendency is to believe that God may truly love other people, while we secretly question in our doubting hearts that God could truly, unconditionally love us.

John the apostle lived in close, personal fellowship with Christ for all three years of Jesus' ministry. He heard Jesus talking every day about the love of God, about His love for His followers. John even wrote down some of the greatest quoted lines ever from Jesus that give us many of our keenest insights into the length and width, height and depth of His love for us. "As the Father has loved me, I have also loved you" (John 15:9). "Love one another as I have loved you" (v. 12). "Greater love has no one than this, that one lay down his life for his friends" (v. 13 NASB).

John heard all this. He'd been exposed to all this. He'd literally stood at the foot of the cross. He'd peered into the empty tomb, had seen the clothes lying there that Jesus was buried in. How could John not have *known* how deeply he was loved?

But writing years later in 1 John—a letter that speaks of God's love in almost every other verse—he wrote, "We have come to know and believe the love that God has for us" (1 John 4:16). Even *he* had to "come to know and believe." It's so hard to fit the ocean of God's love into the cup of our limited comprehension. The enormity of God the Father's love for John just continued to grow and expand over the years as his heart and mind and spirit kept growing in strength and in the knowledge of God.

Love that is this deep and wide simply goes against what we've all experienced and observed, to some degree in life—people who said they loved us, promised they loved us, but didn't end up loving us like they said they would. God, however, is a faithful God who has no problem keeping His Word. Being who He is comes so easy for Him.

"God is love, and the one who remains in love remains in God, and God remains in him" (1 John 4:16b). One of the greatest ongoing revelations for your life is that, in Christ, you are a beloved child of God. This truth far exceeds any earthly titles or positions. It should minimize the pain of the insults and failures of your life. It should fill you with faith and assurance that you still have an eternal purpose in the midst of your pain, and value in the face of the vicissitudes of life. It should energize you and strengthen you. During every trial, during every dark day, let the Holy Spirit whisper the Father's voice in your heart that YOU ARE MY BELOVED CHILD.

> In all these things we are more than conquerors through him who loved us. For I am persuaded that neither death nor life, nor angels nor rulers, nor things present nor things to come, nor powers, nor height nor depth, nor any other created thing will be able to separate us from the love of God that is in Christ Jesus our Lord. (Rom. 8:37–39)

Accept by faith today what may feel sometimes next to impossible for you to believe. Feelings don't guide you. God's faithfulness does. *You are loved.* You are "in the Beloved" (Eph. 1:6). You've been chosen and adopted by your heavenly Father, who loves you wide, loves you long, loves you deeper than the ocean, loves you higher than the sky—like no one has ever loved you before—because that is exactly and permanently who He is in you. And who you are in Him.

---

At the end of each chapter, throughout these next two parts of the book on your *identity* and your *inheritance,* we're including an affirmation specific to the theme of that chapter. We hope you'll say it—out loud—believe it in your heart, and continue to repeat it in the coming days, thanking God by faith for what His Word says is true of you. Here's today's declaration:

*Because Jesus is my Lord, and because I am in Christ,*
*I am beloved as God's adopted child. I know I don't deserve it,*
*but I receive it by faith from my loving heavenly Father,*
*who has set His love upon me, chosen me, and adopted me.*

*Father, Your love for me is more than I can comprehend. After all the things I've done and been, I don't see how You could love me at all, much less love me so immeasurably. But I believe Your Word and choose to trust what I don't always feel. Help me walk in the assurance of Your love for me. Cause a smile to break out on my face as I consider the depth of Your faithfulness and generosity toward me as my Father. I love You, and I thank You for Your love, in Jesus' name.*

## TAKE IT DEEPER BY STUDYING
John 15:9–17 • Romans 8:31–39 • 1 Peter 2:4–10

*Love consists in this: not that we loved God, but that he loved us and sent his Son to be the atoning sacrifice for our sins. (1 John 4:10)*

# CHAPTER 14

# *You Are Blessed as God's Spiritual Son*

*Blessed is the God and Father of our Lord Jesus Christ, who has blessed us with every spiritual blessing in the heavens in Christ. (Eph. 1:3)*

A sking God to bless us, or to bless another person, is among the most common prayers believers pray. And that's fine. It's wholly appropriate—and biblical—to ask for God's blessing, to seek His favor on "the work of our hands" (Ps. 90:17).

But in asking Him to give His blessing, remember this: you are already blessed "with every spiritual blessing in the heavens in Christ."

Peter said it this way: "His divine power has given us everything required for life and godliness through the knowledge of him who called us by his own glory and goodness" (2 Pet. 1:3). Paul said it this way: "Don't worry about anything" (Phil. 4:6), because God's blessing is already assured. Instead, as you make your requests of God, realize you can pray with your thanks predetermined, expecting that "the peace of God, which surpasses all understanding, will guard your hearts and minds in Christ Jesus" (v. 7).

Because in Christ, no matter what happens, you already know you're covered.

The entirety of Scripture yields evidence not only of God's unlimited *ability* to bless but also His eager willingness and desire to bless.

His blessing is not a wish. It's not hopeful thinking. When God blesses, it means He has already made arrangements for success. When God blesses, He provides everything necessary to complete what He has called us to do.

When God created the first man and woman, for instance, the Bible says He "blessed them, and God said to them, 'Be fruitful, multiply, fill the earth, and subdue it'" (Gen. 1:28). He not only gave them a command but equipped them with all the resources they needed for fulfilling it.

He even "blessed the seventh day" after He'd completed His work of creation (Gen. 2:3). What an amazing thing for Scripture to say. From the beginning of time, He was already making gracious provision for us to live with the blessings of rest and worship that each of us needs for fulfilling our callings. And though today we often feel overwhelmed by the sleepless, nonstop demands of life, our identity as a child of God means He has already given us sufficient tools for being able to maintain the kind of pace, rhythm, and availability that keeps us primed to follow His Word and His will.

He's thought of absolutely everything. "Everything required for life and godliness." "Every spiritual blessing." That's what He has for you.

But as with His unconditional love, our hearts are naturally suspicious that God would choose to pour out blessing on us. Maybe in small doses. Maybe in short bursts every now and then. But we don't tend to default to the expectation that blessing is already rushing toward us with river-running, open-hydrant profusion. That's what *some* people get. That's what *other* people get. Not what *we* get.

Because if God was blessing us at *that* level, we think, surely we wouldn't be dealing with some of the stuff we're going through. If He really wanted to bless us, we could tell Him some places and areas where He might want to start first.

But again, your identity calls for looking at life through new eyes. You process life now with a whole new operating system. Some of the same types of awareness and adjustments that go into keeping yourself reminded by faith that you are loved, chosen, and adopted are the same changes of perspective that help you remember . . . wait, I am blessed with every spiritual blessing. And there's not a circumstance in the world that can change it.

Abraham and his wife Sarah were unable to conceive a child—more than twenty years after God had said to him, "I will make you into a great nation, I will bless you, I will make your name great, and you will be a blessing" (Gen. 12:2). So he probably didn't *feel* too blessed during that time, hearing the dim memory replay in his mind—almost like a taunt now—back from when God had said, "Look at the sky and count the stars, if you are able to count them. . . . Your offspring will be that numerous" (Gen. 15:5).

But could God not be trusted for what He had promised? Did the frustrating years that fell in between get to make the call on whether or not Abraham was blessed? Looking at his life on balance now—with King David, even King Jesus Himself in His physical lineage (Matt. 1:1–16)—do you see anything but blessing embedded there?

Does anyone or anything else—including yourself—ever possess the authority or jurisdiction to deem you lacking in the blessing department, if you're a child of God?

No. God's Word reveals what life is certain to bear out. Far from being stingy with His blessings, God pours them out in abundance—from the Garden of Eden to the current events of this day. That's because the treasury of His blessing—unlike anything we know on the earth—is truly bottomless. He never needs to borrow from anyone, "as though he needed anything" (Acts 17:25). "If I were hungry," He said, "I would not tell you, for the world and everything in it is mine" (Ps. 50:12).

And He has no desire to hold them back. "He did not even spare his own Son but offered him up for us all. How will he not also with him grant us everything?" (Rom. 8:32).

There's that word again: *everything*.

This is no measly operation He's running. Living for Christ is no cut-rate experience. Even in times when Paul said he'd been forced to "make do with little," he was still able to do "all things through him who strengthens me" (Phil. 4:12–13). He reported how churches in Macedonia, who were going through a season of severe trial and affliction, were able to live simultaneously with both "extreme poverty" and "abundant joy" (2 Cor. 8:2). They continued to give of themselves generously even in times of shortage because they never doubted God's blessing was just going to keep on coming right behind them.

Here's one other thing that's worth noting. If you were a little surprised to see in the title of this chapter that "You Are Blessed as God's Spiritual *Son*," rather than "Spiritual Child," allow us a quick explanation. In the culture of biblical times, the firstborn son of a family was set apart to receive extra blessing. Just as each generation has its own customs and assumptions that seem odd if viewed from the distance of centuries, this perceived inequality of gender and birth order strikes us as being off. But to those who were reading Paul's original letters, they knew exactly what being a firstborn son entailed: *primo blessing.*

So when Scripture says Christ came to "redeem those under the law, so that we might receive adoption as sons" (Gal. 4:5), God was saying to both men *and* women that their status in His kingdom—because of their faith in God's *own* Son—was like that of the favored son in a family. It meant they were entitled to the big blessings, the superior blessings, the kinds of blessings everyone would want if they could have them.

Well, you've *got* them. You are blessed. Being blessed is who you are. And for this reason, there's nothing—literally nothing—that ever has the power to deplete you as a believer, since the God you serve is "able to do above and beyond all that we ask or think according to the power that works in us" (Eph. 3:20). When you feel as though you're under the pile, with no reserves to draw from, remember that you are blessed with every spiritual blessing. This is who you are.

———

*Because Jesus is my Lord, and because I am in Christ,*
*I am blessed as God's spiritual child, with the full blessings*
*of sonship. God has given me everything required for life*
*and godliness, every spiritual blessing in the heavens in Christ.*

*Heavenly Father, You have made me truly blessed. You have blessed me in the past by sending Your Son to redeem me. You are blessing me in the present by knowing what I need before I ask it. And You give me confidence that You will continue to bless me in the future, now and forever, without fail. Help me live as someone who never doubts Your love and provision, but trusts You to supply every blessing. May I use them and share them for Your glory, in Jesus' name.*

**TAKE IT DEEPER BY STUDYING**
Numbers 6:22–27 • Matthew 25:31–34 • Galatians 3:7–9

*The person who trusts in the LORD, whose confidence indeed is the LORD, is blessed. (Jer. 17:7)*

CHAPTER 15

# *You Are Saved as God's New Creation*

*If anyone is in Christ, he is a new creation; the old has passed away, and see, the new has come! (2 Cor. 5:17)*

God really wanted you saved. He wanted you *rescued.*

That's the precise language the Bible uses to describe the heroism of what's happened to you, and to all of us that He has chosen, loved, blessed, and set His heart upon to redeem. "He has rescued us from the domain of darkness and transferred us into the kingdom of the Son he loves" (Col. 1:13).

To be "rescued," in the original language, carries with it the idea of someone rushing across enemy lines and pulling a person out of danger by force to liberate them. That's what Jesus did for you through the violence of the cross. The whole Bible, really, is the story of God rescuing His lost and endangered people, delivering them from the life-threatening peril they were caught in and setting them free.

He rescued Noah and his family from His own wrath and the destruction of the Flood. He rescued Lot from the fire-and-brimstone devastation of Sodom and Gomorrah. He rescued Joseph from both the slave pit and the prison house. Most notably of all for Israel, as Moses' father-in-law summarized, "Blessed be the LORD . . . who rescued you from the power of Pharaoh. He has rescued the people from under the power of Egypt!" (Exod. 18:10).

But every rescue throughout Scripture—the shepherd David being rescued "from the paw of the lion and the paw of the bear" (1 Sam. 17:37); Daniel being rescued from the lions' den; his friends being rescued from the fiery furnace—each one of these stories foreshadows the gospel story of Jesus going to the cross to rescue us from . . .

From what? From what danger?

From the greatest danger of all. From the just and holy wrath of God on sin (Rom. 6:23).

Let's just be daring enough to say it. We can choose, if we like, to pretend we're living in a fairy-tale land where only the worst villains get what's coming to them, while the rest of us get the kindly grandfather treatment from God, who waves off our wickedness and sins with a wink and a nod and a gentle, forgetful smile.

But the "wages of sin is death" (Rom. 6:23). "If you do not believe that I am he," Jesus said to His doubters—the living Son of God—"you will die in your sins" (John 8:24). That's reality. Sin and death go hand in hand. Sin incurs the righteous wrath of God, who "will not leave the guilty unpunished" (Exod. 34:7).

*Wrath of God.* We don't like thinking about those words and what they mean, but we *must.* Jesus said not to "fear those who kill the body but are not able to kill the soul; rather, fear him who is able to destroy both soul and body in hell" (Matt. 10:28).

What then do we see, when we see the wrath of God?

We see Jesus hanging on a cross. Take note of how He died. The gruesome physical torture, the bloody wounds, the quivering muscles, the shame and humiliation of being held up to naked, open, public shame and ridicule. Nothing about execution by crucifixion was quick and painless. It wasn't like receiving a lethal injection or even quickly losing one's head on a guillotine. Crucifixion was designed to maximize the intensity of the pain and then drag it out as long and as cruelly as humanly imaginable. That was the cross. In fact, the Latin *excruciare* (from which derives our English word *excruciating*) was coined to describe the horror of crucifixion.

In Jesus' case, however, there is the addition of His spiritual agony to the physical torment. We all can testify to the weight that sags inside of us when feeling heavy guilt for merely *one* strain of sin inside a single human heart. Imagine your soul bearing the weight of someone's entire lifetime of sin, all at once—multiplied by all the sin, of all God's people who'd ever lived or *would* ever live. And this is not a calloused, uncaring, unfeeling heart. This is the holy, loving, tender heart of Christ. Now you're getting closer to the crushing spiritual burden Jesus was carrying there, and also having to carry it apart from the supporting presence of His Father: "My God, my God, why have you forsaken me?" (Mark 15:34 ESV).

Want to see the wrath of God on sin? There it is. There's what we all deserve, and what He in no way deserved. Everything He endured on the cross is a glimpse of what the wrath of God will look like and feel like for all eternity on those who die in their sins.

Unspeakable, eternal, ever-dying death.

You may say, "Well, I don't believe that. I don't think God would allow people to suffer in hell." But consider this. Do you not know that the higher the status of a victim, the greater the consequence to the criminal for a crime? Assaulting a friend is wrong. But assaulting an officer of the law brings even greater consequence. How about assaulting a governor? How about a king or a president?

Then we must ask the key question. How high and holy would God need to be for the just and due punishment of humanity's sins against Him to be eternal torment and separation? Because that's how high He is. He is that holy and set apart.

We have a human tendency to exalt ourselves while devaluing God. And in this twisted value system, we don't see God as being that holy, or people as being that evil. So hell doesn't seem justifiable at all to us. And God might agree with you if what you are imagining were reality. But it's a human, prideful fantasy to think we understand the holiness of God, the sinfulness of man, and the just punishment due in light of it.

So the *kindness* of God is great that He doesn't let us toddle along through life without warning us of what continuing on in our sins might cost us. God's desire is for people to be saved and forgiven (1 Tim. 2:3–4), to repent and believe, to be redeemed, changed, and set free.

"Do you despise the riches of his kindness, restraint, and patience," Paul implored in his letter to the Romans, "not recognizing that God's kindness is intended to lead you to repentance?" (Rom. 2:4). "Do I take any pleasure in the death of the wicked?" says the Lord. "Instead, don't I take pleasure when he turns from his ways and lives?" (Ezek. 18:23). It's because God doesn't want "any to perish but all to come to repentance" (2 Pet. 3:9) that He continues to express His enduring patience with us. Over and over again.

As part of His patient nudge, however, He is already revealing signs of His wrath "against all godlessness and unrighteousness of people who by their unrighteousness suppress the truth" (Rom. 1:18). Look around at what's happening in the world. The sexual immorality. The disease and disaster. The scandalous, public failures of powerful people. The futile thinking and living that's going on all around us, in which people still wake up on certain eye-opening mornings, wondering, "What am I doing with my life?"

These are all being used as God's warnings to us. Shots across the bow. They're the hunger in the belly of the prodigal that makes him wonder if he can somehow make a meal from pig slop. They're God's gracious ways of getting people to come to their senses and plead for His rescue.

Imagine if He hadn't done that for you. Imagine if in trying not to interrupt your sin or cause you any temporary discomfort, He hadn't warned you about the dire nature of your condition. Imagine if He decided to show zero percent of His wrath to us on the earth, only to surprise us with all 100 percent of it in coming judgment. *That* might seem like God is being cruel. What we see today is God being merciful. Putting out the warning signs across the road. Truth is always better.

And the truth, also, is that those who've heard the gospel and trusted their lives to Christ have been rescued from *all* of that by the loving and sacrificial payment of Christ. "The wages of sin is death," yes, "but the gift of God is eternal life in Christ Jesus our Lord" (Rom. 6:23).

> We were by nature children under wrath as the others were also. But God, who is rich in mercy, because of his great love that he had for us, made us alive with Christ even though we were dead in trespasses. You are saved by grace! (Eph. 2:4–5)

All the wrath that was due to you, the Father poured it out on His Son. Christ's status as the pure and spotless Lamb of God is so high that His suffering and blood sacrifice is even more powerfully effective and redemptive. And when the wrath of God was placed on the cross, that level of suffering through the body of Jesus resulted in a river of grace and love and acceptance and forgiveness that's being poured into your life now. Hallelujah!

Everything becomes new when a hopeless sinner is rescued by Christ's work on the cross. "The old has passed away, and see, the new has come." As black as things appeared—and actually *were*—that's how brilliantly bright and new you are now. "Though your sins are scarlet, they will be white as snow; though they are crimson red, they will be like wool" (Isa. 1:18).

Are you still finding all of this hard to believe? That's because God is simply that great and incredible . . . *mind-blowing* in who He is and what He does. Every time you've ever wanted a fresh chance—every time you've ever wished you could start all over again—now you can. You never need to view yourself from the "worldly perspective" (2 Cor. 5:16) of needing to prove yourself, earn your opportunities, and walk around in shame and defeat until enough time has gone by.

"He died for all so that those who live should no longer live for themselves, but for the one who died for them and was raised" (2 Cor. 5:15)—the One who rescued you from wrath and makes you now and eternally safe. You are saved and new in Him!

*Because Jesus is my Lord, and because I am in Christ,
I am saved from God's justified wrath on my sin, and I am
a brand-new creation through Jesus' blood. God has rescued
me from darkness and has made me safe with Him forever.*

---

*Lord, I should be facing nothing but Your wrath today. Your
judgment is all I deserve. And yet You have saved me. You've
taken away the old and broken, the useless and unsustainable,
and You have made me new in Christ. I worship You today from
a heart brimming over with joy and thanksgiving, with fresh
hope and promise. Work through this new creation You've made
of me, Lord, to show everyone who sees me what Your grace can
do. In Jesus' name, amen.*

---

## TAKE IT DEEPER BY STUDYING
Romans 5:6–11 • 2 Timothy 1:9–10 • Revelation 21:5–7

*If, while we were enemies, we were reconciled to God through
the death of his Son, then how much more, having been
reconciled, will we be saved by his life. (Rom. 5:10)*

CHAPTER 16

# *You Are Forgiven*
# *as God's Redeemed Saint*

*In him we have redemption through his blood, the forgiveness
of our trespasses, according to the riches of his grace. (Eph. 1:7)*

Forgiveness is a fundamental, necessary key to unlock these Ephesians blessings—these "every spiritual" blessings that we're assured of receiving from the Father when we believe in Christ for salvation. Forgiveness is what completely changes the calculus on how our sins are tabulated against us. It's how we go from having a debt to our Creator that is mathematically impossible to pay down (Matt. 18:24–25) to having an account ledger that reads "Paid in Full." Nothing owed. Zero balance.

Walls removed. Access accepted.

But can that really be true?—that God isn't holding *anything* over our head? Because it doesn't always *feel* true to us on Earth that we're as forgiven and in the clear as we've been told has happened in heaven.

God's Word answers this question much better than we can.

"As far as the east is from the west, so far has he removed our transgressions from us" (Ps. 103:12). Paul said, plain as day, that "Christ Jesus came into the world to forgive sinners" (1 Tim. 1:15), that "in him we have redemption, the forgiveness of sins" (Col. 1:14). "For he chose us in him, before the foundation of the world, to be holy and blameless in love before him" (Eph. 1:4). "Anyone who believes in him," Jesus said about Himself, "is not condemned" (John 3:18).

At one time, of course, you *were* under that sentence of death for your sins, hopelessly stained by them. "But you were washed, you were sanctified, you were justified in the name of the Lord Jesus Christ and by the Spirit of our God" (1 Cor. 6:11).

So, yes, it's a hundred percent true. *You are forgiven.* Or to put it in biblical language that might sound more official, you are . . .

*Justified.* Justification is a legal term that's equal to a judge declaring a defendant in court "not guilty." Rendered innocent. All charges dropped. "What the law could not do, since it was weakened by the flesh, God did. He condemned sin in the flesh by sending his own Son in the likeness of sinful flesh as a sin offering, in order that the law's requirement would be fulfilled in us" (Rom. 8:3–4). Therefore, "who can bring an accusation against God's elect? God is the one who justifies. Who is the one who condemns? Christ Jesus is the one who died" (v. 33–34).

So here's how it works, in the new-creation economy of grace. God looks at your report card, and then He looks at Christ's report card. Yours, like ours, looks terrible and dismal. Failing grades everywhere. The Ten Commandments? Nobody's perfectly followed them except Christ.

So Jesus' report card looks perfect. Straight A's. But then, in a move that's as shocking and loving as it could be, God in His great love for us has nailed our report card to the cross of Christ and given us His report card instead. By faith we have received God's plan for our forgiveness, and the Father accepts Jesus' spotless record as if it were ours. He passes over the sins that we've committed (Rom. 3:25), and through the righteous sacrifice of Jesus on the cross, He declares us righteous in Him, in Christ (v. 26). He considers us "justified freely by his grace through the redemption that is in Christ Jesus" (v. 24)—"the righteous for the unrighteous" (2 Pet. 3:18). Totally forgiven. Totally undeserved. All to the praise of the glory of His grace!

And it's all absolutely just, God says. "If we confess our sins, he is faithful and just to forgive us our sins and to cleanse us from all unrighteousness" (1 John 1:9 ESV).

But again, how can that really be? Sounds too good to be true.

It's *perfectly* fair and justified . . . because of the first two words in Ephesians 1:7.

"In him."

The fact that we are "in him"—"in Christ"—means everything that's happened to Him has spiritually happened to us. He was crucified; we've been crucified (Rom. 6:6; Gal. 2:19–20). He was dead and buried; we are dead and buried. He was raised; we are raised (Rom. 6:4; Col. 2:12). He is seated in heavenly places; we are seated in heavenly places (Eph. 1:6). The Father "made the one who did not know sin to be sin for us, so that in him"—see that?—"we might become the righteousness of God" (2 Cor. 5:21).

So, actually, because we're in Christ, it would be unjust of God *not* to forgive our sins, since Jesus has died for them, and fully paid for them, and we've believed on Him for salvation. God would consider it wrong not to forgive sins that His Son had already paid for on the cross for those who are "in Him."

---

Lean in, for a second, while we tell you something that maybe you haven't heard or believed in a long time, perhaps ever. We wonder if maybe you're someone who, like so many, just cannot get past some of the things you've done, even after receiving Christ and trusting Him for redemption, even after being given the identity of a forgiven sinner.

The enemy, you know, is a certifiable liar and advanced accuser. And when he attacks, you can be sure of this: he will always be pushing the identity button. *You? Forgiven? Holy? Blameless? You think God looks at you and sees "holy and blameless"? After what you've done? After who you've been? After who we all know you to be?*

How dare you believe that! Because if you're not walking by faith in the assurance of your forgiveness, if you're going around hanging your head, if you're continually or routinely punishing yourself for sins that you've confessed and repented of, and that Christ has paid for and buried, here's what you're saying with your posture and actions: you think that Jesus apparently needs you to help Him pay for your sins. All that blood and suffering He invested into this redemption mission was incredible, yes, but it still came up a little short. *Nice try, Jesus, but You didn't quite do it well enough. You must not have accounted for needing to cover the kind of sins of somebody like me.*

You're not forgivable, you think. You're too far gone, like the devil says—that even though God does forgive some people, He just can't forgive you. The accuser reminds you that since you've *been* a sinner in the past, you still *are* a sinner in God's eyes and in heaven's record books. That's just who you are and will forever be, the enemy claims. Sound familiar?

Then allow us to share another identity statement from Ephesians—a word that appears *all over* the Scripture, and it refers directly to you, and to us, and everyone who "calls on the name of the Lord" for salvation (Rom. 10:13).

You are a "saint."

That's not us talking; that's God talking.

Are you shaking your head "No"?

Yes. Anybody who's been forgiven by Christ is one of God's redeemed saints.

Ephesians 1:1—"to the faithful saints in Christ Jesus at Ephesus." Ephesians 2:19—"You are no longer foreigners and strangers, but fellow citizens with the saints." First Corinthians 1:2—"those sanctified in Christ Jesus" are "called as saints, with all those in every place who call on the name of Jesus Christ our Lord—both their Lord and ours."

When we hear the term "saint," as applied to an individual, most people think of someone who lived as a prominent religious leader, and who *performed* holy deeds at a mysterious level, or *performed* such amazing works of compassion that they *earned* a title they obviously *deserved*, commensurate with their religious devotion to Christ. *That's* a saint, someone who's done everything just right. Right?

But did you see those words? *Earned? Performed? Deserved?* To be honest, those are not the kind of words that highlight and bring praise to the glory of the *grace* of God. They bring praise to the *performance* of men. "But if it is by grace, it is no longer on the basis of works, otherwise grace is no longer grace" (Rom. 11:6 NASB).

A saint is a person who is called out and holy. But being a saint is not based on anything you've done, only on what Christ has done *for* you and *in* you. And how in the world could God get away with calling His people "saints" so often in His Word if His plan for us "saints" is still to condemn us in our sins?

Does that sound like God to you?

Being "holy and blameless," you understand, doesn't mean you're perfect in the world's eyes. It means, as Jude 24 says, that God causes you to be "without blemish" as you repent and trust fully in His Son. It's not a permission slip or invitation for you to run back into sin. It's an opportunity and command for you to walk in freedom, truth, and the light (1 John 1:7)—in confession of sin and in faith, not in denial and rebellion.

"If we say, 'We have no sin,' we are deceiving ourselves, and the truth is not in us" (1 John 1:8). Let's be honest. We've all rowed in that boat too many times. "But if anyone does sin, we have an advocate with the Father—Jesus Christ the righteous one," who "himself is the atoning sacrifice for our sins" (1 John 2:1–2). And it's time we started agreeing with God that this identity statement is true.

Do you understand that the devil wants you to live and think as if Jesus did not die, as if His blood was not enough, as if you are not in Christ, and therefore you're not forgiven? At the same time, God wants you live in joy and freedom, in the straight-shouldered confidence that His Word is absolutely true, and that you've been washed clean and have nothing to fear. The old you—the one who did all those things—is gone. And the new you—the redeemed saint of God—is now on the scene.

Consider yourselves to be dead to sin, but alive to God in Christ Jesus. Therefore do not let sin reign in your mortal body so that you obey its lusts, and do not go on presenting the members of your body to sin as instruments of unrighteousness; but present yourselves to God as those alive from the dead, and your members as instruments of righteousness to God. For sin shall not be master over you, for you are not under law but under grace. (Rom. 6:11–14 NASB)

So if you are in Christ, and if Jesus is where your hope lies, then there's nothing for God to look down on you now, nothing punishable to see in you or leverage against you for deeming you unworthy of His grace and mercy. Because you're in Christ now. And when your Father looks at you, He sees Jesus on the cross taking your place.

Therefore, far from receiving the *back* of His hand—far from receiving the dismissive *wave* of His hand—you can see instead your *name written* on His hands (Isa. 49:16), because of the nails that pierced the hands of the One who is "not ashamed to call [us] brothers and sisters" (Heb. 2:11).

There is now no condemnation for those in Christ Jesus, because the law of the Spirit of life in Christ Jesus has set you free from the law of sin and death. (Rom. 8:1–2)

In Him, you are forgiven.
Being His redeemed "saint" is who He says you are.

---

*Because Jesus is my Lord, because I am in Christ,
and because of His death on the cross as full payment for my sins, I
am completely forgiven and justified, every sin paid. God sees me
now with the righteousness of Christ as His redeemed saint.*

*Father, forgive me—not only for my sin against You, but also for not always trusting in Your forgiveness. Help me believe in my heart that if I confess my sins, You are faithful and just to cleanse me of all my unrighteousness. Help me believe that You have forgiven me completely—that I am clean in You, washed in You, and renewed in You. Show me that I can move on, beyond my sin, into the living reality of my identity as a redeemed saint—all because of Jesus, amen.*

## TAKE IT DEEPER BY STUDYING
Psalm 130:1–8 • Matthew 26:26–28 • Romans 5:12–21

*He has not dealt with us as our sins deserve or repaid us according to our iniquities. (Ps. 103:10)*

# CHAPTER 17

# *You Are Prized as God's Dwelling Place*

*. . . that Christ may dwell in your hearts*
*through faith. (Eph. 3:17)*

We can honestly say: God doesn't *need* another place to live.

"The heavens, indeed the highest heavens, belong to the LORD" (Deut. 10:14). "The earth and everything in it . . . belong to the LORD" (Ps. 24:1). "The LORD is high above all nations; His glory is above the heavens. Who is like the LORD our God, who is enthroned on high"—*so* high, in fact, that He "humbles Himself" even to "behold the things that are in heaven," much less the things that are "in the earth?" (Ps. 113:4–6 NASB).

So God is not struggling through the housing market. He "lives in unapproachable light, whom no one has seen or can see" (1 Tim. 6:16). He has spread out the sky "like a canopy, laying the beams of his palace on the waters above, making the clouds his chariot, walking on the wings of the wind, and making the winds his messengers, flames of fire his servants" (Ps. 104:2–4). Clearly He's got it all together and is enjoying all the features and accessories He wants.

Why, then, with physical and spiritual real estate holdings that encompass the entire universe, would God ever decide that He would like to come and live in . . .

In *you?*

And yet He's been acting on this seemingly incomprehensible, delightfully gracious impulse toward His people from the earliest days. After freeing Israel from bondage, He began instructing Moses about a tabernacle He wanted built, "a sanctuary for me so that I may dwell among them" (Exod. 25:8). And once it was set up and completed and prepared for God's arrival, the cloud of His presence "covered the tent of meeting and the glory of the LORD filled the tabernacle" (Exod. 40:34). "The cloud of the LORD was over the tabernacle by day, and there was a fire inside the cloud by night, visible to the entire house of Israel throughout all the stages of their journey" (v. 38).

The infinite God of the universe was *dwelling* among His children in a specific place at a specific time in an ever-present fashion.

The portable tabernacle eventually gave way to the cornerstoned temple, a more permanent structure where His people could come and meet with Him. At the dedication of the temple, fire literally descended from heaven and consumed the sacrifices they had come to offer Him, as again "the glory of the LORD filled the temple of the LORD" (2 Chron. 7:2).

This is God's way. He graciously settles down with us.

But the tabernacle and the temple, though transformed beyond the value of their raw materials by the presence of the Lord, were still only buildings, built of nonliving matter.

People had to *come* there, make plans to *show up* there, leave their homes and *travel* there. The shadow of the Almighty was definitely in their midst, yet He was foreshadowing something even more amazing to come.

The first hint we get of this further aspect of His plan was on an otherwise quiet day in Nazareth when the angel Gabriel appeared to a young virgin girl named Mary, telling her, "The Holy Spirit will come upon you, and the power of the Most High will overshadow you" (Luke 1:35). God Himself—Jesus, the Son of God—would be coming down to dwell inside her, making her womb His earthly home for these important months of His physical development. "How can this be?" she asked (v. 34).

She asked it for herself, of course, but her question leaves us with questions of our own: What must it have been like to know you were carrying the Son of God around inside of you? How much differently would you feel when you awakened to the reminder of this knowledge in the morning or sensed Him stirring within you throughout the day? How special, sobering—holy—it must have felt to realize God had made your body His dwelling place?

And yet as believers in Jesus Christ, that's *who you are*. This also is part of your identity. The Spirit of Christ, the Spirit of God, has come to dwell in your heart "through faith" (Eph. 3:17), through your faith in Him. "Don't you yourselves know that you are God's temple and that the Spirit of God lives in you?" (1 Cor. 3:16). The omnipresent One whose "house" exists on every planet and star and throughout every galaxy, who resides in heavenly places beyond the human imagination, has chosen to call you one of His cherished homes on the earth. "Christ will make his home in your hearts," Paul said, "as you trust in him" (Eph. 3:17 NLT). Do you feel humbled? Do you feel valued? Do you feel loved? You should.

As with Mary, this reality should leave a shocking and humbling impact on you—not so much fearful misery, but awestruck worship. When Mary considered it, she erupted in overwhelming praise toward God for how He had "looked with favor on the humble condition of his servant" (Luke 1:48). And so should you. The One who has no rival or equal, who has prized you favorably enough to want to come settle down inside of you, is worthy of all worship, from every corner of the universe, and from every corner of your life and being.

In fact, speaking of worship, this "dwelling" that God has chosen for Himself is greater than merely your own personal heart, though He has certainly made you priceless in your own right, and He intends you to think of yourself in those terms. Yet when Paul spoke in Ephesians of God's Spirit coming to inhabit us, He also had in mind the bigger, larger plan of the entire body of Christ, the church.

In him the whole building, being put together, grows into a holy temple in the Lord. In him you are also being built together for God's dwelling in the Spirit. (Eph. 2:21–22)

We are each individually God's temple. And we, the worldwide body of Christ, are also being made into the corporate, holy temple of God. Far from lowering your relative value, far from making you merely a lone face in a large crowd, this desire of God to fill His church with His presence expands your influence. It makes you part of an active force of gospel grace and truth on the earth that not even the "gates of hell" (Matt. 16:18 ESV) can keep from advancing. The living God who inhabits you gives you loving, caring, supportive "fellowship" within the Christ-honoring unity of these other believers also, even as He gives you fellowship "with the Father and with his Son Jesus Christ" (1 John 1:3).

God's Spirit among you, teaching you, unifying you, and tying your hearts together with other believers, is what helps keep you inspired toward "love and good works," as well as "encouraging each other, and all the more as you see the day approaching" (Heb. 10:24–25).

"Shout for joy and be glad," the Old Testament prophets wrote of this day, "for I am coming to dwell among you" (Zech. 2:10). "I will make a covenant of peace with them; it will be a permanent covenant with them. I will establish and multiply them and will set my sanctuary among them forever. My dwelling place will be with them; I will be their God, and they will be my people" (Ezek. 37:26–27).

What an amazing privilege for the people of Israel, from their early years as a nation, being chosen as the dwelling place of God. What an amazing privilege for Mary, such an out-of-the-way, unlikely vessel for carrying a treasure of such worth, of being the dwelling place of the Son of God.

And what an amazing privilege for you, having His Spirit right here inside of you—"the Spirit of truth who proceeds from the Father" (John 15:26). He will "never leave you nor forsake you" (Heb. 13:5 ESV). "The LORD will not leave his people or abandon his heritage"

(Ps. 94:14). Throughout all time, in fact, throughout time and beyond, "God's dwelling" will be with His children, "and he will live with them. They will be his peoples, and God himself will be with them and be their God" (Rev. 21:3).

He has found a house in your country, in your city, on your street, in your home, and in your heart, and has chosen you and prized you as His own. If you truly believed this, if you received Him as a gracious gift, how would it affect the way you live every day and every moment?

In Christ, you are the dwelling place of God.

---

*Because Jesus is my Lord, and because I am in Christ, His Spirit now dwells in me. I am the dwelling place of God. I've been bought with a price, the high price of my Savior's blood, and He has deemed me worthy to have fellowship with Him.*

*Heavenly Father, thank You for the gift of Your Son, and for the indwelling prize of Your Spirit. This home, this heart where You've chosen to dwell is only pure, I realize, because You have made it so. But help me, Lord, continue to trust in You to keep me pure and holy. I want my heart to be open at all times to welcome You, to continually be aware of Your presence, to be honoring and worshiping You. Settle here with me, and may my restless heart always be satisfied with Your fellowship, in Jesus' name, amen.*

**TAKE IT DEEPER BY STUDYING**
Deuteronomy 12:1–7 • Matthew 1:22–23 • 1 Peter 2:4–10

*I will dwell and walk among them, and I will be their God, and they will be my people. (2 Cor. 6:16)*

CHAPTER 18

# You Are Gifted
# as God's Specialized Worker

*We are his workmanship, created in Christ Jesus for good works,*
*which God prepared ahead of time for us to do. (Eph. 2:10)*

S alvation is a new beginning. New in Christ. New creation.

But it's not as though you just now showed up on God's radar. Let's go back to what Psalm 139 says—how He knit you together in your mother's womb. How He saw you *in utero* with more precise detail than the most advanced ultrasound technology. How all your days were known and planned "before a single one of them began" (v. 16). He's known about you and how He's wanted to employ you for a long time.

Or stay in Ephesians, where Paul says God chose you "before the foundation of the world" (1:4). Long before you were even conceived, He had already decided—based on His unique, comprehensive knowledge of you—exactly how He wanted to use your life for His glory.

So while it's true that big changes happened to you when you passed from death to life in Christ, God's long-term *preparation* for you—your "workmanship"—was just continuing forward.

Take Paul, for example. Jesus saved him on the road to Damascus in Acts 9. And from there, he became the majority writer of the remainder of the New Testament. But for many years prior to that—completely without Paul's awareness of it—God had a plan for him at that time in history to be His "chosen instrument to take my name to Gentiles, kings, and Israelites" (Acts 9:15).

Think of it. He was a Roman citizen; he understood the Gentile mind. But he was also rigorously trained in the Hebrew tradition, so he understood the Jewish mind as well. He had the intelligence and background to articulate the gospel in ways that people of either stripe could understand (if they wanted to understand). And he had the tenacity to stand his ground against ferocious opposition . . . because when he saw zealous rage in someone else's eyes, he could remember how it felt. He knew the terrible things it could make someone do. But he also knew how Jesus, by His grace, could transform even the hardest soul.

God took Paul's strengths, redeemed his sinful ways, and made him perfect for the job.

The same thing could be said of so many others in Scripture. David was trained as a shepherd. He knew how to protect a flock from dangerous predators, how to care for the daily, often demanding needs of his herd. So God "chose David his servant and took him from the sheep pens; he brought him from tending ewes to be shepherd over his people Jacob" (Ps. 78:71).

Rahab had been a prostitute. She knew how to hide a man within her place of business so he couldn't be found by someone banging on the door suspicious he might be inside. Who else, then, was better suited in Jericho to hide the Israelite spies who'd snuck into town to scout out their enemy's positions? Was it really any surprise that they ended up at Rahab's house (Josh. 2:1), or that God's real desire for utilizing her street smarts was to absorb her into the family of His people (Josh. 2:8–13), to establish a redemptive relationship with her?

When God gave detailed instructions for how the original tabernacle was to be constructed and furnished, He'd already been preparing a particular man to lead the effort. His name was Bezalel. And from what little we know of him, we know all we *need* to know. God had filled him with His Spirit, "with wisdom, understanding, and ability in every craft to design artistic works in gold, silver, and bronze, to cut gemstones for mounting, and to carve wood for work in every craft" (Exod. 31:3–5).

He couldn't do what Moses did. He couldn't do what Aaron did. So he could've easily concluded that his skills were of no real use in serving God. But he'd be wrong.

Because he was God's workmanship.

And so are you. God has a plan for you, and He can use your strengths and redeem your faults.

Maybe, like Bezalel, the Lord has given you certain kinds of abilities, skills, or passions, and yet you've not really considered how you could offer them to Him, for *His* use—art, or acting, or computers, or construction, or baking, or baseball coaching. But if He's placed an interest in you, or a specific form of competency, or a passion for a certain subject, know that "it is God who is working in you both to will and to work according to his good purpose" (Phil. 2:13). How might you be able to influence or serve or build relationships with other people while investing yourself in *these* particular areas, where God has already been building the foundation for it within you?

We know He also gives to His people, in addition to their natural talents, an assortment of spiritual gifts for "equipping the saints for the work of ministry, to build up the body of Christ" (Eph. 4:12). Among these emerging capabilities are things like serving, teaching, exhorting, giving, leading, encouraging, hospitality (Rom. 12:4–8)—all kinds of different opportunities that God will start (or has already started) revealing to you. You can join now then, with all the rest of us, in heeding Peter's instruction: "Just as each one has received a gift, use it to serve others, as good stewards of the varied grace of God" (1 Pet. 4:10).

Perhaps more unexpectedly, though, is how God can co-opt from your heart the various experiences, burdens, even failures that you've carried throughout life, and transform them into "good works" that bring blessing to yourself and others, even if those things once brought only pain.

We're thinking of former drug addicts and pushers that God has rescued from years of using, but now they're equipped like few others to help addicts break free from whatever's keeping them bound and defeated. Or we're thinking of people who've personally experienced abusive situations in their homes or other settings, and can now spot a fellow victim from a mile off. A hundred people may be in the same room, but this person's sensitivity to another's cues draws them into action and compassion.

It's God's *workmanship* in them, redeeming the past for His glory.

Even the specific sins that have been your most potent enemies in life can now become weapons that you turn against the enemy, as you minister to others who've been battling the same experiences, strengthening each other in your broken places.

It's how you put your workmanship into godly practice.

No, you're not *saved* by works (Eph. 2:8–9). We've been through all that. But after you're saved, your whole redeemed life becomes a work of art—the Savior's masterpiece—to do good works in a masterful, Spirit-led way.

The verse there (Eph. 2:10) implies that you simply start walking in them, offering every part of yourself up to His service and control. You see needs; you meet needs. You recognize opportunities; you seize opportunities. You do like Jesus did, as He traveled around from place to place. You use your abilities to serve and sacrifice for others, in whatever way those openings present themselves.

Our father, Larry Kendrick, has been a lifelong example to us for how Christians can invest their experiences, talents, and burdens toward the accomplishment of truly "good works."

Having grown up extremely poor, insecure, and fearful, he struggled with his own identity. He viewed himself as a skinny kid who had few if any usable talents. His alcoholic father was a giant of a man who was very intimidating to his son, and whose abrasive attitudes only reinforced the bundle of self-doubts and sensitivities that our dad carried around as a boy.

But his mother heard the gospel, gave her life to Christ, and began taking her three children to the nearby country church. As a teenager, our father became a believer as well.

After marrying Rhonwyn, the young woman who would become our mother, Dad embarked on a career as a public school teacher, while also serving as a youth pastor in our church. The struggles he'd brought with him out of childhood gave him a burden for students. It also inspired in him a desire for being the kind of husband and father that a godly man's wife and children really need. And knowing how crippling the effects of insecurity can be on a child's heart and sense of identity, he deliberately and consistently encouraged in each of us a "can-do" mentality, challenging us to think like winners and never be afraid to step out in faith.

In 1984, our father was diagnosed with Multiple Sclerosis. His body began to deteriorate. And his mind faded into a long depression—a dark, despondent season that lasted more than a year. But through our mom's unconditional love and the prayer support he received from the church, God reached in and rescued him out of the depths. He brought him into a flourishing, fruitful season of launching a Christian school, which he served as headmaster for more than twenty years.

Dad's time spent in secular teaching environments had given him a passion for Christian education. His gifts enabled him to oversee the school with wise management skills, coupled with a humble, gracious spirit of servant-hearted leadership. His experiences with serving in the church had given him insight into building teams and advisory boards. And his physical struggles against MS, while obviously challenging, gave him a heart for others who battled limitations, while also magnifying the volume of his influence. People knew he believed in what he was doing, that their kingdom mission together was vitally important, and they loyally joined him.

God had been uniquely preparing his life, before our dad even knew Him, to serve, give, and "stand tall" from his wheelchair. God redeemed his past, took his fears and sense of failure, and used them to minister to others. He is the one person our thoughts go toward first when we think of someone who exemplifies living as the workmanship of God.

But it's who you are as well.

And there is *nothing* keeping you from living it, if you choose to trust God.

*You* are the ideal, uniquely gifted, uniquely prepared person to do certain things for the kingdom that are probably right in front of you. We can think of specific people that God has led us toward when casting our films, for example, who—when we met them—God made it overwhelmingly clear, *this* is the right person for that role, as if they were just *made* for it. The Lord had been redeeming their past and equipping them for that moment, for that season, through the experiences of many years.

And with so many needs in people's hearts today, with so many places where "the harvest is abundant, but the workers are few" (Luke 10:2), the opportunities for your skills, your past, your gifts, and your burdens to come together for significant impact are plentiful and powerful.

This is who you are. This is what you can do.

And God has prepared you well to do it.

You are His workmanship.

---

*Because Jesus is my Lord, and because I am in Christ,*
*I am His workmanship. I have been created in Him for good*
*works, which He has already prepared for me to do. Every skill*
*and experience He's given me is His to use at His command.*

*Father in heaven, You've encouraged me today with the knowledge that nothing has been wasted in my life. The skills You've given me, the experiences You've allowed me to go through—You are able to use all of them, in ways that can make me effective in serving You. So I offer them up, asking You by Your Spirit to open my eyes to the people and opportunities where You want me plugged in and working. Help me bear fruit for Your kingdom today, each day, in Jesus' name, amen.*

**TAKE IT DEEPER BY STUDYING**
Ephesians 3:1–9 • 2 Timothy 2:20–21 • Hebrews 13:20–21

*"Pray to the Lord of the harvest to send out workers into his harvest." (Matt. 9:38)*

# PART III

# INHERITANCE
*What You Have in Christ*

# CHAPTER 19

## *You Have Resources and a Rich Inheritance from Your Father*

*I pray that the eyes of your heart may be enlightened so that you may know what is the hope of his calling, what is the wealth of his glorious inheritance in the saints. (Eph. 1:18)*

The radical difference between *who you were* (before Christ) and *who you are* (because of Christ) is an eternity-altering identity shift that, sadly, not every believer is aware of or takes the time to embrace. But our hope and prayer for you, as you read this book, is that God is encouraging you and deepening your knowledge of Him and His grace. And that He is transforming your heart and mind to line up with heaven's eternal perspective concerning who you really are in Him.

The warfare of doubt concerning this reality is probably being engaged in your mind already. The enemy, the accuser, hates everything you are and have in Christ. And he doesn't want you to understand it or be strong in it.

But God's blessings toward you (Eph. 1:3) in making you holy and blameless before Him (v. 4), His desire to set His love upon you (v. 6) and to forgive your every sin (v. 7) are truths that, if believed, will make your everyday life a different kind of experience.

Because when you as a follower of Christ stand firm in who you are, spiritual victory becomes yours. Strong and settled. And the spiritual assurance you're able to take with you now into each day can bring a lot of things down to Earth (fears, worries, insecurities) that once seemed hazy in your mind and hopelessly out of reach.

It's all because of what God has done.

And yet God doesn't stop at *doing*. Your Father keeps on giving.

He doesn't just change who we are. He grants us all the power and resources we need, which come as part of our new identity in Him. Our adoption of Mia did not just change her name and country of residence, but also provided a rich inheritance of relationships, resources, and provisions that were available to her because of who she is. The same is true of our identity in Christ. God does not just save and forgive us. He blesses and resources us as well.

> Blessed be the God and Father of our Lord Jesus Christ. Because of his great mercy he has given us new birth into a living hope through the resurrection of Jesus Christ from the dead. (1 Pet. 1:3)

"New birth . . . a living hope . . ." *AND* . . .

> And into an inheritance that is imperishable, undefiled, and unfading, kept in heaven for you. (1 Pet. 1:4)

So the Father has given you "new birth." That's who you *are*. You're saved. You're born again. But He has also given you an "inheritance." That's what you *have*. He has made you an heir to His abundant spiritual wealth.

This is how Paul, too—like Peter—chose to present this same teaching when he wrote about it in Ephesians. He first said that we are redeemed and forgiven, that God's grace has been "richly poured out on us" (1:8) and has resulted in blessing and acceptance. Then, as if beginning a new paragraph:

> In him we have also received an inheritance, because we were predestined according to the plan of the one who works out everything in agreement with the purpose of his will. (Eph. 1:11)

In light of what the Father has caused you to *be* in Christ—His beloved, adopted child—you've now been cleared for Him to take what's already unimaginable and completely transport it to the next level. "The Spirit himself testifies together with our spirit that we are God's children, and if children, also heirs—heirs of God and coheirs with Christ" (Rom. 8:16–17).

This "inheritance" includes the living Word of God (1 Pet. 1:23) as daily nourishment, wisdom, transformation, truth, and guidance (2 Tim. 3:16–17; Ps. 119:105). And it includes all the promises God has made to you in Scripture, all the things the Bible says are now yours—continual access to the throne of grace; the authority to ask, seek, knock, and expect in prayer through the name of Jesus; the family of God as your eternal spiritual family; the internal enabling and empowerment of the Holy Spirit; the promise of eternal life, starting right this moment and continuing on into heaven—a future with God that will only deepen and expand as we enjoy Him and serve Him together into eternity.

And these are just some of the larger categories of your inheritance. Inside these huge depositories of blessings are all kinds of cabinets and drawers and discoverable hiding places where His goodness and faithfulness and provision and protection and a million other favors, both seen and unseen, are yours to withdraw each day.

But withdrawing is an inaccurate mental picture because, as you've surely noticed in Scripture, the extent of your Father's wealth requires a whole new paradigm of *rich*. "For every animal of the forest is mine," He says, "the cattle on a thousand hills. I know every bird of the mountains, and the creatures of the field are mine. If I were hungry, I would not tell you, for the world and everything in it is mine" (Ps. 50:10–12). The famous quote from Abraham Kuyper, prime minister of the Netherlands at the turn of the 1900s, well applies: "There is not a square inch in the whole domain of our human existence over which Christ, who is Sovereign over all, does not cry, 'Mine!'" Not greedily but righteously.

So a believer doesn't draw *down* on God's estate, lowering the balance in His account by whatever's been taken out. The biblical phrase (in Ephesians and elsewhere) that gives us a better idea of the kind of inheritance we're talking about is this one: "according to."

Paul says you're able to be strengthened in your spirit "according to the riches of [God's] glory" (Eph. 3:16). Grace is given to you "according to the measure of Christ's gift" (Eph. 4:7). The extent to which the Father is "able to do above and beyond all that we ask or think" is "according to the power at work in us" from His boundless supply.

God is not, for example, sitting on fifty thousand blessings of various shapes and sizes today that He's wanting to hand out, to whoever gets their request submitted first, and after that, they're all gone. The inheritance we receive from Him doesn't come *out* of the river. The inheritance He gives to us is *like* a river. It's in keeping with the immense strength and supply of a river. It's "according to" the size of a river—His glorious river of riches.

And you, the Bible says (again), are not merely an "heir" of this inheritance that flows like a river from the unlimited wellsprings of heaven. You are "coheirs" with Christ—"joint heirs," the old King James Version says. To be only an heir would be as if a set of parents willed five acres of land to their five children, and each of the kids received one acre apiece. To be coheirs, however, would mean all five children own all five acres jointly. Or to use another example: if a husband and wife maintain a joint banking account, *he* doesn't own half and also *she* owns half. Both of them own it all.

God's Word doesn't say that believers are merely heirs, but joint heirs! Being a joint heir with Christ is another mind-blowing demonstration of His grace. Your right of inheritance—because you're now a blessed and beloved child of God—is the same as the Son's right of inheritance. Is that not incredible?

Because when all's said and done, we would be content living in the back corner of a back closet in a back alley on the back side of heaven. Have you been back there? I'm sure it's still amazing. But instead of merely that, we have been "seated" with Him "in the heavenly places" (Eph. 2:6 NASB). The Father has given us a joint inheritance with Jesus. "Indeed, we have all received grace upon grace from his fullness" (John 1:16). We get it all, basically. And God alone knows exactly what all that means. But from our small perspective, it's still simply unbelievable to consider.

Except it's true. He owes us nothing, yet gives us everything—this One who "works all things after the counsel of His will" (Eph. 1:11 NASB), who "richly provides us with all things to enjoy" (1 Tim. 6:17). We have His Word on it.

That's why you can give thanks in all things now (1 Thess. 5:18), rejoice in all things (Phil. 4:4), bear all things, believe all things, hope all things, endure all things (1 Cor. 13:7)—because you have been given all things by your infinitely rich, indescribably loving Father in heaven.

That's why you can pray for everything you need in Him. And that's why He's promised that He will supply all of your needs as His children, even now, "according to his riches in glory in Christ Jesus" (Phil. 4:19). You are not asking a stranger for a handout on the street. You are asking your extremely wealthy heavenly Father to be glorified by supplying all you need.

He can do exceedingly and abundantly above all that we can ask or imagine (Eph. 3:20). And we can ask for and imagine a lot! So let's ask for great things knowing that if we abide in Him and His words abide in us, we can ask for our heart's good desires, and He will honor them in His perfect timing (Ps. 20:4).

The One who supplied a river in the Garden of Eden, and animals for Noah's ark, and manna in the wilderness, and ravens with food for Elijah, and twelve baskets full of leftovers for the disciples, and abundance for the Macedonian church in the midst of their poverty, and movie production ideas and resources to South Georgia ministers, can also supply everything you will ever need in Him (2 Pet. 1:3).

It does not weary God or drain Him to pour into us so freely and generously. It is His nature and delight because He is the Source of every good and perfect thing. Providing for His children has been His plan all along from before time began. Our salvation is richly blessed with an eternal inheritance in Him. So you can lift your head in thanks and praise to Him, "who has enabled you to share in the saints' inheritance in the light" (Col. 1:12).

*Because Jesus is my Lord, and because I am in Christ, I have a rich inheritance as a blessed child of my heavenly Father that is imperishable, undefiled, and unfading. It is kept in heaven for me, but is mine in Christ. My Father has graciously made me a coheir with His beloved Son.*

*Father, the enormity of Your blessing on me is more than I can grasp. Your gifts and promises to me as Your child are just beyond me—overwhelmingly gracious, kind, and loving. But even when I feel the most staggered at the undeserved immensity of Your inheritance, help me not walk around like a pauper estranged from my Father, who is withholding His love from me. Help me stand here today knowing instead that I am an heir to the riches of heaven, and that You will always supply everything I need to do Your will on earth. In Jesus' name, amen.*

### TAKE IT DEEPER BY STUDYING
Proverbs 8:18–21 • Galatians 3:27–29 • Hebrews 11:8–10

*Didn't God choose the poor in this world to be rich in faith and heirs of the kingdom that he has promised to those who love him? (James 2:5)*

# CHAPTER 20

# You Have Access and Authority through the Son

*Through him we both have access in one Spirit to the Father.*
*(Eph. 2:18 ESV)*

Everything we have from God the Father is *through* the Son. Do not rush past that statement. It is a crucial truth to understand.

The Trinity, of course—the three-in-one union of Father, Son, and Spirit—is a reality that the human mind cannot completely wrap itself around. But among the subtle deceptions of our age, perhaps of every age, is the skepticism that says God's holiness is not *really* as radioactive as we've been led to believe. Maybe He's more approachable than we think. Maybe drawing close to Him is less like being vaporized by the sun, and more like being absorbed into a warm, comfortable embrace.

But God is the same God "yesterday, today, and forever" (Heb. 13:8). Nothing has changed to alter what He said to Moses: "You cannot see my face, for humans cannot see me and live" (Exod. 33:20). The distance between God's white-hot purity and our dark, corrupted sinfulness is not subject to change, only to remedy.

And the only remedy is through Jesus Christ.

"Through Christ," we can be "reconciled" to God (2 Cor. 5:18). *Through Christ*, we can be pleasing in God's sight (Heb. 13:21). *Through Christ*, we can be "pure and blameless . . . filled with the fruit of righteousness" (Phil. 1:10–11). *Through Christ*, we receive the Holy Spirit, can be "justified by his grace," and "become heirs with the hope of eternal life" (Titus 3:7).

In fact, it's even more elementary than that. Creation itself took place through the Son. "All things were created through him" (John 1:3)—"through him and for him" (Col. 1:16). God "made the universe through him," and even now the Son is "sustaining all things by his powerful word" (Heb. 1:2–3).

So without the Son, we literally have nothing.

Without the Son, there *is* nothing.

But *with* Him—*through* Him—we not only have our existence, but we have the manifold blessings of what the Bible refers to as "access" to God.

And having access to God is, in many ways, our most valuable asset in life.

In terms of the first-century world into which Paul was writing Ephesians, part of the "access" he was talking about was the inclusion of Gentiles into the family of God. The "mystery" of the gospel that Paul mentions so frequently (Eph. 3:3–9) was that no longer was there any spiritual distinction between "Jew or Greek, slave or free, male and female," but that "all are one in Christ Jesus" (Gal. 3:28).

So while at one time these Gentile brothers and sisters "were without Christ," Paul said, "excluded from the citizenship of Israel, and foreigners to the covenants of promise, without hope and without God in the world," they now—"in Christ Jesus"—had been "brought near by the blood of Christ" (Eph. 2:12–13).

> He came and preached peace to you who were far off and peace to those who were near. For through him we both have access in one Spirit to the Father. (Eph. 2:17–18 ESV)

*Access.* It's part of our heritage. *And* our inheritance.

It's hard to grasp exactly how foreign this concept sounded to the religious ears of that time. The possibility of a Gentile being able to achieve access to God was like a football team being four touchdowns behind with fifteen seconds to go. Just wasn't going to happen. It was like being stuck ten miles away from your office in deadlocked traffic, trying to get to a critically important meeting that starts in two minutes.

But Christ became "the mediator of a new covenant" (Heb. 9:15). Through His cross, He spanned the impossible divide "so that those who are called might receive the promise of the eternal inheritance" (v. 15b). The only reason that "we have boldness and confident access" to God is because we have it "through faith in him" (Eph. 3:12).

Again, without the Son . . . nothing.

But because of Him . . . everything.

With access to God through Christ comes a treasure trove of privileges.

Did you ever stop to think that God, even in choosing to save us by grace, could have decided He'd already done more than enough? And that the Son, after dying for sin, returning to life, and going back to heaven, could have left us here to figure out the rest of it by ourselves as best we could? Can you imagine how different life would be if that were the case?

It makes a person wonder why we often find reading and studying our Bibles to be such a chore, when we consider how precious the Scripture is, and how it represents the graciousness of our God toward us. As hard as we find living the Christian life to be, imagine being forced to try navigating it without having the revealed truths of Scripture to guide us.

Or without prayer. What if the Son had not provided us access to the Father through prayer? What if the only ones we could talk with about the concerns and questions of our hearts were each other? What if God truly wasn't listening?

Thankfully, incredibly, we never need to know the answer to that question . . . because Christ has given us access. The Son is our certainty that our prayers are being heard.

"We have boldness to enter the sanctuary," the Bible says, "through the blood of Jesus" (Heb. 10:19). He is our "great high priest over the house of God" (v. 21) who enables us to "draw near with a true heart in full assurance of faith" (v. 22). "For we do not have a high priest who is unable to sympathize with our weaknesses, but one who has been tempted in every way as we are, yet without sin" (Heb. 4:15).

Therefore, through the Son, we're invited at any moment of the day to "approach the throne of grace with boldness, so that we may receive mercy and find grace to help us in time of need" (Heb. 4:16). We make our prayer in His name—"the one who died, but even more, has been raised," the one who "is at the right hand of God and intercedes for us" (Rom. 8:34). "Whatever you ask in my name," He promises us (John 14:14), He will do it. He will do what brings glory to the Father, through the Son, through our lives.

That's the power and beauty of access. We don't come to a God who cannot be touched—"to a blazing fire, to darkness, gloom, and storm, to the blast of a trumpet, and the sound of words" (Heb. 12:18–19). We come instead to "Mount Zion and to the city of the living God, the heavenly Jerusalem . . . and to Jesus, the mediator of a new covenant, and to the sprinkled blood" (vv. 22, 24 ESV).

This is how your Father wants it to be. This is why He raised His Son from the dead and seated Him "at his right hand in the heavens—far above every ruler and authority, power and dominion, and every title given, not only in this age but also in the one to come" (Eph. 1:21). The access He provides for us enables the Son's authority to be seen by the world through the church—through us—"his body, the fullness of the one who fills all things in every way" (v. 23).

When Jesus walked the earth, He gave evidence to the extent of His authority that had been given to Him by the Father. He demonstrated authority over demonic spirits (Luke 4:36) and the authority to forgive sins (Matt. 9:6). His teaching, unlike that of the religious professionals, contained an instantly recognizable level of tone and authority (Mark 1:22). The devil arrogantly acted as though he could *give* Jesus authority in exchange for His worship (Luke 4:6–7), though as Jesus said to Pilate at the hearing before His torture and crucifixion, "You would have no authority over me at all if it hadn't been given you from above" (John 19:11).

"All authority has been given to me in heaven and on earth," Jesus declared to His followers immediately before His ascension. And it's by this same authority that "what is impossible with man is possible with God" (Luke 18:27). It's by this authority that Paul could say, "I am able to do all things through him who strengthens me" (Phil. 4:13). It's by this authority that we have the confidence of knowing, "If we ask anything according to his will, he hears us. And if we know that he hears whatever we ask, we know that we have what we have asked of him" (1 John 5:14–15).

You have all-the-time access to God by the above-all authority of the Son. It's your inheritance as a child of the Father.

***

*Because Jesus is my Lord, and because I am in Christ,*
*I have access to the Father, not only for my salvation,*
*but for every need in my life today. He will accomplish by*
*His authority everything I need according to His Word.*

*Father, I come to You today as You have invited me to come—in the name of Your Son Jesus and through the authority You have given to Him. May I never take for granted this privilege of being able to approach Your throne of grace and to be heard and received as a beloved child. Thank You for Your power and holiness that is so far above me, and for Your desire and willingness to draw so close to me. I bring all my praises and petitions to You now, in Jesus' name, amen.*

## TAKE IT DEEPER BY STUDYING
John 14:12–14 • Colossians 1:15–20 • Hebrews 7:26–28

*"Ask, and it will be given to you. Seek, and you will find. Knock, and the door will be opened to you." (Matt. 7:7)*

# CHAPTER 21

# You Have the Seal and Strengthening of the Holy Spirit

*I pray that he may grant you, according to the riches of his glory, to be strengthened with power in your inner being through his Spirit. (Eph. 3:16)*

The only conclusion that can really be drawn, if you read the Bible through the eyes of faith, is that God just decided He was going to give His children . . . well, *everything.*

It's the way He's always been. Wholehearted. All in.

"See if I will not open the floodgates of heaven and pour out a blessing for you without measure" (Mal. 3:10). "You will be blessed in the city and blessed in the country . . . blessed when you come in and blessed when you go out" (Deut. 28:3, 6). All these blessings, He said, will "come and overtake you" (v. 2). There's *nothing* we need that our Father has not done for us or is not doing for us (2 Pet. 1:2–3).

"He who did not spare His own Son, but delivered Him over for us all, how will He not also with Him freely give us all things?" (Rom. 8:32 NASB). "Everything is yours, and you belong to Christ, and Christ belongs to God" (1 Cor. 3:22–23).

The generosity of the gracious heart of God is uninhibited and overwhelming.

What else could He really give beyond this?

And yet in those untimed moments of eternity past, as God was preparing to roll out His eternal plans for our world and our salvation—as He was delighting in all the gifts and all the grace that He was going to pour out on us—He still had something else in mind. He knew He was going to be glorified by doing even more for us than that.

As we sit here today, with our arms and hearts overrun with the vast spiritual treasures that our heavenly Father has so richly "lavished" on us (Eph. 1:6), it's almost inconceivable that He would've said, *That's still not enough.* But in order for our lives to bring so much more "praise to His glory" (Eph. 1:12), He decided in concert within the Trinity that He wanted to include *Himself* as part of the riches of our inheritance.

In fact, the grand opening introduction to our great spiritual inheritance is the gift of Himself through His Holy Spirit. Marvel at that.

> Having also believed, you were sealed in Him with the Holy Spirit of promise, who is given as a pledge of our inheritance, with a view to the redemption of God's own possession, to the praise of His glory. (Eph. 1:13–14 NASB)

If anyone has ever felt satisfied in just writing a check or sending a gift through the mail, then consider the amount of God's bounty that He's given us—from Creation forward—and know that it is beyond enough to verify His generosity, by anyone's measure. But along with all this inheritance that He's given and prepared for us, we even have *Him* here with us . . . never leaving us, never forsaking us, always helping us, daily strengthening us, willingly encouraging us, constantly guiding us, walking intimately with us.

Words are simply not enough. And the fact that this plan for blessing and equipping us has always been in the works—"before the foundation of the world"—merely testifies that God is always faithful to do what God says He will do. As Jesus said . . .

> "I will ask the Father, and He will give you another Helper, that He may be with you forever; that is the Spirit of truth, whom

the world cannot receive, because it does not see Him or know Him, but you know Him because He abides with you and will be in you." (John 14:16–17 NASB)

The Greek word for *Helper* indicates that the Holy Spirit is "another one of the same kind." Just like Jesus was a walking and ever-present Helper to His disciples in the first century, the Holy Spirit is an ever-present Helper to us in all of our circumstances.

Think of the Spirit as a promise. A promise kept.

As Jesus said to His followers in some of His final words on the earth, "I am sending you what my Father promised. . . . Stay in the city until you are empowered from on high" (Luke 24:49). He commanded them "not to leave Jerusalem, but to wait for the Father's promise" (Acts 1:4).

And when the Promise came, He blew the lid off whatever fears or limitations or inadequacies the disciples may have felt concerning the mission Jesus had given them: to "be my witnesses in Jerusalem, in all Judea and Samaria, and to the end of the earth" (Acts 1:8). He showed up in awesome power and quickly changed the world through His followers.

Today we, too, have this "promised Holy Spirit" (Eph. 1:13). He is the power that ignites our service to God and to others (Acts 1:8). He is the guide who leads us into opportunities where God can use us most effectively for His kingdom (Mark 13:11). He is the master control who steers us away from sin and compromise, into the freedom of loving God without even needing to be horse bridled to do it by the law (Gal. 5:16–25). He is the one who "helps us in our weakness," translates our feeble words into effective prayers, and "intercedes for the saints according to the will of God" (Rom. 8:26–27). There's nothing this Holy Spirit of promise can't do.

And each time He performs one of His wonders and daily activities in you—whether it's putting His hand on your shoulder in a painful situation, or putting His hand on your conscience in a moment of decision, or one of hundreds of ways both great and small that He makes His presence known—let it be a reminder to you that God, even yet, has only barely cracked open the door on the *everything* that still awaits you. He has promised you *much* more than even what you see of your inheritance from Him today.

And the Spirit in you is the guarantee of it.

You are "sealed in him [in Christ] with the promised Holy Spirit" (Eph. 1:13). "You were sealed by him for the day of redemption" (Eph. 4:30).

The imagery here is both strong and beautiful. The "seal" in ancient cultures was a visible sign that guaranteed a person's chosen action or agreement. Often applied with a signet ring or similar instrument, the seal meant that the contents of a document and whatever it ordered must be carried out regardless. The seal made it irrevocable.

Haman's plot against the Jews, as described in the book of Esther, was "sealed with the royal signet ring" (Esther 3:12). That's what made Esther's courage so bold and daring in approaching the king to expose the truth, because "a document written in the king's name and sealed with the royal signet ring cannot be revoked" (Esther 8:8). And it wasn't revoked, though another edit was added to allow the Jews to defend themselves (v. 11).

You'll recall in the book of Daniel, too, how the king had been persuaded to issue a command saying that no prayers could be made for thirty days to anyone but himself, on pain of death in the lions' den. When he realized what he'd done, and how his friend Daniel had acted in violation of it by praying to God, the king tried to think of some way to deliver him. But the deed must be carried out. He'd "sealed it with his own signet ring" (Dan. 6:17). "The order stands" (v. 12).

In similar fashion, we have been "sealed" by the Holy Spirit "until the redemption of the possession" (Eph. 1:14). God has "put his seal on us and given us the Spirit in our hearts as a down payment" on the promise of our future inheritance in heaven (2 Cor. 1:22).

The Holy Spirit in your life is proof of that seal. He now represents another promise that will one day be fulfilled. He is the down payment on that promise that has been sent ahead and paid. Money is in the bank. He's like an engagement ring from the Bridegroom to His bride, to His Church, as He prepares a home for us in heaven.

It means that everything God has promised you is really going to happen. "If the Spirit of him who raised Jesus from the dead lives in you, then he who raised Christ from the dead will also bring your mortal bodies to life through his Spirit who lives in you" (Rom. 8:11). God's guarantee is for those trusting Christ by faith.

---

The Bible, in speaking of our salvation, sometimes refers to it in the past tense. "In this hope we were saved" (Rom. 8:24). We can look back and remember when we believed on Him and received His promise by faith. Yet it's still doctrinally true that, as God grows us and matures us and sanctifies us by His Spirit, we remain in the process of "being saved" (1 Cor. 1:18). Paul said to "work out your own salvation" (Phil. 2:12), to carry it to its proper conclusion and watch it take shape in your life. "Our inner person is being renewed day by day" (2 Cor. 4:16), "being transformed into the same image from glory to glory; this is from the Lord who is the Spirit" (2 Cor. 3:18).

But a day is coming, as sure as tomorrow's sunrise, when we who've been "declared righteous by his blood will be saved through him from wrath" (Rom. 5:9)—*will* be saved, future tense. And the reason we know that we know, that God *will* surely save us in the end, is because of the "down payment" He's already made on His promise. It's because He's put "skin in the game" which, even as we speak, is living inside that skin of yours.

> For all who are being led by the Spirit of God, these are sons of God. For you have not received a spirit of slavery leading to fear again, but you have received a spirit of adoption as sons by which we cry out, "Abba! Father!" The Spirit Himself testifies with our spirit that we are children of God. (Rom. 8:14–16 NASB)

Since God is going to keep His promises, the only question is whether you're going to believe it, receive it, and stand upon His promise until it is fulfilled. You have the Holy Spirit in you to help you do just that.

Now and forever.

*Because Jesus is my Lord, and because I am in Christ, I have the seal of the Holy Spirit in my heart and life. He is the fulfillment of the promise Jesus made that He will not abandon me but will be with me in all circumstances. He is my Helper, Counselor, Comforter, and Strength, the guarantee of my spiritual inheritance in Christ, and the sign of a promise to be fulfilled when Christ returns for me.*

*Father, I come to You in Jesus' name to thank You for all that You have given me in Christ. I worship You in light of the riches of Your glorious grace poured out on my life. Open the eyes of my understanding to grasp the fullness of my inheritance in You. Help me not worry about the future but to trust, access, and utilize everything You have provided for me. Thank You for the presence and power of Your promised Holy Spirit. Help me honor Your Spirit, trust Your promises, and glorify You in all circumstances. In Jesus' name, amen.*

## TAKE IT DEEPER BY STUDYING
1 Peter 1:5–9 • 1 John 2:24–27 • Revelation 7:1–4

*You are being guarded by God's power through faith for a salvation that is ready to be revealed in the last time. (1 Pet. 1:5)*

# CHAPTER 22

## *You Have Hope and a Home in Heaven*

*We have this hope as an anchor for the soul, firm and secure.*
*(Heb. 6:19)*

Non-Christians can experience a fleeting measure of happiness in this life. They can express a worldly, temporary version of love and gratitude. They can also feel compassion and loyalty and can drum up human endurance.

But they cannot have true hope.

Not *real* hope. Not genuine, eternal hope.

Hope is such an incredible part of our inheritance as God's children.

It is associated with the marriage of two other words: *desire* and *expectation*. You don't hope for things you don't want, and you don't hold out hope if you know something is never going to happen.

The world has a twisted version of hope. First, because their hope is often not for God-honoring things. And second, because their hope is not sure. It's more like a worldly wish to the wind, like hoping you'll win the lottery, or hoping to elect a president who will solve all the world's problems. Hope makes an impressive campaign slogan, but only God can see the future, rule over the universe, and truly guarantee us true and lasting hope.

He gives us hope in Christ—hope that is beautiful, meaningful, lasting, and sure.

"In this hope we were saved," Paul wrote (Rom. 8:24)—"the hope of eternal life that God, who cannot lie, promised before time began" (Titus 1:2). "This hope will not disappoint us, because God's love has been poured out in our hearts through the Holy Spirit who was given to us" (Rom. 5:5).

It's the only real hope anyone on Earth can have. It soars beyond the hope of this weekend or this year; it reaches up past the stars and into eternity. And you have it—you *have* this hope—if you've put the entirety of your hope in Jesus Christ. You have a blessed and priceless "hope reserved for you in heaven" (Col. 1:5).

At one time, as we've heard Paul say already, we were "without Christ," outside the family, "without hope and without God in the world" (Eph. 2:12). But now "our citizenship is in heaven, and we eagerly wait for a Savior from there, the Lord Jesus Christ" (Phil. 3:20).

He is preparing a place for us—an amazing, majestic place beyond our wildest dreams. And He is coming again to gather us up and to carry us there, where we will live with Him forever. This kind of *otherworldly* expectation is at the heart of what real hope is anchored in.

———

To fear is to believe and expect that something terrible is going to happen. But to hope is to believe—with greater intensity—that something marvelously good is going to happen. *Because it truly is!* As Jesus said to His followers:

"In My Father's house are many dwelling places; if it were not so, I would have told you; for I go to prepare a place for you. If I go and prepare a place for you, I will come again and receive you to Myself, that where I am, there you may be also." (John 14:2–3)

Christ's promise and imagery here is that of a bridegroom going back to prepare a permanent place for his bride to come live with him. He is the church's Bridegroom (Matt. 25:1–13), and has given us a promise that He is coming again.

And when He comes, it won't be a letdown.

> For the Lord himself will descend with a shout, with the archangel's voice, and with the trumpet of God, and the dead in Christ will rise first. Then we who are alive, who are left, will be caught up together with them in the clouds to meet the Lord in the air, and so we will always be with the Lord. (1 Thess. 4:16–17)

Wrongs will be made right. Evil will be confronted. Our bodies will be made new.

No more sadness or separation, the Bible says. "He will wipe every tear from their eyes" (Rev. 21:4). In heaven, "death will be no more; grief, crying, and pain will be no more, because the previous things have passed away" (v. 4b). No more words of exhausted desperation: "How long, LORD? Will you forget me forever? How long will you hide your face from me? How long will I store up anxious concerns within me, agony in my mind every day? How long will my enemy dominate me?" (Ps. 13:1–2).

The inward, frustrated cry of Paul in Romans 7, "What a wretched man I am! Who will rescue me from this body of death" (v. 24), will never cross our minds or lips again. The heartache regarding our sinful nature will be over, and the battle against our most hated weaknesses and temptations will be gone. No more continually tripping our feet and butting our heads against Romans 3:23, sinning and "falling short of the glory of God."

We shall be changed and be like Him . . . because we are God's children.

> Beloved, now we are children of God, and it has not appeared as yet what we will be. We know that when He appears, we will

be like Him, because we will see Him just as He is. (1 John 3:2 NASB)

He will transform the body of our humble condition into the likeness of his glorious body, by the power that enables him to subject everything to himself. (Phil. 3:21)

So today, as a coheir with Christ, as a blessed and beloved child of God, you can rest and walk in "full assurance of your hope" (Heb. 6:11). You can imitate those who "inherit the promises through faith and perseverance" (v. 12).

Like a pregnant woman who lives with anticipation of seeing the precious face of her newborn child soon for the first time, or like a couple hearing the strain of the "Wedding March," knowing their beautiful covenant is only moments from finally beginning, every believer can also "lift up your heads" today, "because your redemption is near" (Luke 21:28).

The fancy theological word for this exclusively Christian experience is "glorification." And it's as sure as God's love for you, as sure as His work in saving you. "Those he predestined, he also called; and those he called, he also justified; and those he justified, he also glorified" (Rom. 8:30).

It's not something we can see yet. That's what makes it hope. But "when Christ, who is your life appears, then you also will appear with him in glory" (Col. 3:4).

---

That's what people who don't know any better would call "pie in the sky"—those who say, "Where is his 'coming' that he promised? . . . All things continue as they have been since the beginning of creation" (2 Pet. 3:4).

Well, no, not exactly . . . because now that you know of your identity in Christ and your inheritance through Him, you can start experiencing right now the earthbound effects of an ever-strengthening hope, the heritage of those who by God's grace are seated already in heavenly places. And what does this sure hope do for us?

• *Hope gives you constant reason to rejoice.* Having obtained access through Christ into fellowship with the Father, you can "rejoice in the hope of the glory of God" (Rom. 5:2). Circumstances will tell you otherwise, but your heart can choose to dwell in the joy of hope.

• *Hope helps you keep things in perspective.* Paul said, "I consider that the sufferings of this present time are not worth comparing with the glory that is going to be revealed to us" (Rom. 8:18). Funeral homes, hospital beds, family in-fighting, financial worries—they can all sting and stink right now, but they are all temporary and won't be able to hurt you forever or take away the treasures that God has stored up for you in heaven.

• *Hope can spur you to incredible endurance.* "I would have despaired," David said, "unless I had believed that I would see the goodness of the Lord in the land of the living" (Ps. 27:13 NASB). The weight of life, pressing down on us, will eventually overpower us if all we're fighting for is our earthly survival. But the glorious eternity that awaits us, fanned into flame by the power of the Spirit inside us, gives us the Christ-like endurance to run the race before us and take on any tough hurdles ahead of us.

• *Hope motivates us to get our lives in order.* Our hope, because of the gospel, no longer depends on our own hard work and effort. Christ's righteousness is ours, and we can rest our whole lives upon it. But "everyone who has this hope in him purifies himself just as he is pure" (1 John 3:3). The gratitude and expectation, far from making us want to sit down and do less, inspires us "to deny godlessness and worldly lusts and to live in a sensible, righteous, and godly way in the present age, while we wait for the blessed hope, the appearing of the glory of our great God and Savior, Jesus Christ" (Titus 2:12–13).

As we've said before: life is way too short, and eternity way too long, for us to waste the vapor of time that remains to us on momentary and meaningless things. The world with no hope says, "You only live once, so spend your life however you want it." But God's child with a living and eternal hope says, "We only live once, so let's make the best use of our lives and time for the glory of our God!"

With all that's been given to us, and with all that Christ has done in us, and with all the wonderful things being prepared for us, and with all the rewards to be gained or lost at the judgment, how could we not be bursting with hope? How could we not be motivated to live godly lives that matter for eternity and spread the glorious gospel of Christ in this world, so that more and more people can discover and experience the hope we have in Him?

You can live so much differently now . . . because of *who you are, what you have,* and *what's to come.*

---

*Because Jesus is my Lord, and because I am in Him,*
*I have a living and sure hope of Christ's soon return,*
*when I will be transformed into His likeness, receive a new body,*
*and begin enjoying a home in heaven with my Savior and*
*His saints for all eternity. My Father has given me His*
*Holy Spirit as a guarantee and promise of what's to come.*

*Father, I praise You and thank You that I have a living and sure hope in Jesus. Fill my mind and heart with joyful and expectant anticipation of His return. Set my heart in heaven where I have already been seated spiritually with Christ. Fill me with Your Spirit, and help me live each day in anticipation of what's to come. Open my eyes to view my present circumstances through the eternal perspective. Give me strength to endure the trials in life. And help me get my house, my heart, and my life prepared even now. In Jesus' name, amen.*

**TAKE IT DEEPER BY STUDYING**
Psalm 31:19–24 • 1 Corinthians 15:50–58 • Hebrews 10:23–25

*May the God of hope fill you with all joy and peace in believing, so that you will abound in hope by the power of the Holy Spirit. (Rom. 15:13 NASB)*

# PART IV

# IMPERATIVES
*Embracing Your Identity*

# CHAPTER 23

## *You Must Renew Your Thinking*

*Therefore, I say this and testify in the Lord: You should no
longer live as the Gentiles live, in the futility of their thoughts.
(Eph. 4:17)*

Reading the first half of Ephesians is like standing on a spiritual high
dive. You look out over the wide expanse of God's plan and His
eternal purposes; you leap out invigorated, realizing you can be part of
it all; and then you plunge into the depths of it, immersing yourself into
the experience.

It consumes you. It refreshes and excites you. All these things you
discover about your identity in Christ and your inheritance from the
Father—you're deep inside it now. You're chosen, accepted, beloved, forgiven. You're sealed and safe and strengthened. Abundantly supplied.

By the time you reach Ephesians 4, it's as if you've bobbed back up
to the surface, taking a deep breath of air. All these wonderful truths that
you'd once seen only from a distance are now all around you. It feels good
being here, being held afloat by them, confident in the face of old doubts
and fears. It feels like this is where you've always belonged, where you've
always known you should be.

So, what do you do next then? How do you follow up on this feeling,
on this new position where you find yourself?

You start swimming.

It's time to get moving. And so as we push off into this next section, into the back half of Ephesians, that's exactly what we're going to do. Paul concludes his three-chapter dive into the spiritual realities of your salvation by stopping to worship Jesus for a moment—"who is able to do above and beyond all that we ask or think" (Eph. 3:20)—and then he turns his eyes toward the swimming lane in front of you, and says . . .

"Therefore."

Ephesians 4:1—"Therefore I, the prisoner of the Lord, urge you to live worthy of the calling you have received." And beginning at this point, Paul starts to describe for you and imagine with you the kind of life that you as a Christian are meant to live . . . because of who you are, because of what you have. You can be humble and forgiving now. You can be faithful and prayerful now. You can be open and honest, blameless in your moral purity and integrity. All of this is within reach for you, solely because of what God has done to re-create you with a new identity.

But though this life is now achievable, it is also what's expected of you. It's imperative that you do it and pursue it. The Lord has provided so much for you in Christ. He's given you so many things. And He expects you now to use them—to not be like the hunter portrayed in the Proverbs, who kills his game but is then too lazy to roast it (Prov. 12:27), who "buries his hand in the bowl" but "doesn't even bring it to his mouth" (Prov. 19:24).

But don't think of the patterns and practices that are laid down for you in Ephesians 4–6 as if they're some kind of legally worded fine print. They're not the bad news that takes the shine off the good news.

Everything we'll be discussing in these "You Must" chapters carries the added bonus of being your path to life's greatest blessings. Nothing that God requires of you is not good for you. You will *love* the life you're able to experience by importing these imperatives into your daily activities.

So let's start looking at them.

Paul portrays them as being like articles of clothing that you take off and put on. You lay down the old—the grubby and the ill-fitting—and you take up the new. "Take off your former way of life, the old self that is corrupted by deceitful desires"—the parts that are representative of who you *were*—in order to be "renewed in the spirit of your minds, and to put on the new self, the one created according to God's likeness in righteousness and purity of the truth" (Eph. 4:22–24)—the clothes that go with who you *are*.

It's not unlike what Jesus commanded of Lazarus, after He spoke the dead man back to life. Lazarus had been sealed up in his burial tomb for four days. So when he emerged resurrected from the grave, he was still "bound hand and foot with linen strips and with his face wrapped in a cloth" (John 11:44). "Loose him," Jesus said to those who were nearby, "and let him go" (v. 44b NKJV). *Get out of those clothes. Lazarus, and get back to living again.*

It's not impossible for someone who's alive in Christ to still go around wearing the garments of their formerly dead identity. We can put them on at anytime. But why? Think about it. Why would we want to wear them anymore?—those rotten, restrictive old things we always wore—things that left us feeling so bad and brought us so much pain and loss. We look terrible in them. They're filthy and gross. They're fine for people who've given themselves up for dead, but not for you, not for us—not for those who've been given new life in Christ.

To use another example, it's as though your computer has grown glitchy and riddled with viruses. It doesn't do what it's supposed to do anymore. It often locks up and crashes. It works *against* you instead of working *for* you—until one day your father, hearing of this, sends you a new hard drive in the mail to install, complete with new software and a new operating system, with anti-virus protection to prevent your files from future corruption.

There it is! It's in the box, ready to be replaced and uploaded—all new, all bought and paid for. But you can't just sit there looking at it. You can't just lay it beside your old computer for six months, waiting till you feel like doing something with it. The old stuff needs to be taken out—now!—and the new equipment put in.

So we put off lies and we put on truth. We put off bitterness and we put on forgiveness. We put off sexual immorality and we put on purity.

We *were* children of wrath, but now we're the beloved children of God. We *were* our old identity, but now we've been given a new identity.

Ephesians 4 is where we start to see the makeover. But before we can expect to notice any visible difference in ourselves, the first "take off/ put on" change needs to happen in the nerve center—in our brain, in our thinking.

The way a man "thinks in his heart, so is he," the Bible says (Prov. 23:7 NKJV). It all starts there. "Those who live according to the flesh have their minds set on the things of the flesh, but those who live according to the Spirit have their minds set on the things of the Spirit" (Rom. 8:5). If you truly want your life directed by Him—if you truly want your life to be different than it's always been—the first place to focus is your mind.

So ask yourself: What types of influences command the majority of your thoughts? What do you spend most of your time thinking about? Is it your work? The news? Politics? Sports? TV and movies? Social media? Your hobbies? Your money?

If you had a free evening with nothing else to do, how would you most likely spend it? Filling your mind with what? Thinking about what? During those times when you're alone in the car, or passing forty-five minutes between appointments, where does your train of thought most commonly drive you?

"You should no longer live," Paul said, "in the futility of your thoughts"—filling your mind with things that are unimportant at best, ungodly at worst. Not all the things you think about are necessarily bad, of course. But do they possess any lasting value? Are they really worth as much time as you spend on them? If you were given two months to live, how many of them would you continue to find so fascinating?

Part of what Paul is communicating here, in light of what he said about "making the most of the time, because the days are evil" (Eph. 5:16), is not to waste your mind on subject matter that basically *doesn't* matter.

But the "futility of your thoughts" doesn't stop there. The real question to ask yourself is: if your thoughts were driven by your identity in Christ, what would be different?

We must put off the kind of thinking that doesn't square with who we are, the kind of thinking that doesn't match up with what the Lord has called us to be. Are your thoughts filled with worry, despite being blessed with every spiritual blessing? Are they filled with anger and the rehearsing of grudges, despite God not begrudging all your sins and offenses against Him? Are your thoughts dark and self-condemning, despite being told that you are loved, that God finds great pleasure in you?

It's *futile* to think that way—to not be constantly reminding yourself of things that the Lord says are true of you, the way Ephesians 1–3 says they're true of you. Because if you don't, your thinking patterns will have more in common with who you *were*, back when you were "carrying out the inclinations of [your] flesh and thoughts" (Eph. 2:3).

A new identity calls for a new kind of thinking.

God the Father, "according to the good pleasure of his will" (Eph. 1:5), redeemed you from your former manner of living. He now has a "good, pleasing, and perfect will" (Rom. 12:2) for every single aspect of your life—your marriage, your relationships, your work, your everyday interactions with others. All of it. But the secret to being able to "discern" His will in each of these areas, the Bible says, is by committing yourself not to be "conformed to this age, but be transformed by the renewing of your mind" (Rom. 12:2a).

Get your thinking right—line it up with who you are—and you could be living like the new person God saved you to be.

*Lord, help me put this mind You've given me to good use. Cause me to invest my thoughts in worshiping You. Lead me into Your Word, to meditate on it, to love it like rich food for my soul— brain food that my heart needs for its ongoing nourishment and growth. Convict me when I dwell on things that do not honor You, or simply on thoughts about You, myself, and others that are not borne out in the truth of Scripture. Give me a heart that truly knows You, in Jesus' name.*

**TAKE IT DEEPER BY STUDYING**
Mark 12:28–34 • Colossians 3:1–3 • Hebrews 8:10–12

*Let the peace of Christ, to which you were also called in one body, rule your hearts. And be thankful. (Col. 3:15)*

CHAPTER 24

# *You Must Upgrade Your Speaking*

*Let no unwholesome word proceed from your mouth,*
*but only such a word as is good for edification according to the*
*need of the moment, so that it will give grace to those who hear.*
*(Eph. 4:29 NASB)*

Where has our journey with God taken us? From death to life. From lost to found. From separated to near. From enemy to friend. From cursed to blessed. From being a stranger to being God's beloved child. Discovering who we are and what we have in Christ should change everything about our lives.

Especially our speech!

When we brought our adoptive daughter home from China, she only knew how to speak Chinese. But she quickly learned English because it was the language of her new family. More importantly, as members of God's family, one of the biggest changes that needs to take place in our lives involves the words of our mouths. There we encounter an element of ourselves that's only a "small part of the body"—our tongue—and yet "how great a forest is set aflame by such a small fire!" (James 3:5 NASB).

"Death and life," the Bible says, "are in the power of the tongue" (Prov. 18:21). It holds enormous potential, able to cause extensive damage as well as proclaim truth, declare praise, and bring great delight. Both to bless and curse. To wound and to heal. We all know this, and we've experienced both sides of it.

But we will fail at effectively representing the grace and power of our heavenly Father if we refuse to bridle our tongues. "If anyone thinks he is religious without controlling his tongue, his religion is useless and he deceives himself" (James 1:26). Those who more fully understand their worth in Christ and are grateful for His matchless grace poured out upon their lives will not only *act* differently than before, but also *talk* differently than before.

Their mouth becomes a source of life rather than a sewer of rottenness. Truth replaces lies. Encouragement dethrones slander.

Instead of hearing them say, "I can't do it," you're much more likely to hear them say, "I can do all things through Him who strengthens me" (Phil. 4:13 NASB). Instead of bemoaning how nobody likes or appreciates them, they can freely say, "I'm a blessed and beloved child of God." They will say things that reflect the truth of their new identity as a chosen, accepted, forgiven, ambassador of the King.

In fact, although the devil is adept at convincing us that beating ourselves up verbally is somehow pleasing to the Lord—that we're practicing the truest, most honest form of humility when we declare how much of a failure we've been—those words are simply not true for a believer.

We've sinned, yes. But we are now saints in Christ. We've done shameful things against Him and His Word, but we are now forgiven in Him. At Christ's great expense, He has chosen to cleanse us for all eternity and give us hope and a future. So to say we're no good, that we're pathetic, hopeless, unloved, unwanted, unable to do things by His power—in the face of what Christ has done for us—is just an outright lie.

And lying, of course, is only one of the things we need to clean up in our speech. Ephesians calls out several more: "foul language" (4:29); "bitterness, anger and wrath, shouting and slander" (4:31); "obscene and foolish talking or crude joking" (5:4). We're familiar with the things on that list. We're well aware that these parts of speech are not meant to be included any longer in a Christian's vibrant vocabulary.

But the power to truly overcome bad habits will never be found in just telling ourselves to work on it and do better. Our amazing, life-changing identity in Christ, His awesome plan for us, His powerful purposes in saving us, and His putting us to work for His kingdom—*that's* what should overhaul the way we speak. That's what turns our words into affirmation, into wisdom, into biblical truths, and into encouraging blessings, the kind that brightly reveal us to be a living, walking, talking child of the light.

This is part of our identity: "You were once darkness, but now you are light in the Lord; live as children of light" (Eph. 5:8). *Talk* as children of light.

———————————————

We discussed earlier how all people, whether they're believers or not, are made in the image of God. Each person possesses priceless value, simply by virtue of being created by Him with loving care and intention. We are all image-bearers of Almighty God.

So it's interesting how James, whose short New Testament book speaks often about our mouths, chooses to warn us against the twisted hypocrisy of using this same tongue of ours for both helpful words and hurtful words, for praise of God as well as putdowns of others. He says: "With the tongue we bless our Lord and Father, and with it we curse people who"—notice carefully—"are made in God's likeness" (James 3:9).

See the difference that makes? In how you talk to them?

Every person you deal with each day is someone to whom God has given great intrinsic value. So every time you step into their presence, the words you say should make them feel honored and valuable. They've been made in His image, just like you. Their ears and hearts are vessels to be appreciated and edified, not toilets for you to fill with verbal sewage.

So when you see and interact with them—both verbally and nonverbally—are you mindful of communicating to them and acknowledging them in accordance with what God says is true of them?

"Let your speech always be gracious," Paul said, "seasoned with salt, so that you may know how you should answer each person" (Col. 4:6).

It's not just the right thing to do; it lines up with who they are, and with who *you* are.

―――――――――

One of God's central purposes in drawing us to Himself, He says, is to show forth how He reconciles all different kinds of people, from all different kinds of views and backgrounds, into a single, unified body. "You who were far away have been brought near by the blood of Christ" (Eph. 2:13). He has "torn down the wall of hostility" that naturally exists between people (v. 14), and in His own flesh He has brought enemies together as fellow members of His household.

Unity. *God loves unity.* He is unified within the Trinity, and He wants us to be agents of unity as His unified children.

As you study the Word, notice how much of what God says in Scripture about the proper use of our tongues orbits around this theme of unity. The reason He wants you talking the way you should is, to a large degree, because it builds up and unifies your brothers and sisters. *Unity* is one of the ways we bear the most compelling witness of Christ's character to the world.

"By this everyone will know that you are my disciples," Jesus said, "if you love one another" (John 13:35). And this kind of unity is often best achieved by how we speak to one another, more effectively than any other way.

Let's put it to the test.

Paul said the wardrobe change we should make with our tongues is to shift away from words that are careless and "unwholesome," and to choose words instead that are "good for edification according to the need of the moment." We're to throw off the "filthiness and silly talk," the "coarse jesting" and so on, and replace it with the "giving of thanks" (Eph. 5:4 NASB).

So take a situation where perhaps you would be tempted to gossip, or run people down, or tell an off-color joke, or make a crude or foolish comment of some sort.

What's honestly your motivation behind that? Love? Not likely. It's usually a desire for attention, for being thought of as a funny, popular person. You want people to like you. It's selfishly driven. Not building up others, but building up yourself. Pride.

But think about the end result, even after the laugh. They actually will respect you less and see less of Christ in you. God is not glorified with that kind of speech because His attributes of truth and love are being filtered out by a self-centered tongue.

But what happens if you do what God's Word says instead? What if you "give thanks" while you're engaging in conversation? What if, instead of sharing unwholesome words, you dare to talk about how grateful you are for what God has been doing in your life? Or how you're grateful that *they're* in your life, or in your workplace, or in your family, or that they're one of the people you're privileged to know and call a friend? Thank them. Or share how you see Christ in them. Or tell them how you are hopeful of great things for their future.

Not only will you make a favorable impression on them (which dirty humor totally fails to do), but you'll also be building them up, along with building your relationship and tying your hearts closer together. Their respect for you will go way up too! You'll be allowing someone to hear words they rarely hear from anyone, and are likely longing to hear from someone, while you're honoring God with the beauty of love, truth, grace, and *unity* in action.

Let's shift gears. Here's another one. Let's take that single phrase from Ephesians 4:29 that counsels you to edify "according to the need of the moment" (NASB). In any conversation—it doesn't matter who it's with or where it takes place—the other person is always carrying a bundle of needs of some kind. Physical needs, perhaps. Emotional needs. Worries they're dealing with. Questions they need answered. Comfort they may need. Counsel. Direction. Only God knows.

And they're likely carrying multiple needs in their hearts *in that moment*, as you're talking with them. So rather than being primarily concerned with how you're coming off in the conversation, use it to ask questions about how *they're* doing, about what's going on in *their* lives.

Then listen carefully. Because inside their answer, almost every time, one or more needs of the moment will bubble up and arise. And God's Spirit can give you the discernment, compassion, and wisdom to then speak truth and life and love toward meeting their need.

Maybe one of their family members recently died. Maybe they're struggling to make an important decision. Maybe they're stressed on multiple fronts, grappling with a situation that's beyond their ability to cope right now. Then here's your chance to turn a potentially worthless, forgettable conversation into a priceless, memorable, life-changing moment.

Jesus did this all the time. The woman just wanted some water (John 4:7). But He saw her need, spoke the truth, and changed her life forever.

Seemingly random conversations become priceless encounters with God. The word of encouragement you share, the similar experience of yours that you bring up, the caring counsel you offer—it all speaks to the need of the moment. And the powerful choice you make to stop what you're doing, right then, and pray with them about their need . . . that's "light" happening. Love. Unity. You may have no advice to give, but just tell them you understand or that you're sorry, and that you'll be praying for them.

That's offering up the words of your mouth for God to translate them into joy and compassion. Because that same moment, if not for how you handled it, could so easily have been hijacked into a stupid, senseless, pointless conversation. A waste of time and a waste of breath. Instead it became something beautiful, personal, and uplifting, an experience of God's glory.

Jesus said, "On the day of judgment people will have to account for every careless word they speak. For by your words you will be acquitted, and by your words you will be condemned" (Matt. 12:36–37). Frightening to hear? Yes, we'd all hate to hear some of the things we said in life, being repeated before God and held up against us.

But if you confess to God your verbal sins of the past, He is faithful to cleanse and forgive. If you ask Him to sanctify your speech as a weapon of His truth and love, then He will honor that prayer. If you let your words line up with your identity in Him, along with His heart for extending unity and grace to everyone within talking range, you'll be thankfully hearing your words come back to you on that day of judgment.

You'll be glad for what you said, and what you didn't say. You spoke as a changed, redeemed soul who had love in your heart and eternity on your mind, one who had a genuine gratitude for the Lord and for others, a person who deemed them worth blessing with fresh fruit from your sanctified lips. Now *that* sounds like who you are!

---

*Father, thank You for the gift of speech that You've given to us, the ability to express our hearts and to hear from others. I receive it, Lord, as a stewardship. I receive it as something for me to use not for my own pride or at my own whim but to surrender to Your authority. Speak the truth in love through me. Communicate Your gospel and wisdom and knowledge and hope through my mouth. May I see this gift of words as the daily opportunity to honor You, draw people to Christ, and encourage others in their journey. In Jesus' name, amen.*

---

### TAKE IT DEEPER BY STUDYING
Colossians 3:16–17 • James 1:26–27 • 1 Peter 4:11

---

*May the words of my mouth and the meditation of my heart be acceptable to you, LORD, my rock and my Redeemer. (Ps. 19:14)*

CHAPTER 25

# *You Must Cleanse Your Heart*

*Don't grieve God's Holy Spirit. You were sealed*
*by him for the day of redemption. (Eph. 4:30)*

We all prefer clean drinking water. We like wearing clean, fresh-smelling clothes. We enjoy the crisp feeling of settling down at night into clean sheets on a clean bed. We want a clean bill of health from our doctor.

But if one thing happens to disturb any of those nice, clean experiences—a bug in your glass, a lunch stain on your shirt, a bad reading from your blood work—suddenly the whole thing is upset. It's not right anymore. It's distressing. Disappointing. Frustrating.

The life that God wants for you is one of pure joy and peace. Close and clean. Consistent and connected. And you can experience these kinds of privileges every day—the real-time blessings of knowing you're loved and forgiven, approved by God, freed from guilt, and richly cared for. You can walk confidently into any situation, filled with the incomparable contentment of "a pure heart, a good conscience, and a sincere faith" (1 Tim. 1:5).

There's nothing else like it.

And it's all yours because of the Holy Spirit, who dwells in you, fills you, and powerfully intercedes for you whenever circumstances war against you. It's a clean, joyful life that God has made for you, living with His Spirit inside you.

However, there's something you should know about the Holy Spirit—a certain, specific quality of His—that if you're not tuned in to it, the everyday freedom that you long to know and experience will evade you.

The Spirit of God can be grieved. His sensitivity to human sin, based on the fullness of His holiness, is at a high level. Therefore, when we—who have the Holy Spirit inside us—insist that He must share living space with the hidden, cherished sins of our hearts, He reacts. He feels disturbed.

He grieves.

Paul wanted us to see our sin in just that light. Our own tolerance for sin may allow us not to feel it or notice it so acutely, to be able to live with it inside us and not be overly bothered by it. But maybe we wouldn't be so flippant and dismissive about some of the things we're doing, Paul said, if we could see how completely illogical our sin appears when viewed alongside the Holy Spirit we've been given.

Take sexual immorality, for example—the unwillingness to control our own bodies "in holiness and honor" (1 Thess. 4:4) but rather being enslaved to our "lustful passions," same as people "who don't know God" (v. 5). Is that wrong? Of course it's wrong. We know it's wrong. "God has not called us to impurity but to live in holiness" (v. 7). But are we horrified by it, when we see this sin in ourselves? Are we desperate to repent of it? *Grieved* by it?—because anyone who isn't, Paul said, "does not reject man, but God, who gives you his Holy Spirit" (v. 8).

Do you see what he's saying? We may be able to hear the warnings of Scripture or the warnings of the pastor in church on Sunday, and still not be motivated to clean out the things from our lives that are polluting our relationship with God. But the fact that *His own Spirit* is in us, and feeling grieved within us, ought to open our eyes to how offensive our sin against God truly is.

Paul knew we needed to understand this, because he remained focused on this same theme in 1 Corinthians 6. "Don't you know," he asked of those who continued to practice fornication, "that your body is a temple of the Holy Spirit who is in you, whom you have from God?" (1 Cor. 6:19).

In other words, no sin is ever committed in isolation, because God's Spirit is there, seeing it. No sin is ever a private matter alone, because God's Spirit is there, feeling it. When we violate the Lord's standards, we can be sure His tender, loving Spirit is grieving and grimacing at those things, whether we're grieving ourselves or not. Because He knows they can never satisfy us. And it hurts Him to see us thinking they will.

But at His right hand "are pleasures forevermore" (Ps. 16:11 NKJV). In His hand, extended freely toward you, are all the blessings of the clean, clear life you really want, if not for the sin that you keep allowing to linger—sin that keeps promising so much but giving back so little.

Love Him for having such a tender heart toward you.

Ask Him to give *you* that kind of heart as well.

---

Apart from Christ, our hearts were hard, darkened, and calloused. They allowed us to give ourselves over to "every kind of impurity with a desire for more and more" (Eph. 4:18–19). But then God promised you this:

I will also sprinkle clean water on you, and you will be clean. I will cleanse you from all your impurities and all your idols. I will give you a new heart and put a new spirit within you; I will remove your heart of stone and give you a heart of flesh. I will place my Spirit within you and cause you to follow my statutes and carefully observe my ordinances. (Ezek. 36:25–27)

That's who you are now. That's who God has made you to be. Clean and new. With His Spirit inside you. And with each new day, it's who you can continue to become and grow into.

But it's also why sin is such a big deal, even after you've been saved from it, and why every bit of it—every inch of it—needs to be purged from your life.

You can do it by being "tender-hearted," Paul said (Eph. 4:32 NASB), by cultivating the Holy Spirit's brand of sensitivity toward your sin, toward *all* sin. "Search me, God, and know my heart; test me . . . see if there is any offensive way in me" (Ps. 139:23–24).

Seek to have a heart like Joseph, who, in resisting the adulterous temptations of Potiphar's wife, said, "How then can I do this great wickedness and sin against God?" (Gen. 39:9 ESV). Just the *thought* of it! It should be *abhorrent* to us. It should be *incomprehensible* to us. Sinning against God and against His Spirit should make absolutely no sense to us.

Can you imagine it being that way? It can be. You're *made* for it to be that way, "to lay aside every hindrance and the sin that so easily ensnares us" (Heb. 12:1), and simply start walking this clean, clear path that His Spirit has laid out in front of you.

So will you do it? Are you ready? Then let's do it right now. Bring before Him all your unconfessed sin, those "works of the flesh" that are so obvious to you: "sexual immorality, moral impurity, promiscuity, idolatry, sorcery, hatreds, strife, jealousy, outbursts of anger, selfish ambitions, dissensions, factions, envy, drunkenness, carousing, and anything similar" (Gal. 5:19–21). They're doing you no good. They're taking you nowhere. Worst of all, they're grieving the Holy Spirit, whose desire is to have you for His dwelling place.

Imagine, though, seeing Him replace those harbored sins—all of them—with "the fruit of the Spirit" (Gal. 5:22), with things that truly *can* satisfy and enliven you. "Love, joy, peace, patience, kindness, goodness, faithfulness, gentleness, and self-control" (vv. 22b–23). Doesn't that list sound a whole lot better and brighter? More promising? More fulfilling? Happier?

Cleaner?

The Bible speaks of how we as God's people, for some insane reason, go looking for relief and refreshment in dry wells, in "cracked cisterns that cannot hold water" (Jer. 2:13). And yet as Jesus told us, "The one who believes in me, as the Scripture has said, will have streams of living water flow from deep within him" (John 7:38). "He said this about the

Spirit," John added in his Gospel, because "those who believed in Jesus were going to receive the Spirit" (v. 39).

And one of those people now is you . . . with clean, clear water available to you. Why would you want to pollute it with even trace amounts of sin, with even one drop of sin's poison?

So cleanse your heart of anything that's grieving the Holy Spirit—any of those old ways of thinking and speaking, of acting and reacting. Drink to the full from what God has freely given. And see if your walk with Him doesn't feel a whole lot more peaceful and unobstructed.

*Lord God, thank You for Your patient, tender, abiding Holy Spirit, living inside me. Thank You for not tolerating and condoning my sin but seeking to free me from my sin, and from all its painful consequences. Forgive me for being so hard to convince. Forgive me for being so resistant to You and to Your loving plan for me. I confess my sins before You now, and receive from You the healing refreshment of Your mercy and the power to truly change, in the name of Jesus, amen.*

TAKE IT DEEPER BY STUDYING
Psalm 51:1–17 • James 4:4–10 • 1 John 3:2–3

*Repent and turn back, so that your sins may be wiped out, that seasons of refreshing may come from the presence of the Lord. (Acts 3:19–20)*

# CHAPTER 26

## *You Must Walk by the Spirit*

*I say then, walk by the Spirit and you will certainly
not carry out the desire of the flesh. (Gal. 5:16)*

The Spirit told Philip, 'Go and join that chariot'" (Acts 8:29).
Philip, one of the leaders of the first-century church, had already
followed God's unexpected instruction to "get up and go south to the
road that goes down from Jerusalem to Gaza" (v. 26). That's what had
put Philip in position to be near this chariot in the first place, in which
an Ethiopian government official was traveling back to his homeland
and—remarkably—"reading the prophet Isaiah aloud" (v. 28).

The Holy Spirit was the only One capable of connecting all these
dots and placing one of Christ's followers in the direct path of someone who was right on the doorstep of becoming one himself. The divine
appointment that followed was amazing, transformational, and sent the
gospel to Ethiopia.

But the reason it all came together was because Philip was walking
by the Spirit, being led by the Spirit, in tune with the Spirit, willing to
go in whatever direction the Spirit told him to go. The Spirit does not
negate our obligation to obey God's Word; the Spirit is the *secret* to
obeying God's Word!

"Three men are here looking for you," the Holy Spirit said to Peter. "Get up, go downstairs, and go with them with no doubts at all, because I have sent them" (Acts 10:19–20). Peter, just prior to this moment, had been praying, and then a party of travelers knocked on the door, sent there by a Roman military leader named Cornelius.

The Holy Spirit was again overseeing a divine-appointment situation. Peter would soon find himself at the house of an "unclean" man—a Gentile—who, against all logic and background, was eager to hear about what Jesus had done to forgive his sins and give him eternal life. God was declaring that Cornelius, and *all* Gentiles, though once thought to be outside of His family, were part of His gospel plan for the world. The Spirit guided and empowered Peter to obey the Word of God.

But the reason these two men were able to make contact at all was because Peter was walking by the Spirit, being led by the Spirit, following the Spirit wherever, and to whomever, the Spirit told him to go.

What you're witnessing here is the biblical pattern for how God wants His people to follow Him: being led by the Holy Spirit that we've been given as part of our identity and inheritance in Christ.

Sadly, many church leaders and believers avoid talking much about the Holy Spirit. They're so guarded against any potentially confusing behavior, or looking weird, or associating with anyone that might be given to extremes, that they run away themselves to the opposite extreme. Their new version of the Trinity might seem to be the Father, the Son, and the Holy Bible. They want to follow Jesus and obey the Word of God, but they forget that Jesus Himself was led by the Holy Spirit, that the Word of God was written by people led by the Spirit (2 Tim. 3:16), and that it is still the "sword of the Spirit" today (Eph. 6:17).

If we ignore the Holy Spirit's role in our daily lives, then we will tend to rely upon our own strength, our own self-discipline, and our own understanding to try to obey God's Word. This is exhausting and will end up being a lot of work, with little to no fruit to show for it.

Too many pastors in too many pulpits, after teaching a passage of Scripture, basically end up telling their congregations to "try harder, do better, and be more committed" in order to obey it. "If you want to reach your community, love your wife like Christ loved the church, or be a man or woman of integrity, then you just need to get up earlier and get out there and muscle it forward. Go do it! I believe in you." But that's like pushing a car up the road without ever engaging the engine. As if it's all up to you.

The *Holy Spirit* is the engine of the Christian life. Jesus said the Spirit is the power source (Acts 1:8), the One who helps us understand the Word as we read it and live out our spiritual identity (Rom. 8:14; Gal. 5:18). Obeying God faithfully and successfully is impossible without the indwelling power of the Spirit, without the tag-team partnership of the Word of God in our hands and the Holy Spirit in our hearts. If a tree branch is lying on the ground, not producing fruit, do you tell it to "try harder, do better, and be more committed"? No, it needs to be plugged back into its source of life to truly bear fruit.

Our identity in Christ is repeatedly connected to the work of the Holy Spirit. Having been "sealed" by the Spirit when we believe the gospel at salvation (Eph. 1:13), we're also commanded not to "grieve the Holy Spirit" (Eph. 4:30), to continually be "filled by the Spirit" (Eph. 5:18), to pray "at all times in the Spirit" (Eph. 6:18), to be "led by the Spirit" (Gal. 5:18), and to "walk by the Spirit" (Gal. 5:16). This is to be your daily habit—to take the Word of God, pray in surrendered obedience, and then go out and obey the Word by staying in step with God's Spirit.

As you ask Him to fill you and lead you by His Spirit, He'll begin to prompt you at different times to be His hands and feet in a situation. To reach out in love. To share your faith. To serve a need. To share this verse with that person. To give a gift. It's not an audible voice but a gentle thought, a desire, an inner inclination or prompting to serve in some type of specific capacity. It may be just, "Go talk to that person"

. . . and you won't know why until after you do. But the Spirit is never in disagreement with the Word of God. And as you follow His lead, then He will continue to prompt you more and more.

———————

The Bible says, "Don't get drunk with wine, which leads to reckless living, but be filled by the Spirit" (Eph. 5:18). Becoming drunk, we know, has a direct influence (in a "reckless" way) on how someone speaks and thinks and walks, when they're filled with and being led by alcohol. Likewise, the Christian life entails being filled with and controlled by the Spirit, to surrender to Him in thinking and speech, to develop a heightened, awakened, alertness to Him . . . because He is not a Spirit of fear, but of power, love, and sound thinking (2 Tim. 1:7).

When He leads you to step, you learn to step. When He tells you to stop, you stop. When He prompts you to go encourage or share the gospel with someone, or to delay a certain meeting, or to give this amount of money at this time, or to pray for this person now, or to hire *this* person and not hire *that* one, you trust that He can see the future and knows what's best.

We've had so many Spirit-prompted, family, ministry, and movie-related "miracles" happen when we've just made ourselves available to obey God as He led us. He has blessed us so much when His Spirit has prompted and we've obeyed. Mia's adoption in the introduction to this book is an example of that. God has also protected us multiple times from potential danger or a bad business or relationship decision by giving us a strong lack of peace about something that we needed to avoid (Col. 3:15).

Too many believers today don't know what to make of this dynamic. Sounds too risky. Sounds dangerous. Sounds confusing. Sounds like it could lead them into some places that are potentially shaky, not to mention embarrassing.

That's what Jesus' disciples thought about Him on a regular basis as He was being led by the Spirit. *Why are You talking to this Samaritan woman? What do You mean, 'who touched You in this crowd?' You want us to pay our taxes how? What do You mean someone is going to betray You? What do you mean You need to go to Jerusalem and be crucified?*

If you follow how Jesus did His entire ministry, the Spirit was always directing Him from place to place. He was filled with the Spirit at His baptism (Luke 3:22) and was "led by the Spirit in the wilderness for forty days to be tempted by the devil" (Luke 4:1). Then He entered the synagogue and read, "The Spirit of the Lord is on me" (Luke 4:18), who would be leading Him to the fulfillment of His mission. Jesus was constantly walking in the Spirit.

Yes, we realize we're at a different place in history today. We have the full Bible now and we're commanded to follow it. We must! We're not saying to add to the Word of God. We're just talking about how to *obey* the Word of God. And it's the Word of God that commands us multiple times to follow and walk by the Spirit (Gal. 5:16).

Should the devil be the only spiritual being who's able to whisper ideas into our heads? His promptings are accusations, temptations, and bad ideas, and we're to resist him with the Word in those situations. But shouldn't the Holy Spirit be speaking to us too? Even *more* clearly? Helping us to know how to *obey* the Word in our daily interactions in life?

If He is truly real and alive and living inside us, should we not reasonably expect Him to be leading us and showing us where to walk, in ways that align with God's will and with the work He's commissioned us to do?

Philip and Peter would say yes. As would Paul, who once told of being "forbidden by the Holy Spirit" (Acts 16:6) from ministering somewhere that apparently wasn't on God's agenda. People may say that God never does anything but through His Word, and yet *in His Word* we see Him leading His children by His Spirit, and teaching us to be led by the Spirit ourselves. We've just seen too much of it in our own lives to believe otherwise.

For example, during the weeks leading up to the filming of the movie *Overcomer,* we traveled to Columbus, Georgia, scouting for a suitable hospital location for scenes needed in the movie. We prayed and asked the Holy Spirit to lead us where He wanted us to go. We arrived at a hospital that we heard was a good option to consider. Going inside, we randomly chose the fourth floor to casually walk around and imagine how this backdrop would look on camera. In the process of telling the staff what we were doing, we ended up meeting with one of the administrators, who said, "Yes, I know you all from *War Room*. I loved that movie! You're welcome to use this whole wing, if you want it." Great! Big answered prayer.

And yet it didn't end there.

Completely unbeknownst to us, our aunt Carole, the sister of our mother, who lives in Columbus, had been at home praying, just doing her morning devotions, when the Lord prompted her to get up and go to St. Francis Hospital where we were. She didn't really know why.

At the same time, in a coffee shop across town, a local pastor was engaged in mid-conversation with someone, when he sensed the Lord telling him to get up and go immediately to the hospital to visit some of his church members, which he promptly did.

Within minutes, our aunt showed up—on the fourth floor of the hospital—and surprised us with her arrival. As we talked, the elevator door opened again, and out walked Pastor Thomas—who would have been a stranger in our eyes, except for our aunt recognizing him and calling him over to meet us. To make things even more uncanny, Pastor Thomas said he'd arrived there with the intention of going to another part of the hospital, but the Lord had specifically impressed him to go to the *fourth floor*.

Here we stood, all of us, having made no plans to meet and be together that day. And yet, this "chance" meeting became one of the most significant unplanned moments of the summer. We met the key man in the community that we ended up needing to help us make the movie. Later that night, he told of other pastors who'd be interested in helping us, and then volunteered to set up multiple leadership meetings with them, which became significant to what we were doing. He also offered us the use of his own church building, which became our production office. The property behind their church proved to be the perfect setting for scenes we needed to film.

The benefits of that elevator meeting on the fourth floor went on and on during the summer. We can't fathom how these "coincidences" came together in any other way than that God's Spirit was prompting different believers that day to converge on one unplanned location, all at one time. None of us could know; we could only be led. And how could we be led into such clear answers to prayer unless the Holy Spirit was doing the real-time, real-life prompting?

Jesus said, "When the Holy Spirit comes, he will guide you into all the truth. For he will not speak on his own, but he will speak whatever he hears. He will also declare to you what is to come" (John 16:13). And when He does, "He will glorify me, because he will take from what is mine and declare it to you" (v. 14).

Thankfully He's given us His Word to guide us through universal truth and principles, but He's also given us His Spirit to make the Scripture come alive for us, to help us know how to obey it in our context, to strengthen us to proclaim the Word, and to show us specifically where to put it into practice today . . . as we walk by His lead.

The worst, most frustrating way for anyone to try living the Christian life—the worst way for anyone to try living out their identity—is by relying on the limited energy of their own flesh and by deeming their own smarts and intuition sufficient enough to fulfill God's will.

The power of Christian living comes from the engine of the Holy Spirit. And the daily insight needed for recognizing the specifics of any situation can come only from His leadership and guidance.

We want to encourage you to surrender your life to Christ, to obey Jesus and be baptized in the name of the Father and the Son and the Holy Spirit, and to ask God daily to fill you with His Spirit. Be sure to get any sin out of your life, knowing it would grieve God's Spirit. Stay daily in God's Word, keep praying about everything, and ask Him to lead you by His Spirit. Then fasten your seatbelt and get ready for Him to work in you and through you as He prompts and empowers you for His glory.

Be filled with the Spirit (Eph. 5:18).

Be led by the Spirit (Gal. 5:18).

Walk by the Spirit (Gal. 5:16).

It's what you've been saved, commanded, and should be excited to do!

*Father, thank You for sending Your Holy Spirit to guide me, and for choosing to include me in the work You're doing all around me. Open the eyes and ears of my heart to recognize what the Spirit is saying. And please motivate my will and my feet to follow where I'm led. I've seen the results of following my own way, of being my own boss, of directing my own steps. You alone will always lead me exactly where I need to be, doing exactly what I need to be doing. I trust You. Help me follow You—to walk in the Spirit, in Jesus' name.*

### TAKE IT DEEPER BY STUDYING
Acts 1:4–8 • 1 Corinthians 2:10–16 • 2 Corinthians 3:4–6

*We have not received the spirit of the world, but the Spirit who comes from God, so that we may understand what has been freely given to us by God. (1 Cor. 2:12)*

CHAPTER 27

# *You Must Walk in Love at All Times*

*Be imitators of God, as dearly loved children, and walk in love,*
*as Christ also loved us and gave himself for us. (Eph. 5:1–2)*

G od is love.

Within the Trinity is perfect love and unity. Always has been; always will be. So when God made man in His image, there was love and unity in the garden. But then when sin and death entered the world, hate and selfishness entered the heart of every person.

Then Jesus came to the earth as a living, complete demonstration of the love of God. He was dearly loved by His Father, filled with God's Spirit, and a walking channel of God's love to others (John 3:16; Rom. 5:8; John 15:9). This was His focus every day: being a constant demonstration of the love of His Father. That's one of the reasons Jesus never sinned. He was God, yes, but He also focused on loving others. And love does not sin against others. Love is the fulfillment of the law.

He then taught His disciples how to become a channel of God's love as well:

"Just as the Father has loved Me, I have also loved you; abide in My love. If you keep My commandments, you will abide in My love; just as I have kept My Father's commandments and abide in His love. These things I have spoken to you so that My joy may be in you, and that your joy may be made full. This is My commandment, that you love one another, just as I have loved you." (John 15:9–12 NASB)

He received the Father's love for Him and poured it out on them—then said He wanted them to receive His own love for *them* and pour it out on *others*.

Then we come to Ephesians 5, where we're told as God's "dearly loved children" that we, too, should be "imitators" of Him and walk in love toward others wherever we go. Remember, He has called us from death to life and has given us endless resources, including His Holy Spirit which pours out the love of God into our hearts (Rom. 5:5). We now have an endless supply of God's love—something that everyone else in the world desperately needs and wants. And we have this river of spiritual resources and the amazing privilege of glorifying our God (who is love) by loving everyone we come into contact with. Whether you view someone as your friend, your neighbor, or your enemy, Jesus said you still need to love them.

Imagine two landowners. One builds his home in the desert; one builds his house next to a river. The person's land in the desert has no trees, no crops. He has nothing but sand to share with guests who come to visit him. And he's constantly thirsty, always asking his *visitors* for water rather than sharing it with them.

In contrast, the landowner by the river has lush trees, a gorgeous yard, beautiful fields of fruitful crops, an endless supply of fish, and lots of fun outdoor opportunities for everyone who comes. He's able to generate electricity from the river, share freely from the produce of his gardens, and in the future he'll always have all the water he'll ever need. Anyone's welcome to visit, drink as much water as they want, and even take buckets home with them.

When we give our lives to Christ, God's Spirit becomes like a river within us. A river pouring out God's love. He wants us to allow this love to flow in us freely by faith, and for us to freely and generously share

His love with everyone we meet, all the time. Our lives can become so much more joyful and fruitful in a million ways if we become a channel of God's love to everyone we encounter.

This simplifies so many things for us. Sometimes life feels as though it has too many things to remember. Too many variables. Too many instructions to keep up with. Even your Christian life can feel this way— as if every day means figuring out how to apply a whole Bible's worth of wisdom to each individual encounter or situation you face. It can be frustrating, trying to choose the right thing for any given moment.

But Jesus boiled it all down to "Love the Lord your God" entirely and "Love your neighbor as yourself" (Matt. 22:37–39). Well said. Amen. That's obviously true. And yet He knew He was speaking to an audience that, when anyone laid down a challenge before them about following a rule, they would add it to their performance list of things to do and to check off so that they could look good and feel better about themselves.

Which never works when it comes to love. That's *not* how love works.

And so when talking with His friends, His followers, Jesus told them something else. He boiled down Christian living to one single focus: *abide in Him.* "Remain" in the One who has made you *who you are.* "As the Father has loved me, I have also loved you. Remain in my love" (John 15:10).

So the answer to simplifying how to handle your relationships with others—at home, at work, and elsewhere—is, yes, to approach them with love. "Above all, put on love, which is the perfect bond of unity" (Col. 3:14). "Above all, maintain constant love for one another, since love covers a multitude of sins" (1 Pet. 4:8). But do it the only way love can actually be done. Believe and receive love first before trying to pour it out. Allow your identity in Christ as God's beloved child to be how you do it. Get into that river where He has poured His love into you through His Spirit, where He has transformed you from lost to found. And with His love sweeping in from behind you, let it rush through you like a channel or a giant garden hose, spraying the refreshing love of God into people's hearts everywhere you go.

The Bible says, "This is the command as you have heard it from the beginning: that you walk in love" (2 John 6). And this is how you follow that command, Jesus said: "Love one another as I have loved you" (John 15:12).

Because here's what happens when you do. *Life gets fun.*

This same life of yours that once felt so overwhelmingly complicated, or so dull and routine, now becomes a daily, Spirit-led adventure in loving other people with the love of Christ.

When you go into the grocery store, or when you pull up to the drive-thru, or when you're talking to your spouse or to one of your kids at night, or when you're dealing with a coworker or an employee who's having a hard time, think of it first as an awesome opportunity to show Christ's love to them.

That's how Jesus lived. He kept stepping into the moment, discerning the need of whoever was in front of Him, and then serving that need and shining God's love on them. People were overwhelmed when they encountered Him. If they were hungry, He fed them. If they were ignorant, He taught them. Weary? He encouraged them. Hurting? He comforted them. Sick? He healed them. Demon possessed? He cleansed them.

One thing—LOVE—but a million applications.

As you're sitting there and learning to *abide* in the love of God for you, *resting* in His love that changed you into a new creation in Christ, it's time to ask Him to also use you and your life—through your countenance, your cheerfulness, your encouragement, your service, your words, your resources, your prayers, anything—to redirect that love into a person's heart around you that probably really needs it. Try staying sensitive to how the Holy Spirit might prompt you to be the love of Jesus to someone.

If you don't feel any love in your heart, then you either don't know Christ, or you might be holding on to some things we talked about a couple of chapters ago that are grieving His Spirit and blocking the flow. In the verses in Ephesians immediately preceding the command to walk in love, Paul writes:

Don't grieve God's Holy Spirit. You were sealed by him for the day of redemption. Let all bitterness, anger and wrath, shouting and slander be removed from you, along with all malice. And be kind and compassionate to one another, forgiving one another, just as God also forgave you in Christ. (Eph. 4:30–32)

Bitterness and unforgiveness are the opposite of love. They're like hating someone in your heart. And since we've been forgiven of all of our sins in Christ, we're commanded to forgive everyone who sins against us as well.

Refuse to let *anything* stand in your way from being someone God can pour His love, grace, and blessing through to others.

———

Let me share a personal story. This is Stephen writing for a minute. Soon after setting up our production office in Columbus before filming *Overcomer*, I'd stepped into a planning meeting. Walking in, I saw and greeted a few of the people we'd hired to help us throughout the summer.

I'd just been reading in Scripture about the subject of this chapter, how Christ wants us always abiding in Him, being led by His Spirit, and looking for how we can walk in love toward others. And, as if out of nowhere, I suddenly sensed the Spirit impressing on my heart to go specifically encourage one of the new staff members there—a woman named Becky. I didn't really know her or why this would be important.

So after I noticed she'd finished up with some paperwork, I said, "Becky, can I speak with you for just a second?" I motioned her over to a hallway just around the corner, where I thanked her for joining our crew, and then quickly asked, "How are you doing today?"

She looked at me, then looked away, and then immediately started to cry.

For the next few minutes, just pouring out her heart, she told me how she loved the Lord but had been struggling with her faith in recent months, that she was dealing with some family difficulties and had been battling depression. She went on to tell me, too, that her marriage of twenty years had recently ended in a divorce, and she was having a hard time getting over it. The rejection had left her feeling like she was not worth fighting for, she said.

As soon as those words came out of her mouth, I began to see why the Spirit had led me to her. Here we were, making a movie about our identity and value in Christ. And here in our production office, the Lord was putting us into situations where we could immediately apply it to our team.

"Becky," I said, "first of all, you told me your husband was not a believer, which means he doesn't possess the capacity for loving someone unconditionally, the way only Christ can enable us to do. And second, this thought that Satan has put in your head that you're 'not worth fighting for' is a lie, and it's a direct attack against your identity. Because the truth is, God *made* you and Jesus *died* for you. That's what *He* says you are worth. Don't let the enemy convince you of something that's not true about who you are."

She looked down for a moment and then back up at me. "Just this morning," she said, "one of the first things that popped into my head, for some reason, was the thought, 'I don't think the Kendrick brothers even like me.'"

I was sort of taken aback by that. We'd just barely gotten started with pre-production, and I hadn't even been around the office all that much up to this point because of everything else we were doing. "Well, isn't that interesting," I said, "that almost as soon as I walked in here, the Lord said to me, 'Go encourage Becky today.' What does that tell you about what *God* thinks of you?"

I walked away from that ten-minute conversation and the prayer we shared together, thinking, "You are so awesome, Lord, that You would encourage *me* today by letting me be part of how You wanted to encourage someone else." And nearly a year later, Becky told me how God had used that one conversation to be a breakthrough in her spiritual life and in her understanding of His great love for her. In the last year, I've had so much fun stepping into situations, just asking God to love others through me. It's less stressful, more joyful, and much more fruitful. I never want to go back to living for myself!

Walking in love, everywhere we go, can do some amazing things.

---

*Who is God?* God is love. *Who are you?* You are beloved. *And what's the most important thing you can do each day?* To love.

Everywhere you go, you should be stepping into that context saying, "Lord, here am I, Your beloved. Fill me and use me to pour out Your love everywhere I go." Start with your spouse and your family. Fill yourself up with God each day, and then fill up your home with God's love. Then expand out to your friends and church, to neighbors and then strangers.

Be aware and be ready. Where's the person who's hurting? Go comfort them. Where's the person who's worried? Go pray with them. Where's the person who's fearful? Go affirm them. Where's the need? Join God in being a part of the answer.

I dare you now to get up from what you're doing today, and go have some fun by walking in love. It's who you are. And there's no greater way to live!

*Heavenly Father, I praise You, my God of love, for loving Your Son and loving the world through Your Son. I thank You for saving me and making me Your beloved child! I thank You for the gift of Your Holy Spirit, who pours out Your love in my heart. Take my life, Lord, fill me up, and make me a powerful and fruitful channel of Your unconditional and sacrificial love everywhere I go. Give me a servant's heart. Help me die to my pride and selfishness. Help me always get all of the sin and bitterness quickly out of my life. And use me to change the world and glorify Your name in all I do. In Jesus' name, amen.*

## TAKE IT DEEPER BY STUDYING
Romans 13:8–10 • Philemon 4–7 • 1 John 4:18–21

*Do not owe anyone anything, except to love one another. (Rom. 13:8)*

# PART V

# IMMOVABLE
*Standing Strong*

# CHAPTER 28

# *You Can Be Strong during Spiritual Attack*

*Take up the full armor of God, so that you may be able to resist in the evil day, and having prepared everything, to take your stand. (Eph. 6:13)*

Have you ever had one of those days or weeks or seasons of life when everything seems to ambush you all at once? The same week your Check Engine light comes on, a strange health issue sabotages your family, unexpected bills arrive in your mailbox, your workload causes sleepless nights, and then a relationship problem blows up out of the blue over a confusing issue. Isn't it ironic how inconveniently timed it all seems?

There are many reasons why these kinds of crises can "group hug" you. But don't discount the real possibility that you're experiencing what Ephesians 6 refers to as "the evil day." It's when the devil has blitzed you from all sides in hopes of taking you down. We're talking about a 100 percent, genuine, spiritual conspiracy here—a precise, enemy attack that the Bible indicates will periodically happen and we should basically expect.

But because Satan knows a hit-and-run play probably won't be enough, he schedules a barrage of fiery arrows to try wearing you down. Whether the difficulty is mechanical or medical, financial or relational, this type of attack is out of the ordinary and meant to strike you at a place much deeper than your wallet, schedule, or job security.

You must remember that Satan hates God's children. Jesus said he comes to steal, kill, and destroy (John 10:10). Since you are made in God's image, saved by His Son, indwelt by God's Spirit, and destined for God's glory, Satan puts a target on your back and declares war. So don't take it personally. It's a family feud, and you are a highly favored child.

What is he after? Satan wants to steal your joy, hijack your faith, sabotage your morality, and ultimately derail your testimony. And he will definitely try to slander your grasp of your own identity. He is after your deepest core, the headquarters of your mind and heart where your faith is anchored and your fellowship with God abides. He will use whatever tool he can find to plant doubt, deceit, and discomfort inside you so that you'll want to give up. He wants you to question your faith in God's goodness and love, what His Word says is true about you, and whether or not you can make it through this round and get back up for another attack.

But here's what we came to tell you: *YOU ABSOLUTELY CAN.* You can totally prepare for it. You can stay strong throughout the full battle and keep going because of the unchanging nature of your God, because of His resurrection power at work within you, and because of the endless resources you have in Christ. You are not relying on your own strength, your kung fu skills, or the contents of your canteen. You have the Spirit of God within you, the Word of God in your hand, and a protective Father and victorious Lord standing on both sides of you.

You must remember that Jesus has already disarmed the enemy and taken the bullets out of his gun through the cross (Col. 2:13–15). The devil is threatening you now with an unloaded gun. So you can stare him in the teeth during the next attack, unafraid to call his bluff, and then "take your stand" and resist him.

---

The Old Testament account of Job clearly shows Satan as capable of wreaking havoc on a good person's life. Within a short space of time (Job 1:13–19), Satan orchestrated and unleashed a wide range of attacks on Job to arrive on the same day. Invading thieves showed up and stole a portion of Job's livestock from the field; a fire broke out in one of his sheep pens, killing the entire herd as well as some of his servants; worst of all, a windstorm came past his oldest son's house, where the rest of his children had gathered for a family meal. The whole structure collapsed, burying all of them. It was an evil day.

From Job's perspective, it was the worst moment of his life. It felt random. Just accidents? Mere coincidences? The results of climate change? Not so. The Bible describes this specific attack as being strategically, satanically planned and highly organized (Job 1:9–12). Satan's clear goal was to get Job to abandon his faith, to judge God as being evil for allowing it, and then to curse God to His face.

But as the dust settled, Job fell to the ground with a broken heart and surprisingly did the opposite of what Satan had hoped. He worshiped God in the midst of his pain, saying, "The LORD gives, and the LORD takes away. Blessed be the name of the LORD" (Job 1:20–22).

Satan lost round one. So he turned up the heat and attacked Job's health. Then Mrs. Job walked up to her husband and taunted him to "Curse God and die!" (Job 2:9). Wonder where she got that script from? Her counsel was precisely what Satan was pushing Job to do. But Satan lost round two as well. In all, Satan tried to find an opening into Job's heart through his possessions, his kids, his health, then his wife, and finally his discouraging friends.

But Satan lost every round, and his plan became an epic failure. Because when everything was against him, Job still clung to God with a loyalty that, in retrospect, beautifully reflected Jesus on the cross. Job said, "Though He slay me, I will hope in Him" (Job 13:15 NASB), and then, "I know that my Redeemer lives" (Job 19:25).

Job stood firm through it all. And listen, dear friend, so can you. The devil's attack, no matter how it feels, is never so overpowering that it automatically gets to succeed against you.

But we know Satan hasn't stopped using this same playbook. In the New Testament, Peter describes him as "prowling around like a roaring lion, looking for anyone he can devour" (1 Pet. 5:8). That's what he's still doing today—in your country, in your community, at your church, and around your family. He, or one of his demonic representatives, is prowling. Looking. Intent on invading somewhere. Waiting for the best time to interrupt your peace. He'll wait for the moment when you're most vulnerable. When you're exhausted. Angry. Afraid. Lonely. Or when you've gotten so comfortable that you lower your shield and let your guard down.

You may not recognize it now. Today may be an impressively sunny day. That's great. Enjoy it. When life is going well, you're probably not thinking about how the devil may be plotting. You don't need to be worried or afraid, but you also don't need to be deceived or naïve.

Instead "be sober-minded, be alert," Peter said (1 Pet. 5:8), aware that Satan is only biding his time. Waiting. Scheming. And when he's got you in the position he wants you—perhaps a bit overconfident or apathetic or sufficiently distracted—he'll launch a surprise attack, as subtly or suddenly as he thinks will be most effective.

But how? It might be a well-timed temptation. Sometimes his weapon is to stir up deception in your thinking, division in your marriage, or discouragement and depression over some loss. Or sometimes, like in the story of Nehemiah from the Old Testament, it's just a well-timed distraction.

When Nehemiah was leading the wall-rebuilding project around Jerusalem, he was constantly being invited away from his priority mission. Carnal people kept inserting themselves into his schedule, demanding attention to veer him off task. On one day, it might be people plotting "to come and fight against Jerusalem and throw it into confusion" (Neh. 4:8). On another day, it might be the claim of a "widespread outcry" from the locals (Neh. 5:1), clamoring about economic injustices. Then it would be his enemies demanding he travel to a vital meeting, seeking to stall Nehemiah's progress if not do him bodily harm (Neh. 6:1–4). And then of course, there was the day people spread rumors "trying to intimidate us, saying, 'They will drop their hands from the work, and it will never be finished'" (Neh. 6:8–9).

Every time it happened, it likely felt like the "evil day." But Nehemiah refused to give up or give in. He kept responding by praying for help, rallying his team, ignoring his accusers and their latest emergency, and then staying on track until the wall was done. Satan kept dialing, but Nehemiah kept blocking his calls.

The attack of distraction is one of Satan's signature strategies—gnats of annoyance and interference. Have you felt it? Have you recognized it? If taken at face value, distractions may just seem like life being coincidentally unfair. Or it may seem like they're all worthwhile opportunities calling for you, even though in running off to do these secondary things, they're taking you away from God's one main thing (Luke 10:41).

Your natural reaction to the frustration of it may be to blame the people involved. *They're* the ones distracting you. *They're* the ones you're mad at. You think the problem is the carnal knuckleheads in your life. And God's the One who could've stopped all of them from doing it, and He didn't.

Can Satan really plant bad ideas, malicious assumptions, or harsh accusations in other people's minds against you? Absolutely. The word Satan means *accuser*, and false accusation is his specialty. Remember, he incited Judas to betray Jesus (John 13:2). Does Satan really have the power to influence the forces of nature? Go read Job. Can Satan at times be the impetus behind sickness and disease? He did it in Job's life. That's not to imply there's a demon behind every difficulty or that Satan sparks every sniffle. We don't believe that at all. But Scripture reminds us to stay aware of his devices (2 Cor. 2:11).

As a personal testimony, we've watched bizarre things show up "on schedule" with almost every Christian movie we make. While making *Fireproof*, our marriages started having weird issues. Right when we started producing *Courageous*, our godly father started hearing blasphemous voices in his head. We've experienced strange illnesses, heavy dark oppression, betrayal, confusing crew division, bizarre distractions—all uniquely timed.

Listen, "our struggle is not against flesh and blood, but against the rulers, against the authorities, against the cosmic powers of this darkness, against evil, spiritual forces in the heavens" (Eph. 6:12–13). *There's* the real source of problem—not the people Satan is manipulating as his tactical tools. Jesus didn't treat Judas as the enemy.

There is a real, formidable enemy behind this, who likes to threaten you with fear tactics to make you feel weak, who wants to whisper in your heart that you just can't do it, that you're too inadequate. Under-supported. Under-supplied. Under-prepared. He hopes you'll feel betrayed by your God—abandoned!—though He's never left you or stopped loving you for even one moment.

But guess what: you're more prepared now. You've got the "full armor" of a true, newer understanding of your identity fortifying you. You've been prepared by Christ with both the watchfulness and the wherewithal to "be able to resist in the evil day."

When it arrives and Satan attacks, don't panic or run away in fear. Don't even flinch. Just rally the body of Christ in prayer, stand your ground, proclaim the Word of God, speak the truth in love to those around you, then obey what God has told you to do. And keep moving forward by faith, obeying the mission you've been assigned by God. Build your wall, Nehemiah! When the devil aims low, you stand firm, cling to the Lord, and honor God in the midst of any pain. "Do not be overcome by evil, but overcome evil with good" (Rom. 12:21 NASB).

God has "seated us with him in the heavens in Christ" (Eph. 2:6). Even when under harsh attack from every quarter imaginable, your life is able to "display the immeasurable riches of his grace through his kindness to us in Christ Jesus" (Eph. 2:6–7).

For the rest of your life, as you walk with the Lord, you can continue to stand strong . . . because of who you are, whose you are, what you have, and who is powerfully living inside of you.

*Heavenly Father, thank You that You have not given me a Spirit of fear, but of power, love, and a sound mind. And because of who I am in Christ, I have strength in You to stand against the attacks of the enemy. Thank You for the promise that You will faithfully love me and never leave me. Give me discernment to recognize how the enemy is attacking. Help me put on the full armor of God, stand firm with confidence in Your Word, and prayerfully be victorious in each spiritual battle. Prepare me to walk in truth with my head up, my eyes alert, and my heart in tune to Your voice. You have overcome, and Your Spirit is alive in me. In Jesus' name, amen.*

### TAKE IT DEEPER BY STUDYING
1 John 5:18–20 • 1 Peter 1:5–7 • Jude 24–25

*We know that everyone who has been born of God does not sin, but the one who is born of God keeps him, and the evil one does not touch him. (1 John 5:18)*

## Be Strong in the Lord

*(An interview with the apostle Paul based upon 2 Corinthians 6:2–10.)*

**What difficult circumstances are you living in?**

In much endurance, in afflictions,
in hardships, in distresses,
in beatings, in imprisonments,
in tumults, in labors,
in sleeplessness, in hunger.

**How are you living your life and
staying strong in the midst of all of this?**

In purity, in knowledge,
in patience, in kindness,
in the Holy Spirit, in genuine love,
in the word of truth, in the power of God;
by the weapons of righteousness . . .

**Knowing your extremely difficult circumstances, how is your identity
and inheritance in Christ helping you to stand strong for God?**

We know and remember that we are . . .

regarded as deceivers (on Earth) and yet true (in Christ)
as unknown (on Earth) yet well-known (in Christ)
as dying (on Earth) yet behold, we live (in Christ);
as punished (on Earth) yet not put to death (in Christ)
as sorrowful (on Earth) yet always rejoicing (in Christ)
as poor (on Earth) yet making many rich (in Christ)
as having nothing (on Earth) yet possessing all things (in Christ).

# CHAPTER 29

# You Can Be Triumphant during Temptation

*God is faithful; he will not allow you to be tempted beyond
what you are able, but with the temptation he will also provide
a way out so that you may be able to bear it. (1 Cor. 10:13)*

In order to warn us about the dangers of sin, God has given us dozens of real-life temptation testimonies. They run up and down the halls of Scripture. Nearly every Bible character who makes an appearance of any significant length in God's Word is seen grappling with one temptation or another.

Three of these stories, however, are epic in nature. Two of them end in colossal failure, while the third ends in well-fought victory.

The first is Adam and Eve (Gen. 3:1–7). Here we see the enemy's common use of *deception*. Deception is his stock-in-trade, as effective today as on that long-ago day. And it's a tactic we can be expecting and prepared for by seeing it for what it is. Deception is essentially a cloaked, compelling way of attacking God's identity.

"Did God really say, 'You can't eat from any tree in the garden'?" (Gen. 3:1). These are the first words of Satan that we hear in Scripture, and already they're questioning God's love and goodness toward the first man and woman. The truth is, God had said they were "free to eat from any tree of the garden" (Gen. 2:16), with the exception of only one: "the tree of the knowledge of good and evil" (v. 17)—because the fruit of *that* tree, God knew, would kill them. So in reality, God had given them bountiful room for being nourished by a whole orchard of food, by a forest of deeply satisfying options. And even in what He commanded them to avoid, He did it from a Father's heart of protection and concern for their well-being. That's who God is, as we've seen—one who blesses in abundance, one who desires to keep us from hurting ourselves.

But there's a part of us that suspects this isn't true, that this is *not* who God is. And in Genesis 3, you see your enemy doing to Eve what he still does to you—causing you to wonder if maybe you've been wrong about God. Because according to the serpent, here was the real story about the fruit of that forbidden tree: "God knows that when you eat it your eyes will be opened and you will be like God" (v. 5).

That's twisted truth. Their eyes would be opened, only not in the way they thought. But the fruit did look good. It sure did seem to hold something desirable, not something that could kill you. Isn't that how temptation always works? He dangles something you want; he hopes you won't see or remember what taking a bite from it always ends up taking from you. But that's just the surface of the deception, the part you see—the pornographic image, the junk food, the pint of whiskey, the pull toward your own preferred escape from life's pressures. Underneath it—the reason he's able to tempt you to do the opposite of what God has told you to do—is the deceptive question of why a good, loving God would keep something so luscious from you. Nothing could be further from the truth.

The second story is from David's life (2 Sam. 11:1–5). Witness Satan's use of *opportunity*, of what the Bible calls "an opportune time" (Luke 4:13 NASB).

As you know, times of extreme difficulty and frustration can often be the justifying permission we give ourselves for indulging in sin as a form of pain relief. Always expect Satan to show up when you're tired or angry or upset or under pressure. But be equally as wary of those times when something really good is happening—when you're getting praise, when an unusual amount of money has come in, when you've accomplished a goal that you'd set for yourself and can afford to kick back and rest a little.

That's where temptation found David one evening, up on his rooftop, just taking it easy. David had been successful—successful enough, in fact, that "in the spring when kings march out to war" (2 Sam. 11:1), he chose the luxury of staying home, sitting it out. But because he wasn't where he was supposed to be—because he wasn't living within his identity—he was an easy target for the enemy. Just get him upstairs, Satan knew. Get him where he can look down and see something to stir his heart—the sight of a woman nearby, in the soft light of evening, visible through her window as she was bathing herself. The rest is scandalous history.

David's life and his kingdom would soon be rattled to their foundations. And he never saw it coming—because he wasn't on guard. He wasn't reminding himself that times of ease and achievement are like the scent of fresh prey to the enemy's senses.

Watch out for those high-mountain moments when you're feeling really good about something you've been able to do, about a great blessing you've experienced or been part of. Celebrate it, thank God for it, but do expect Satan to be lurking around somewhere in its afterglow, just when you thought you could take the night off. Even a good time can be an opportune time for you to forget who you are, to forget what you have. Be careful.

Then finally, triumphantly, there's Jesus, being tempted by the devil in the wilderness (Matt. 4:1–11). Look at each of these temptations, and you'll see they're an attack on *identity*.

It's hardly coincidental that directly beforehand, in the final verse of Matthew 3, Jesus was being baptized by John in the Jordan. Right here at the launch of Jesus' earthly ministry, as we've seen before, the voice of His Father boomed out from heaven, "This is my beloved Son, with whom I am well-pleased" (Matt. 3:17). He would need to remember that.

Because, again, Jesus' temptation, like your temptation, is first and foremost a challenge to identity. *Prove it,* the enemy was saying to Him. *Let's see it. Let's see if You're who God says You are.* "If you are the Son of

God, tell these stones to become bread" (Matt. 4:3). "If you are the Son of God, throw yourself down" from the "pinnacle of the temple" (vv. 5–6).

If Jesus had not known who He was—if He'd not remained firm in His identity as the well-beloved Son of His heavenly Father—any of these temptations could have derailed Him from His mission. Satan tried twisting God's Word around to make his logic sound more convincing, but Jesus used the true Word of God to make His defense absolutely immovable.

And you can do the same thing. In moments of temptation, *remember who you are*. "I am unconditionally loved by God. I am chosen and adopted and a new creation in Him. I'm free, I'm redeemed, I'm valuable, and empowered by the Spirit. My old self is buried with Christ, and I am raised to walk in newness of life. I have the helmet of salvation to protect me, and a great inheritance waiting in heaven for me. So, no, Satan, I don't need your moldy bread to satisfy me. I can do all things through Him who strengthens me."

Wonder what would happen to the enemy's success rate if he knew *this* is what he'd be hearing the next time he pulled out another temptation on you?

*Lord, thank You for giving so many examples in Your Word, both positive and negative, that expose the enemy's well-worn strategies against me in times of temptation. And thank You for giving me a new identity that can stand up to them all, no matter how deceitful or ill-timed. You are my strength, my rock, my refuge, whenever I'm accosted by Satan's schemes and lies. Keep me alert, Lord, to his tactics, and keep me triumphant in battle. In Jesus' name, amen.*

### TAKE IT DEEPER BY STUDYING
1 Timothy 6:9–12 • Hebrews 2:14–18 • James 1:12–18

*Fight the good fight of the faith. Take hold of eternal life to which you were called and about which you have made a good confession in the presence of many witnesses. (1 Tim. 6:12)*

CHAPTER 30

# *You Can Be Constant during Criticism*

*Who can bring an accusation against God's elect?*
*God is the one who justifies. (Rom. 8:33)*

We already know Satan is a deceiver. Crafty and opportunistic. He tempts, distracts, and raises doubts. But these aren't the only highlights on his résumé. He is also "the accuser of our brothers and sisters, who accuses them before our God day and night" (Rev. 12:10).

Satan *accuses*. Often *falsely* accuses. He will slander God's love in your mind and build a harsh case against you in your own heart. He takes whatever God has said specifically about who you are in Christ and then launches a campaign to convince you of the exact opposite. Twisting truth. Flipping it upside down. Inserting a question mark in each place where God has put a period. Dismissing who you are *now* and trying to convince you that you're still who you *were* before Christ.

His tactics are toxic. He will misquote Scripture out of context, hoping you don't catch it (Luke 4:9–11). He will present truth out of balance, stating that the wages of your sin is death, but not mentioning that God's gift to you is eternal life through Jesus (Rom. 6:23). He will swing your thinking to extremes, presenting all law with no grace, or lifting up grace as an excuse to run back into sin (Rom. 6:1–3).

But he's sly and subtle. He doesn't make himself known.

If Satan rang your front door dressed like a demon, and offered you a slimy envelope with "LIES TO BELIEVE" written on the cover, you would bolt the lock, start dialing Psalm 91:1, and tell him to get off your property in Jesus' name.

So he disguises himself as a trustworthy messenger, an angel of light (2 Cor. 11:14), and repackages his messages not as Satan speaking but as if it's your own brilliant thinking. And he will present a lie to you as if you're discovering some secret about yourself that no one else in the world truly realizes or understands, just you alone. Then he'll replay the message on a condemning loop *ad nauseam* to wear you down.

If you don't realize what's going on, you'll feel like swallowing what he's serving, even though it's the opposite of what God's Word says—how you're such a loser, how you'll never amount to anything, how you're doomed to fail, how you can never be forgiven, how you're unloved and unusable. Then he'll muster up any past failures, half-facts, and fearful feelings as his *proof* that what he's telling you must be true.

But it sounds so true, doesn't it? Especially if the words match how you feel and you can remember an experience or two that might back it up. Now, then, is the moment when you must make a decision. Believe them or not? And whether you realize it or not, the moment you believe Satan's lies is the equivalent of taking off your armor in battle, letting the enemy shoot fiery arrows directly into your head and heart. Every lie you receive is devastating. Enslaving. Confusing. Taking you down into depression.

And if the arguments and evidence he's put in your head are not taking root, he can easily employ the people around you to reinforce his message *for* him.

---

He knows that a well-timed verbal slam from someone you know at just the right time might do the trick. As Job could attest, you should be aware that Satan will strategically try to use unsuspecting people as his resident mouthpiece. They may be good people in trusted relationships. But if someone's lips are unbridled and available, and if he can get them angry or frustrated enough, Satan will readily try to plant an untruthful or unloving script in their minds that quickly flies out of their mouth before it's even processed. Ready, shoot, aim! And if you, the listener, are not on your guard, and your identity is not currently grounded by faith in Christ, then things could quickly go south and become debilitating.

How great a fire can rage from the sparks of careless words (James 3:5–6). It's from careless words that many hearts get broken, temperatures rise, fights break out, and bitterness blooms. It's here that relationships reel, marriages struggle, and families can fall apart. Even big churches can crumble when leaders don't know who they are in Christ. This is spiritual warfare, and people often don't recognize it until it's too late.

In your life, it's so important to keep your spiritual armor on and filters on your ears to discern whether people's words are from the Spirit or the flesh, from the throne of heaven or the pit of hell (James 3:6). It doesn't matter how loving, wise, or respected someone is, their words should not be instantly ingested as gospel truth at all times.

Consider what Jesus did in the city of Caesarea Philippi. In one historic moment, Peter boldly proclaimed Jesus as the Messiah and Son of God. Crystal clear and rock solid. Jesus immediately discerned Peter's words as being from God and praised him in front of the other disciples. But seemingly in the next breath, Peter let his mouth run wild, declaring that Jesus was never to die on a cross. Jesus quickly discerned the source of this statement and immediately rebuked Peter as now being the mouthpiece of Satan (Matt. 16:13–23).

Jesus modeled mind-blowing discernment here. To think that in one moment a person can be a fountain of truth and a minute later a poisonous well. This experience should not only flag how we listen but how we speak. Any of us can be a walking blessing one moment and toxic the next if we are not guarding our tongue.

Now let's take this to the next level. How you respond to criticism, rebuke, and false accusation can reveal how grounded you are in your identity in Christ and how armored you are in spiritual battle. When a verbal bomb is dropped on you, how do you respond? Do you tend to handle criticism well or take it hard? Are you discerning or devastated? Do you listen and learn or flail and fall apart? Does your week ever get hijacked by one negative thing that someone says about you? It never has to be that way.

We must remember that criticism and verbal abuse will eventually come at all of us.

All the greats of Scripture were heavily criticized. Joseph's brothers "could not bring themselves to speak peaceably to him" (Gen. 37:4). Moses, within three days of being celebrated for parting the Red Sea, was surrounded by a choir of whiners, verbally attacking him for not having fresh drinking water ready in the desert (Exod. 15:23–24). Job's friends refused to believe anything other than the idea that his calamities must be divine punishment for a hidden sin he must have been refusing to reveal. David was cursed as evil (2 Sam. 16:5–8). Elijah was labeled the "troubler of Israel" (1 Kings 18:17 esv). Paul was stalked from city to city by accusers.

And Jesus—likely more than all the rest—was falsely accused and criticized by His family, His fickle followers, and His jealous enemies. "He's out of his mind," His own family said (Mark 3:21). "He's blaspheming!" the religious elite repeatedly said (Matt. 9:3). "You have a demon!" some would shout at him (John 7:20). "Look, a glutton and a drunkard, a friend of tax collectors and sinners" (Matt. 11:19).

During His journey to the cross, the attacks only intensified. "For many were giving false testimony against him, and the testimony did not agree" (Mark 14:56)—except that "they all condemned him as deserving death" (v. 64). "They spat in his face and beat him; others slapped him and said, 'Prophesy to us, Messiah! Who was it that hit you?'" (Matt. 26:67–68). "He saved others; let him save himself if this is God's Messiah, the Chosen One" (Luke 23:35).

Do you see a pattern here? As believers in Christ, we come from a long lineage of verbal abuse victims. Criticism and false accusation go with the territory. They should be expected. "Don't be surprised," Peter said, "when the fiery ordeal comes among you to test you as if something unusual were happening to you" (1 Pet. 4:12). "If they persecuted me," Jesus told His disciples, "they will also persecute you" (John 15:20).

In His first recorded sermon, Jesus said, "Blessed are you when others revile you and persecute you and utter all kinds of evil against you falsely on my account. Rejoice and be glad, for your reward is great in heaven, for so they persecuted the prophets who were before you" (Matt. 5:11–12 ESV).

He would later indicate that it's actually a bad sign if no one is criticizing you. "Woe to you when all people speak well of you, for this is the way their ancestors used to treat the false prophets" (Luke 6:26). So, believe it or not, we should actually be hoping for some appropriate criticism from the world as a sign that we are on the right track.

But how should we respond? When someone attacks you, criticizes you, or slanders you, be wearing your armor: the helmet of the knowledge of your salvation, the breastplate of being right with God, the shield of your trust in God's Word. Resting in the love, grace, and acceptance of your Father.

Then when criticism comes your way, be quick to listen, slow to speak, and slow to anger (James 1:19). Pause before responding. Filter it through the Word of God. Remember that you are blessed, beloved, chosen, accepted, and forgiven in Christ. If their words are not true, then you can lift your shield of faith, block the fiery darts, and stand firm without flinching. If what they say *is* true, you should receive it with humility, learn and grow from it, but not question your identity in the process.

For criticism that is based upon truth may actually be a gift from the Lord—excellent counsel in disguise. When Moses was serving the people tirelessly from morning to night, his father-in-law walked up and said, "What you're doing is not good. . . . You will certainly wear out both yourself and these people who are with you, because the task is too heavy for you. You can't do it alone" (Exod. 18:17–18).

Moses desperately needed to hear these words. They were not an attack, but they could have *felt* like one if he had been insecure in himself.

Moses could have taken it personally as an assault on his intelligence and leadership ability. But Moses had the humility to listen and consider. Discerning that these remarks were accurate and helpful, he received his father-in-law's counsel like a champ, and it became a breakthrough moment of growth in his life and a blessing to the entire nation.

"Faithful are the wounds of a friend," King Solomon said (Prov. 27:6 NASB). "Reprove a wise man and he will love you" (Prov. 9:8 NASB).

So we should always filter criticism, accusations, and rebukes through the sieve of God's Word, seeing if perhaps they reveal a place in our hearts where we're hiding pride or living in error. Being a believer doesn't exempt us from being wrong. The book of James says, "We all stumble in many ways" (James 3:2). That's why, thankfully, "the LORD disciplines the one he loves, just as a father disciplines the son in whom he delights" (Prov. 3:12). Jesus loved His disciples so much that He willingly rebuked them as often as needed. They learned over time to listen and receive His counsel to help them grow.

So ask yourself: Is a particular piece of criticism genuine—even a piece of self-criticism? Is it true? Then take your medicine, embrace your responsibility, and repent from what has been revealed. Thank the one who rebuked you and grow from it. Step up into your identity as God's beloved child who no longer resorts to sulking, sinning, or self-righteousness in order to feel better about yourself. Because when it's *false* accusation, the appropriate response is not to curl up and pout but to raise up the shield of faith, "with which you can extinguish all the flaming arrows of the evil one" (Eph. 6:16).

Jesus, as always, is your example here. Many times He rested in who He was and chose silence as His comeback. He knew the accusations weren't descriptive of Him, so He didn't take them personally and didn't get distracted by them. And neither should you—"for although we live in the flesh, we do not wage war according to the flesh, since the weapons of our warfare are not of the flesh" (2 Cor. 10:3–4).

Your new identity means you can simply "take every thought captive to obey Christ" (v. 5). Put it behind you. Stay strong and press on. Listen to the wise and grow. But the words of a fool or a liar don't need to find a resting place in your schedule or your thinking. If you keep remembering who you are in Him, and let your Father be your Defender, then regardless of what others say, you can move forward all the stronger and all the wiser for the glory of God (Rom. 12:18–21).

*Father, You are my strength. You are my hiding place. When the accusations of the enemy become more than I can bear—when it's hard for me to clearly see the truth—You are my source of confidence. Your Word gives me assurance. You are my shield of faith. Defend me, Lord, against every false attack. And teach me, Lord, whatever I need to learn. Make me more like Christ every day, more fervent in prayer, more anchored in trust. I pray this in His name, amen.*

**TAKE IT DEEPER BY STUDYING**
Isaiah 54:11–17 • Romans 8:1–4 • 1 Peter 2:21–25

*"No weapon formed against you will succeed, and you will refute any accusation. This is the heritage of the Lord's servants, and their vindication is from me." (Isa. 54:17)*

# CHAPTER 31

# *You Can Be Faithful after Failure*

*A righteous man falls seven times,
and rises again. (Prov. 24:16)*

Peter's denial of Jesus. Most of us remember it well, down to the small details. The mob had come into the garden and taken Jesus away, hauling Him up before the high priest. Peter followed to see what was happening, but only at a distance, afraid of being seen, afraid of what being affiliated with Him might mean in such a volatile situation.

Three times he was recognized around the fire by people in the courtyard—"This man was with him" (Luke 22:56); "You're one of them too" (v. 58); "This man was certainly with him, since he's also a Galilean" (v. 59). Three times he outright told them *No!*—"Woman, I don't know him" (v. 57); "Man, I am not!" (v. 58); "I don't know what you're talking about!" (v. 60). A rooster crowed in the distance. Jesus turned and made eye contact. Recognition passed instantly between them, the memory of Peter's promise that "even if I have to die with you, I will never deny you" (Matt. 26:35). Three of the Gospel writers reported he then "went outside and wept bitterly" (Luke 22:62).

Remember it? Of course you do.

But here's the part we *don't* remember so readily—not only about Peter, but also about ourselves, after our own failures. We remember what happened, we remember the looks in people's eyes, we remember the angry questions we shouted at ourselves: *Why? How could you do this? You knew better! What were you thinking?* But do we remember who we are? Even now? After failure? Do we remember what Jesus did for us "while we were still sinners" (Rom. 5:8), and "how much more then, since we have now been declared righteous by his blood, will we be saved through him from wrath" (v. 9)?

The Peter you see bawling on his hands and knees after making the biggest mistake of his life is the same Peter who was in Jesus' mind the night *before* the denial. As Jesus was praying there, praying for Peter and all His disciples, He said to the Father, "I guarded them and not one of them is lost, except the son of destruction [Judas]" (John 17:12).

Jesus told Peter and his friends to "remain" in Him like branches in a vine, because "just as a branch is unable to produce fruit by itself unless it remains on the vine, neither can you unless you remain in me" (John 15:4). Obedience would always be expected of them. Dependent trust was essential. In fact, to help them produce even more fruit, Jesus promised that His Father would continue pruning them and working with them, to keep them growing a healthy crop of faithfulness. But "you," Jesus said of Peter and the others, "are already clean because of the word I have spoken to you" (v. 3). They'd believed in Him. They'd believed His Word. They'd received the forgiveness of their sins by faith.

That's why Jesus could tell Peter specifically, *pre*-denial, "I have prayed for you that your faith may not fail. And you, when you have turned back, strengthen your brothers" (Luke 22:32). Not only did He know what Peter would do; He was already painting a vision of what Peter's life would look like after repentance.

It's why He could also ask Peter specifically, *post*-denial, "Do you love me?" (John 21:15)—not just once but, symbolically, three times. Apparently His interaction with Peter in the days following the Resurrection had convinced Peter of how thoroughly Christ had forgiven him. Peter was confident enough to say, "Lord, you know everything; you know that I love you" (v. 17). Hearing Peter's confession, Jesus challenged him to "follow me" (v. 19). *You can do it, Peter. I will be with you.* Failure had not finished him; failure had made him ready for a new adventure of faithfulness.

When people fail, when they've really blown it—whether it's David's fall with Bathsheba, whether it's Peter's denial of Christ, or whether it's your own painful example of personal failure that you know so well—there's no secret about how the enemy will react. He'll leverage it as an opportunity to strike hard, below the belt, beating you down with the guilt that your sin has left behind, convincing you that God has ended your chance of ever being useful to Him again. To make things worse, he'll take further advantage of the shame and hopelessness you feel by enticing you toward additional sin—*anything* to stop this heartache, to help you stop thinking about it any longer. *Feed your lust. Feed your stomach. Medicate yourself with drugs, alcohol, or even mindless social media.*

That's the devil's way. That's his predictable response to your failure.

But "if we confess our sins"—if we own what we've done and determine to learn from it—the Lord is "faithful and righteous to forgive us our sins and to cleanse us from all unrighteousness" (1 John 1:9). If you "humble yourselves, therefore, under the mighty hand of God," He will "exalt you at the proper time" (1 Pet. 5:6). You can cast "all your cares on him, because he cares about you" (v. 7).

Many times throughout Scripture—many times throughout all of history—epic failures, when handled with genuine repentance, have resulted in giant leaps of faithfulness. Falling on your face may be what finally positions you in a place where you really start walking with Him, where God draws you into the deepest intimacy with Him you've ever known. The choice to fall forward is often how the pride that's been keeping you stumbling and struggling for so long finally weakens to a whimper.

But only if you start remembering who you are. Not who you *were*, which is the only thing Satan wants you thinking about. You *were* dead in your sins; you *were* following the patterns and priorities of the world; you *were* enslaved in unrighteousness; you *were* without God and without hope of any peace or future. And according to your enemy, you are still all these things. According to him, you're not in Christ anymore after everything you've done.

But that's not what Scripture says. In light of who you *are*, the Bible says you were "buried with him by baptism into death, in order that, just as Christ was raised from the dead by the glory of the Father, so we too may walk in newness of life" (Rom. 6:4). You are free then—even after failure—to "consider yourselves dead to sin and alive to God in Christ Jesus" (v. 11). Nothing except the paralysis of regret or a posture of unrepentance is keeping you from being able to live out your real identity.

Peter was equally as loved *after* his denial as *before* his denial—equally called, equally a disciple, equally seated with Christ in heavenly places. The testimony of his life going forward became a passionate repudiation of the death that he surely thought had started at the sound of that rooster's crowing. Instead, his future of faithfulness was primed to begin. So is yours.

*Father, forgive me. I know You forgive me. Your Word says You've forgiven me. No sin is so heinous that Your grace cannot sink it into forgetfulness and restore me to fruitfulness. I know this. I believe it by faith. So with all humility and in full repentance, I come to You today, relying wholly on Your righteousness, not my own—relying wholly on Your mercy, which is without limit. Shine through me, through what You've redeemed in me, for the sake of Jesus, amen.*

**TAKE IT DEEPER BY STUDYING**
Psalm 73:21–28 • Psalm 85:4–9 • Hosea 6:1–3

*My flesh and my heart may fail, but God is the strength of my heart, my portion forever. (Ps. 73:26)*

CHAPTER 32

# *You Can Be Loyal after Loss*

*Set your mind on things above, not on earthly things. For you died, and your life is hidden with Christ in God. (Col. 3:2–3)*

It used to be so easy to get lost. With nothing but paper maps to rely on, or the scribbled notes someone had written down for you to follow, a journey from home through unfamiliar roadways could be an adventure in U-turns. The confusion you'd feel when unsure about whether to take a left at this intersection, or to pass up this street, could leave you out of sorts and bewildered.

Finally came the advent of GPS technology, and suddenly the path from here to there became a whole lot easier to navigate. Gone were the sketchy instructions that said to look for landmarks and count traffic lights. At each point of the way now, you can see at a glance the one item of information that makes all the difference: knowing exactly *where you are.*

Because when you know your identity—when you're sure of it and can keep referencing it—you significantly limit the opportunities for the lane shifts of life to veer you off the main road. When you deal with setbacks, when you lose abilities, you still have a north-star position to stay anchored on. You know who you are. You know who Christ has made you to be. You know where you stand with Him. Not even the inevitable, uninvited experiences of loss are able to leave you feeling hopeless.

Life for the unbeliever, however, never really gets beyond the paper map stage. The person who lives without Christ travels the road by feel, by their best guesses. But so many things can change or cause conditions to look different than expected. The career and level of income they'd grown accustomed to enjoying, which had maintained a steady, upward trajectory for the past twenty-five years, suddenly starts losing altitude. The parent who'd been their reliable bastion of strength, encouragement, and counsel takes ill and dies. Perhaps even their own health and vitality becomes threatened by an unfavorable report from the doctor. Their moment in the spotlight fades into criticism and collapse.

No matter who you are, then—life will test your identity. You'll find out in unmistakable terms precisely where you've placed your worth and sense of importance. But if your identity is in Christ, you can survive without them. Nothing you lose will keep you from staying filled.

Paul understood and lived out this concept. His motivation for getting up in the morning throughout most of his early life was to pursue religious perfection. His sense of righteousness was based solely on his self-performance. The reason he could square his shoulders in the street was because of what he'd accomplished through his training and pedigree. "If anyone thinks he has grounds for confidence in the flesh," he said, "I have more: circumcised the eighth day; of the nation of Israel, of the tribe of Benjamin, a Hebrew born of Hebrews; regarding zeal, persecuting the church; regarding the righteousness that is in the law, blameless" (Phil. 3:4–6).

Then one day, the Lord dropped him to his knees on the road to Damascus. For the next several years, he began dealing with the reality that all the things he'd counted on for stability and stature were not able to support their own weight. The whole economy of his heart changed to a new currency. "Everything that was a gain to me, I have considered to be a loss," he ultimately determined (v. 7). Only one thing mattered to him anymore: "that I may gain Christ and be found in him, not having a righteousness of my own from the law, but one that is through faith in Christ" (vv. 8–9).

Because even when everything else is gone from you—whether by brave choice or by painful removal—your identity in Christ will be enough. *More* than enough. Knowing and remembering who you are, in Him, is the secret to staying satisfied for a lifetime.

Life, despite the picture painted by television commercials and sappy Christmas movies—or even by the social media feeds of real-life friends and acquaintances—is not, by earthly forms of measurement, a graph of steadily increasing returns. Moses wisely observed that "our lives last seventy years or, if we are strong, eighty years. Even the best of them are struggle and sorrow; indeed they pass quickly and we fly away" (Ps. 90:10).

This is not the depression talking; this is simply reality talking. Life will always involve loss and limitation. We go from being young to being old. We go from being in school to suddenly being stripped of those everyday relationships. We go from the bustle of a houseful of activity to the eventual silence of the evening routine. We go from being the dad who can do a backflip on the trampoline to a man whose joints stiffen when he pulls himself off the sofa.

But somewhere along the line, if we're not careful, we'll knit our identity too tightly into the "before" image of our lives and resent the "after" image. Then on cue, Satan will launch his barrage of insults, disguised as our own voice of self-pity, about how we're washed up, a has-been, worthless, unremembered—how we don't matter, how we can't do anything, how we'll never enjoy another day of contented happiness ever again.

*Not true.* Not for those whose identity is planted firmly in the unshakable Christ and in the assurance of His everlasting love. "The path of the righteous is like the light of dawn, shining brighter and brighter until midday" (Prov. 4:18). "The righteous thrive like a palm tree and grow like a cedar of Lebanon. Planted in the house of the LORD, they thrive in the courts of our God," said one of the psalm writers. "They will still bear fruit in old age, healthy and green, to declare: 'The LORD is just; he is my rock, and there is no unrighteousness in him'" (Ps. 92:12–15). Jeremiah wrote of a future where "young and old men rejoice together. I will turn their mourning into joy, give them consolation, and bring happiness out of grief. I will refresh the priests with an abundance, and my people will be satisfied with my goodness" (Jer. 31:13–14).

Bright. Healthy. Thriving. Joyful.

Abundantly satisfied. Rejoicing and fruit-bearing.

This hardly sounds like a pointless, cheerless future—not for those who've set their mind "on things above, not on earthly things." Not for those who've died to what once held them captive to "the lust of the flesh, the lust of the eyes, and the pride in one's possessions," choosing instead to live by the new identifying belief that "the one who does the will of God remains forever" (1 John 2:16–17). "For if we died with him," Paul said—if we've given up our personal demands and our claims of entitlement, trusting Christ to be our source of meaning and joy—"we will also live with him" (2 Tim. 2:11).

There's simply no losing in this scenario. Nor does it leave us subject to getting lost along the way. We won't just find our way home someday; we'll find something to enjoy and give us meaning throughout every part of the journey.

*Lord, in You I find hope, satisfaction, and fullness that no loss can take away. You fill me with lifelong usefulness and optimism because You've filled me with Your eternal Holy Spirit. I will never stop needing You, Lord, to remind my forgetful, nostalgic flesh that I am passing through only a small section of my life with You while I'm here on the earth. You have guaranteed me an inheritance of blessing that will never fade or lose value. Praise You, Lord, in Jesus' name.*

## TAKE IT DEEPER BY STUDYING
Philippians 4:10–13 • Hebrews 11:13–16 • 2 Peter 1:5–11

*They now desire a better place—a heavenly one.*
*Therefore, God is not ashamed to be called their God, for*
*he has prepared a city for them. (Heb. 11:16)*

# CHAPTER 33

## *You Can Be Glorifying to God at All Times*

*If anyone speaks, let it be as one who speaks
God's words; if anyone serves, let it be from the strength
God provides, so that God may be glorified
through Jesus Christ in everything. (1 Pet. 4:11)*

It didn't matter what circumstance Jesus stepped into, He would always glorify His Father in the midst of it. He lived ready to honor Him in everything. Christ knew He was the beloved Son of His heavenly Father, and He was always walking in sync with the Holy Spirit. He had no sin, hypocrisy, immorality, or bitterness in His life to hold Him back.

Every new sunrise was a fresh opportunity for Him to teach another truth, humbly serve another need, powerfully work another miracle, or graciously reveal another amazing aspect of His Father's character to a dark and needy world.

The Son of God represented and glorified His Father so perfectly that Jesus is described as "the radiance of God's glory and the exact expression of his nature" (Heb. 1:3). It didn't matter where Jesus was, who He was with, or how dark a situation had become, He stepped into it, shined the light of His truth and love into it, served the needs at hand, and then glorified His Father in the midst of it.

Look at the consistent results of His daily interactions with people:

| Mark 2:12 | ". . . they were all astounded and gave glory to God" |
| Luke 7:16 | ". . . and they glorified God" |
| Luke 13:17 | ". . . the whole crowd was rejoicing over all the glorious things he was doing" |
| Luke 18:43 | ". . . all the people, when they saw it, gave praise to God" |

Since God is so worthy of our worship, and we were created and saved to worship Him with our lives, there is nothing more fulfilling and eternally valuable than for us to glorify God in our daily decisions and situations. Jesus was a master at it and invites us to learn how to do it as well.

In His first sermon, Jesus exhorted His disciples, "Let your light shine before others, so that they may see your good works and give glory to your Father in heaven" (Matt. 5:16). Notice that His admonition was not to honor ourselves, but God. That's why Jesus often operated anonymously (Matt. 6:1–6). He wanted His Father to get the glory. It didn't matter if He was being faithfully followed or falsely accused, worshiped or beaten, Christ always responded as the beloved and chosen Son of His Father, faithfully bringing Him glory in every unique context.

He not only glorified the Father by showing mercy and love, but also when He confronted evil, cast out demons, rebuked the religious hypocrites, and threw the greedy money-changers out of the temple. These were not welcomed, peaceful occasions. They likely were very awkward to the watching world. But that was what was needed.

And Jesus knew that sometimes representing the Father meant tough love, *exposing* hidden wickedness, *offending* prideful rebels, or befriending social outcasts that none of His friends liked. But this is how He lived every day. Then leading up to His betrayal and crucifixion, Jesus prayed an epic prayer to the Father saying, "I have glorified you on the earth by completing the work you gave me to do" (John 17:4).

Though He was betrayed, denied, falsely accused, beaten brutally and abandoned, Jesus continued to glorify His Father with His words and attitudes throughout the excruciating suffering and isolation of the cruel cross at Calvary.

Now, after thousands of years, Jesus' life of sacrificial love still remains the absolute best model for any person anywhere to live. His impact on the world far surpasses any other living human being. And His way of living for God's glory at all costs is actually the way God wants each of us to live out the rest of our lives.

Whether you eat or drink, or whatever you do, do everything for the glory of God. (1 Cor. 10:31)

We too, as beloved children of our Father in heaven, and as new creations who've been given grace, forgiveness, and salvation—as those who've been given a rich inheritance and the power of the Holy Spirit—are called to be humble and willing followers of Jesus Christ our Lord, and living and loving imitators of God, our Father in heaven.

Shining His life. Obeying His Word. Living His truth.

Honoring and reflecting His character in every situation.

Helping others experience Him and know Him in their own personal context.

This calling is not a boring burden to bear or a religious chore to be checked off. It is an invitation to the greatest life of all. We serve an amazing, awesome Lord who is the giver of every good thing in life, and He came to give us "life and have it in abundance" (John 10:10). He can see our lives from a big-picture, eternal perspective and has called us out of empty, sinful, self-centered, dead living that wastes us away, into His glorious new life that shouts His wondrous praise to the heavens. He is inviting us into meaningful, powerful experiences that will change us and many other people for eternity.

We are called to represent His grace and love, not just on Sundays at church or when the world is watching us, but every day in every way and all the time—even in the toughest, messiest situations and with the most difficult people. The devil, the world, and your own flesh will tell you that this is an impossible, unreachable, boring way to live. But it's actually the opposite of that. It's what God has been preparing and equipping you to do all along.

Too often, Christians settle for mediocre, lukewarm, empty living. Worshiping God a little on Sundays, but then living for themselves, their pleasure, and their glory during the week. They compartmentalize their faith to the point where *Jesus is Lord* only over a few easy areas, but not over every area or any area that would mean discomfort, awkwardness, or sacrifice.

In contrast, following Him is an awakening to real freedom. Freedom from your sin, yes, but also freedom from hypocrisy and half-heartedness. Freedom from insincere motives, religious performance. Freedom from the need to impress or outshine others. Freedom to simply live closely to Him, loving Him, being loved by Him, and representing Him in good times and bad times.

At all times. That's the freedom you have now in Christ. An *always* freedom.

This is your inheritance from Him. To fully know Him and to make Him fully known.

---

Before your salvation, you were not even remotely equipped for doing this, but now you're completely supplied with everything you need for it—all day long, up-close and consistently—because of who He powerfully is in you and who you are now in Him.

When anyone focuses on glorifying God with their life, then everything they do is raised to a level of higher importance and value. The words *glory* and *glorify* are abstract words that Christians sometimes say and pray, but may be hard to grasp if you don't bring them down to Earth. First, God's "glory" is the *expression* or *unveiling* of one or more of His amazing attributes. It's when His awesome nature goes public and on display. It's when He shows up and shines in some specific way—whether it's His tender mercy after sinning, His perfect justice setting things right, His gracious provision meeting a need, or His powerful protection saving the day.

His glory is the revealing of any of His limitless abilities, majesties, or kindnesses. They will line up with what He has revealed about Himself through His Word. Obviously we've only tasted a sample of this. The Bible says He is "exalted above the heavens," that His "glory [is] over the whole earth" (Ps. 57:5). Just walk outside on a clear starry night and look up if you want to enjoy some of the glory of God always on display.

But the word *glorify* is when something or someone honors, praises, or magnifies the glory being revealed. So when God showed up in Exodus and parted the Red Sea, His *glory* was brilliantly shining. Then when the children of Israel sang, celebrated, and worshiped God because of it, they were *glorifying* Him. When God provided Abraham the ram in the thicket, His *glory* was revealed as the perfect provider. Then when Abraham worshiped God by calling Him his Jehovah-Jireh, he *glorified* God's revealed *glory*.

In the Bible, when Jesus received word that His friend Lazarus was sick, He told His disciples, "This sickness will not end in death but is for the glory of God, so that the Son of God may be glorified through it" (John 11:4). And if you'd been there when Jesus called out, "Lazarus, come forth!" (John 11:43 NKJV), and watched as His dead friend emerged from the tomb, you'd have understood exactly what He meant when He said, "Didn't I tell you that if you believed you would see the glory of God?" (v. 40).

His glory was revealed when people witnessed His resurrection power, ordering Lazarus out of the grave. Jesus can actually bring dead things back to life again. It's another amazing aspect of who He is. So it was *glorious* when everybody saw it. And God was glorified by it. The One who is "the resurrection and the life" (John 11:25) was on awesome display.

But it didn't end there. When Jesus returned to their city of Bethany, they gave a dinner for Him. Lazarus was attending—still living proof of

God's glory—and Mary, one of Lazarus's sisters, "took a pound of very costly perfume of pure nard, and anointed the feet of Jesus and wiped His feet with her hair; and the house was filled with the fragrance of the perfume" (John 12:3 NASB).

As the sweet-scented offering of her worship became evident, the beautiful aroma was an incredible response to her having experienced the glory of God through her brother's resurrection. The fragrance in the air was a glorious honoring of Jesus and the amazing thing He had done. Mary's praise was honoring His glory, and so it *glorified* Him.

Likewise, our worship is one way we glorify Him, but hardly the only way. Paul said "we are the fragrance of Christ" to all people—to "those who are being saved" as well as "those who are perishing" (2 Cor. 2:15). So when you "walk in love, as Christ also loved us and gave himself for us," you are revealing His sacrificial love to others, and so you glorify Him for being "a sacrificial and fragrant offering to God" (Eph. 5:2).

Therefore, we glorify Him anytime we honor our heavenly Father by reminding ourselves or one another of who He is or what He's done. Or anytime we worship His nature and great name. Or anytime we point out and celebrate His goodness or proclaim His gospel of grace. Or anytime we model His character through our words and our lives. Or anytime we love our enemies and forgive our abusers. That's when we're being like Jesus and *glorifying* our Father in heaven. We can do it in thousands of ways. And every day and moment is another opportunity.

It can be when you speak of Him to others, when you freely share what He has done for you, or when you look for ways to serve others in His name. God is always "glorified" by this, Peter said (1 Pet. 4:11). When you walk in sexual purity, you are honoring His ownership and presence in your body, His temple. "You were bought at a price. So glorify God with your body" (1 Cor. 6:20).

The last three chapters of Ephesians are filled with moment-by-moment opportunities to glorify the One who has poured out His love and glorious grace upon you and made all that you have in Christ possible for you.

This includes your darkest days, when you are falsely accused, betrayed by a friend, mocked or attacked, lied to or abused. You can still follow Christ's example and glorify God by choosing to love your enemies, pray for those who mistreat you, forgive as you have been forgiven, and walk in love to represent the One who loved you and died for you.

No one can steal away your opportunities or stop you from glorifying God in any situation. Even if you've sinned and wronged others, you can glorify God's grace and mercy by repenting, confessing, and making things right with those you've mistreated.

When you are humble and gentle, it reflects Christ, who is gentle and humbled Himself for you (Matt. 11:29). When you are patient and long-suffering with difficult people, it reflects your God, who is kind and patient with you (Rom. 2:4). When you keep the unity of the Spirit and live at peace, it glorifies our God, who is one in Himself and has given you peace with Him (Rom. 5:1). The glory of God makes every day matter, and you can glorify Him.

At all times.

Rejoice always; pray without ceasing; in everything give thanks; for this is God's will for you in Christ Jesus. (1 Thess. 5:16–18 NASB)

Don't ever think again that your work is a waste, your responsibilities are enslaving you, or your sufferings are stealing your worth. Nothing is holding you back from seeking and glorifying God today with your thoughts, attitudes, words, prayers, and the decisions you are about to make. You have everything you need in Him. By walking with Him, by resting in who you are in Him, and by relying on what you have in Him, think of each day as a wide-open, clean canvas, for you to throw open the curtains and shine the life of Jesus in this world, painting a portrait with your life of the magnificent and matchless glory of God.

To God be the glory!

*Father, I want to glorify You today with my worship and my work. I choose to speak of the wonderful things You've done for me and the amazing things You are to me. I honor You and stand in awe at Your goodness and wisdom, at Your love and great compassion. Help me throughout the coming days to be like Jesus and glorify You with my lips, my heart, and my life. Thank You for the gift of this lifetime to show forth Your praise in countless glorious ways, in Jesus' name.*

### TAKE IT DEEPER BY STUDYING
Psalm 66 • John 17:1–5 • 1 Peter 2:11–12

*Say to God, "How awe-inspiring are your works!" . . . Come and listen, all who fear God, and I will tell what he has done for me. (Ps. 66:3, 16)*

## Eight Lifestyle Exhortations
### from Ephesians

Here are very practical lifestyle choices adapted from Ephesians 5:15–21 that can help each of us position ourselves to glorify God in our daily lives.

Four things Scripture says God's beloved children should STOP doing . . .

| Verse 15 | Stop being careless. | Wisely approach your day with purpose. |
| Verse 16 | Stop wasting time. | Make the most of every opportunity. |
| Verse 17 | Stop being foolish. | Find out what God's will is and pursue it. |
| Verse 18 | Stop getting drunk. | Find your joy being filled with God's Spirit. |

Four things Scripture says God's beloved children should START doing . . .

| Verse 19 | Start speaking. | Edify others with God-honoring words. |
| Verse 19 | Start singing. | Glorify God with your voice and musical choices. |
| Verse 20 | Start thanking. | Be grateful for all God is doing in every circumstance. |
| Verse 21 | Start serving. | Submit and support instead of being self-centered. |

# CHAPTER 34

## *You Can Be True to the End*

*We are not those who draw back and are destroyed,*
*but those who have faith and are saved. (Heb. 10:39)*

One of the most loving things we can do for anyone is to help them prepare for the Day of Judgment. Everyone who has ever lived is headed toward this awesome encounter. It is the great equalizer. The ultimate reality check. Nowhere to hide. No one else to blame. No way to delay it so that you can go back and prepare. The end will come; the books will be opened, and you will be tasked with giving a personal account to God for how you invested the life He entrusted to you (Rev. 20:11–15).

Eternity runs through a single opening. "We must all appear before the judgment seat of Christ, so that each may be repaid for what he has done in the body, whether good or evil" (2 Cor. 5:10). At this judgment, God will "bring to light the things hidden in the darkness," disclosing the motives of our hearts (1 Cor. 4:5). Jesus Christ will judge the words we have spoken (Matt. 12:36) and the deeds we have done in life (Rom. 2:5–8).

This Day of Judgment is not a religious allegory designed to motivate people. It is a coming reality established by a holy God who will bring about justice in all things (Jer. 9:24). This judgment is already wired into our consciences (Rom. 2:15). Each of us is aware of our own sinfulness, while internally desiring for evil injustices to be exposed and punished, for wrongs to be made right, for innocent victims to be vindicated, and good deeds to be rewarded. All of this will happen as a result of the judgment seat of Christ.

Solomon, the wisest king on Earth summarized all his counsel by writing, "When all has been heard, the conclusion of the matter is this: fear God and keep his commands, because this is for all humanity. For God will bring every act to judgment, including every hidden thing, whether good or evil" (Eccles. 12:13–14).

And yet even there, at your mortal journey's final reckoning place, everything will hinge on your *identity*. Since no one is righteous or sinless apart from Christ, admission beyond this point is reserved for those whose names are "written in the Lamb's book of life" (Rev. 21:27). Your eternity depends on *who you are* (Titus 3:5–7).

God's Word says, "The one who believes in the Son has eternal life, but the one who rejects the Son will not see life; instead, the wrath of God remains on him" (John 3:36).

As terrifying as the thought of final judgment may sound—and *should* sound to those whose identity is found in themselves or their own accomplishments—the Bible says that you, if you remain in Christ, can approach this awesome and sobering day with confidence. Yes, *confidence.* "Remain in Him," John the apostle said, "so that when he appears we may have confidence and not be ashamed before him at his coming" (1 John 2:28). John exhorts us to walk in love and stay close to the Lord in anticipation of the judgment.

He writes, "God is love, and the one who abides in love abides in God, and God abides in him. By this, love is perfected with us, so that we may have confidence in the Day of Judgment, because as He is, so also are we in this world" (1 John 4:16b–17).

Jesus, of course, lived righteously, loved sacrificially, and pleased the Father in totality. Perfect obedience. Faithful love. Complete fulfillment of all God's law. Sinless and flawless. Therefore, the Father readily, justifiably, received Him into heaven at the end of His earthly life (Heb. 4:14). The same result will be true of all of us who are found in Him at the judgment—because Christ's righteousness is our righteousness (Phil. 3:9). We didn't earn this righteousness; it was given to us as a gift of God's grace (Rom. 5:17).

In Christ, you can "put on the new self, the one created according to God's likeness in righteousness and purity of the truth" (Eph. 4:24). For this reason, Christ will be able to present you "without spot or wrinkle or anything like that, but holy and blameless" (Eph. 5:27). This is part of our inheritance as God's beloved children.

So as we prepare to close this book, and as we each look ahead to the remainder of our lives in this world and eternal future with Him, "what sort of people" should we be as we "wait for the day of God and hasten its coming" (2 Pet. 3:11–12)?

Paul said it's time for us to "wake up from sleep, because now our salvation is nearer than when we first believed. The night is nearly over, and the day is near; so let us discard the deeds of darkness and put on the armor of light" (Rom. 13:11–12). "Be alert and sober-minded for prayer," Peter added, because "the end of all things" is fast approaching (1 Pet. 4:7).

*This is serious*, in other words. Life is a vapor. Time is short. Start preparing for the Day of Judgment now. Start living with eternity in view.

"Everyone who has this hope in him purifies himself just as he is pure" (1 John 3:3). But even with your mind "ready for action"—with your eyes wide open, taking on each day with passion and priority and maintaining an intense love for others—"set your hope completely on the grace to be brought to you at the revelation of Jesus Christ" (1 Pet. 1:13). Trust Him to fulfill His promise and do what He said He would do. "He who started a good work in you will carry it on to completion until the day of Christ Jesus" (Phil. 1:6).

But it is important to make sure that He has truly begun a good work in us. There is *not* an indication in Scripture that someone can merely pray a prayer one day, and then forever walk away from Christ, live in unrepentant sin, and die apart from the Lord and still anticipate receiving eternal life. Salvation is through faith in Christ alone, not our good behavior. But a faith that truly saves is also a faith that will later obey and not permanently walk away. There are multiple warnings in Scripture about this.

> This saying is trustworthy: For if we died with him, we will also reign with him; if we endure, we will also reign with him; if we deny him, he will also deny us; if we are faithless, he remains faithful, for he cannot deny himself. (2 Tim. 2:11–13)

And so we cling to Christ alone as our merciful and only hope, surely knowing there is no other way of salvation and no other sacrifice for our sins. "For if we deliberately go on sinning after receiving the knowledge of the truth, there no longer remains a sacrifice for sins, but a terrifying expectation of judgment" (Heb. 10:26–27). "Nevertheless, God's solid foundation stands firm, bearing this inscription: The Lord knows those who are his, and let everyone who calls on the name of the Lord turn away from wickedness" (2 Tim. 2:19).

So, what about you? As we close this book, we want to encourage you toward very hopeful and joyful days. But first, permit us to ask again out of love and genuine concern for your absolutely best in life and in eternity: Is Jesus Christ truly your Lord?

Have you genuinely repented from your sins and placed your faith and trust in Him and His death and resurrection for your forgiveness and eternal life? If you would say *Yes*, did your life truly change, and have you continued to show lasting evidences of faith, love, and obedience? (James 2:17–26). Was it an empty, passing religious decision that faded away? Or was it a genuine trust that resulted in your heart turning, submitting, and clinging more and more to the Lord over time?

If the latter is so, then you are not one of those who has "tasted the heavenly gift" and "shared in the Holy Spirit" and "tasted God's good word and the powers of the coming age" and then fallen away from it to your death (Heb. 6:4–6). You have entrusted yourself to "a faithful Creator" (1 Pet. 4:19) and are not to "throw away your confidence, which has a great reward" (Heb. 10:35). You are not like the people who John said "went out from us" because "they did not belong to us" (1 John 2:19).

Your Father has invested too much of Himself in you—the precious blood of His own Son—to let His beloved children slip away from His grasp.

"I give them eternal life," Jesus said of His people, "and they will never perish. No one will snatch them out of my hand" (John 10:28). We can be like Paul, who said, "One thing I do: Forgetting what is behind and reaching forward to what is ahead, I pursue as my goal the prize promised by God's heavenly call in Christ Jesus" (Phil. 3:13–14).

The relief and confidence that God's children will feel on that day when Jesus says, "Come, you who are blessed by my Father; inherit the kingdom prepared for you from the foundation of the world" (Matt. 25:34), is a hope you can already enjoy, right now. Rather than dreading it, you can be like God's saints in the past who "eagerly wait through the Spirit, by faith, the hope of righteousness" (Gal. 5:5).

Many of us live with that sense that we're still failing, that we have so much more distance we need to cover spiritually, so much more discipline we need in place. We've thankfully been able to let go of many of our sins, but others keep sneaking through the cracks, again and again (1 John 1:8–10; Rom. 7:17). We sometimes feel like the ice skater who takes three or four hard spills during the routine, and then dejectedly waits for the judges to post the scores, fearing the worst.

You may not *feel* so sure of your status before God because of the history of your mistakes. You may still have lots of questions about your ability to obey, to overcome, to walk worthy of your calling. But your *identity* is not based upon your feelings or your performance; it is the result of your faith in Jesus and in His life, death, and resurrection. It is in the salvation and righteousness God freely gives you in Him (Rom. 10:10).

So the Bible tells us to lift up our heads because our "redemption is drawing near" (Luke 21:28 NASB)—to cast our eyes on "him who is able to keep you from stumbling and to present you blameless before the presence of his glory with great joy" (Jude 24 ESV).

Our hope is not in ourselves. We cannot save ourselves or keep ourselves saved, so we walk by faith and cling to Christ alone, the Author and Perfecter of our faith (Heb. 12:2). Jesus is fully "able also to save forever those who draw near to God through Him, since He always lives to make intercession for them" (Heb. 7:25).

Because of His sacrifice and what He has already done in your life, because of His grace toward you and His Spirit within you, you can now live out your identity in Christ, filled with hope and joy, bearing fruit in every good work, living for the glory of God, and looking forward to being found faithful and true to Him in the end.

This is not only the greatest and most fulfilling way to live your life, but also the best way for you to prepare for the Day of Judgment when it arrives. So, with this in mind, and with the remaining sunrises left on the fading calendar of life, may our God and Father help each of us to live wholeheartedly, walking in love and truth as His beloved children.

Let us throw off the remaining rotten hindrances of our old, dead life, and put on the fresh, clean garments and spiritual armor of our new life in Him, never looking back.

As we learn to walk in the Spirit, we will no longer be held back by the sinful desires of our flesh. And we no longer have to be overcome by evil, but in Him we can overcome evil with good. We can be strong in the Lord—in *who we are* in the Lord and in *what we have* in the Lord—and to live by the power of His glorious might (Eph. 6:10–12).

So, because of Him, who we are in Him, and of what we have in Him . . .

- Let us stand firmly, resisting the devil's accusations, attacks, and schemes.
- Let us pray boldly, knowing we have open access to the Father through Jesus.
- Let us shine brightly, as His lights in the darkness, bearing witness to the truth.
- Let us walk worthy, imitating our Father in our thoughts, speech, and relationships.
- Let us work diligently, spreading the gospel and making disciples of all the nations.

- Let us live victoriously, knowing the Holy Spirit is within us and empowering us daily.

Then, we too can join the apostle Paul, and look forward to declaring these words in our final days . . .

I have fought the good fight, I have finished the race, I have kept the faith. There is reserved for me the crown of righteousness, which the Lord, the righteous Judge, will give me on that day, and not only to me, but to all those who have loved His appearing. (2 Tim. 4:7–8)

God's promises to you, which will be fulfilled with certainty in the end, are currently in force in your heart today. You don't need to wait until you stand before Him to know who you are or the inheritance you have in Him (1 John 5:13; Phil. 3:20–21).

In Christ, you are LOVED, ACCEPTED, BLESSED, and FORGIVEN. In Christ, you are SEALED and STRONG and HOLY and BLAMELESS. In Him, you have peace and access with the Father, fellowship with the Son, and a rich and glorious inheritance through the Spirit. In Him, you are the DWELLING PLACE OF GOD, and you will dwell with Him forever and ever. All for the glory of God!

This is you. *Defined.*

To God be the glory!

*Lord, I do not deserve the mercy, forgiveness, and grace You have poured out on me, but I praise You that my life and future is in Your strong hands. I cling to the cross of Jesus Christ alone for my salvation and eternal life. I rest on Your unchanging grace for my identity and heavenly reward. Redeem all of my life in light of eternity. Keep my heart and eyes fixed on You in all circumstances. Lead me daily by Your Spirit, and help me be anchored in my faith, secure in my hope, and undying in my love. Come quickly, Lord Jesus, and use my life mightily for Your glory until that glorious day. In Jesus name, amen!*

## TAKE IT DEEPER BY STUDYING
1 Thessalonians 5:4–11 • Hebrews 12:1–2 • Revelation 14:1–5

*May the God of peace himself sanctify you completely. And may your whole spirit, soul, and body be kept sound and blameless at the coming of our Lord Jesus Christ. He who calls you is faithful; he will do it. (1 Thess. 5:23–24)*

# Group Discussion Questions

**Introduction:** How do you define yourself? What was your favorite part of Mia's adoption story? How is adopting a child similar to the spiritual adoption we have in Christ? Have you ever studied Ephesians? Did you know it was about identity? What are you hoping to get from this study and discussion group?

**Chapter 1:** What is an identity? How was identity a foundation to the life of Jesus? Has your identity changed over time? Why does it affect so many other areas of life? Could you relate to the stories about identity issues? Would it be difficult to look in a mirror and sincerely answer the questions at the end of the chapter? Which questions meant the most to you? Why?

**Chapter 2:** What do people tend to put their identity in? What types of things influence who we think we are as we grow up? What are identity problems you currently see in the culture? Why are feelings an unreliable source of identity? What affects how we feel? How do feelings change depending on what we choose to believe? Why should we not allow other people to define us?

**Chapter 3:** Where should we go to discover who we are? Why is God the most qualified person to define us? Do you believe that God owns you? How would His ownership of you influence who you are? How is God's identity tied to ours? How is it tied to everything else? How does knowing who God is help us discover who we are?

**Chapter 4:** What meant the most to you in this chapter? Do you believe God designed you? Have you ever felt like a mistake? Do you value yourself the way God does? Have you thanked Him for His design in your life? Your family? Your body? Did you pray at the end of the chapter and thank God for making you like you are?

**Chapter 5:** What does it mean to be made in the image of God? How are people different from animals? How does the *imago Dei* give us rich value? Ruling authority? Resemblance to Jesus? Relational depth? Do you value people as if they are priceless and made in God's image? Do you view yourself this way? How would your life change if you honored the *imago Dei* in all people?

**Chapter 6:** What was your favorite part of the Parable of Fred? What were the most important lessons in the parable? How can adults apply this as well? Did you honor your parents' counsel growing up? How did you see it play out in life? Do you honor God's design or resist it?

**Chapter 7:** What is the definition of sin? What qualifies something as sinful? How does resisting God's design dishonor the nature of His glory? Do you recognize sin in yourself? In children? In society? Why is sin always unlike God? In what ways is all of our sin the same, and in what ways is it unique to us? How can God use our past brokenness for redemption?

**Chapter 8:** How are the lost sheep, lost son, and lost coin similar? What things did they all have in common? How does our *lostness* cause us to lose our value? What exactly is the gospel? How is God demonstrated in each parable? Share how God has pursued you relationally in the past.

**Chapter 9:** Why did Jesus tell some people they were going to hell? Why would Satan tell people the opposite of their eternal destination? What are the seven biblical evidences of true salvation? How did you test? How did this chapter speak to you about your own spiritual condition?

**Chapter 10:** What is grace? How is grace unlike the law of God? Why are we saved by grace and not by works? Why is it important to God that we are saved by grace not by works? How is our relationship with God like a river? What does it mean to praise the grace of God?

**Chapter 11:** How are Luke and Blake the same, and how are they different? What did Luke and Blake base their identity on? How did Blake's performance-based identity affect how he viewed himself and others? How did Luke's understanding of God's love and grace affect him as a man? Did you learn anything in this chapter? How did God speak to you through this story?

**Chapter 12:** How does loss and tragedy reveal identity? What is the core of your identity? What was the difference between Job's heavenly and earthly identities? Explain how the book of Ephesians is designed? Why must we believe truth before we can obey commands?

**Chapter 13:** How has God demonstrated and proven His love to us? What does the word *beloved* mean? Why does God love us? How are unconditional love and grace similar? How does our upbringing affect our understanding of love? Why is it hard to really believe God loves us?

**Chapter 14:** What does the word *bless* mean? When and how did God bless people in Scripture? What does it mean that we are blessed in Christ? How does God bless us? Do you consider yourself blessed in Christ or more like the *unfavored* child? Why do you think that way?

**Chapter 15:** Why does God use the word *saved* to describe our salvation? What are biblical illustrations of people being literally saved? What are we being saved from? How do we deserve God's wrath? How does salvation honor the justice and mercy of God?

**Chapter 16:** Why is forgiveness a necessary part of salvation? How and why does God forgive us and still honor His justice? How is grace involved? Share a story about God's forgiveness in your life. Jesus said those who are forgiven of much will love much; why is that true? Why does the Bible call us saints? What qualifies someone to be a saint in God's eyes?

**Chapter 17:** How is our salvation like the Old Testament tabernacle? How is it like Mary carrying Christ in her womb? How does God dwell in us? What does His presence bring us? How is God glorified more by inhabiting us?

**Chapter 18:** What is a workmanship? How is Bezalel an example of this? How does God uniquely design people? How does He use their past, their parents, and their passions for His kingdom? How have you seen God uniquely gift you or someone you know for a specific task? What do you think God has been preparing you to do for His kingdom?

**Chapter 19:** What is the difference between our identity in Christ and our inheritance? What is our inheritance in Christ? How is it similar to an earthly inheritance? How is it different? What is a coheir or joint heir? Share how God has met a unique need in your life in the past?

**Chapter 20:** How is Jesus uniquely able to give us access to God? What does this access provide for us? How did Jesus make it possible for us to approach God? How do you view God when you pray? Do you pray specifically and boldly? Why or why not? Do you pray in faith or in doubt?

**Chapter 21:** What does the Holy Spirit do in the life of a believer? What roles does He play? What does it mean that He seals us in Christ? When does this happen? Why is this a good thing? How is the Holy Spirit another "Helper" like Jesus? How is He the fulfillment of a promise?

**Chapter 22:** What does the word *hope* mean? How is the world's hope different from Christ's? What are we hoping will happen? What does our hope provide for us? How does it help us? What does it motivate us to do?

**Chapter 23:** What do you honestly think about who you are? Is your thinking about yourself in line with the world or with God's Word? Why is it important to renew our thinking concerning our identity? What does Ephesians 4 teach us about changing who we are? What does it mean to put on and put off old thinking and ways? How do we change?

**Chapter 24:** Why are words so powerful? Share of a time when someone's words blessed you or tore you down. How should knowing our identity in Christ affect our speech? What specific things should we stop saying? What should we say instead? How does knowing that we will be judged by our words affect the things we say?

**Chapter 25:** How does God change someone's heart? How are we supposed to cleanse our own hearts? What things does God want us to get out of our lives? What grieves the Holy Spirit? Why is it important that our identity in Christ guide this process?

**Chapter 26:** What does it mean to walk by the Spirit? Why do you think so many people are afraid to talk about the Holy Spirit? What are examples from Scripture or your life about following God's Spirit? How does the Spirit speak to us and lead us? How do God's Word and His Spirit work together? How do we prepare our hearts to be used of Him?

**Chapter 27:** What does it mean to walk in love? How does the Trinity love? How did Jesus love? How is God's love like a river? What does it mean to abide in Christ? What are scriptural examples of walking in love? What are some examples from your own life? How does love summarize so many of the Bible's commands? What blocks the love of God in our lives? How does forgiveness help us walk in love?

**Chapter 28:** How did Satan attack Job? What was his goal? What are different ways that Satan attacks us? How does our identity in Christ help prepare us for Satan's attacks? What are we to do and remember during attacks? How are we to respond to Him? How is God's Word a key to this?

**Chapter 29:** Who tempts us? How? Does God ever tempt us to sin? (see James 1:13). How have you responded to temptation in the past?

How does knowing who you are in Christ affect your thinking during temptation? How did Satan tempt Jesus? How can we be strong during temptation?

**Chapter 30:** How have you been criticized in the past, and how have you responded? How do you usually respond now? Why? How can God use criticism for our good? Who was criticized in Scripture? How was Jesus criticized? Why did Jesus not entrust Himself to man? What else did you learn in this chapter?

**Chapter 31:** How does failure affect our sense of our own identity? How did Peter's failure affect him? How did God use it for good? Share about a failure that was hard to overcome. How does God want us to respond to failure? How does knowing our identity in Christ help us?

**Chapter 32:** What are things people have lost for their faith? What is the greatest sacrifice you have made for your faith? What was Paul willing to lose for the sake of Christ? What are things you will likely lose in life? How does losing a title, position, or relationship test our identity? How does knowing our identity in Christ affect how we view loss? Where is our eternal home?

**Chapter 33:** What does it mean to bring God glory? How did Jesus glorify the Father in all circumstances? How can we? What does God's glory reveal? How was God glorified through Lazarus? Through Mary? What are ways we can glorify Him regardless of the circumstances?

**Chapter 34:** How should the final judgment of God affect how we live? What will God judge? Who will be judged? How are people who abandon their faith and walk away from Christ permanently like Judas? What does it mean to remain in Christ? What are promises we can stand on and rest in concerning our salvation? What are things we can do to help us stand firm in Christ until the end of our lives?

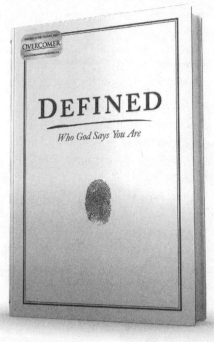

## SHARE THE MESSAGE OF *DEFINED* WITH YOUR SMALL GROUP.

Help your small group know who they are in Christ and understand how their identity in Christ shapes their lives. This 8-session Bible study includes:

- Four DVDs with a promotional video and eight 10- to 15-minute video sessions featuring Alex Kendrick and Stephen Kendrick
- One *Bible Study Book*
- Access to digital video downloads
- Access to additional leader resources available from Wordsearch Bible online platform
- Personal-study opportunities for ongoing spiritual growth
- Content from Priscilla Shirer, Jackie Hill Perry, Cameron Arnett, Eric Geiger, and more

**LEARN MORE AT OVERCOMERMOVIE.COM/RESOURCES OR CALL 800.458.2772.**

FROM THE CREATORS OF **WAR ROOM**

# OVERCOMER

OvercomerMovieResources.com

## TEEN RESOURCES

Alex and Stephen Kendrick, along with writer Troy Schmidt, lead teen guys on a hands-on investigation to uncover who they really are and how Christ has shaped their identities.

**Paperback - $12.99 - 978-1-5359-4988-0**

Beloved author and speaker Priscilla Shirer plays Principal Olivia Brooks in OVERCOMER. Her latest book is written to help teen girls understand they can find their identity in Christ.

**Paperback, $12.99, 978-1-5359-4987-3**

Also available: Defined in Spanish
*Definido: Quién dice Dios que eres*
Paperback - $12.99 - 978-1-5359-66832

**B&H**
**PUBLISHING**

Affirm Films A Sony Company © 2019 Columbia TriStar Marketing Group, Inc.

FROM THE CREATORS OF **WAR ROOM**

# OVERCOMER

OvercomerMovieResources.com

## KIDS RESOURCES

*Wonderful: The Truth About Who I Am* (for Middle-Grade Readers)
Stephen Kendrick and Alex Kendrick, with Amy Parker, wrote this illustrated
book for middle-grade readers to help them discover who they are and how
God has made them to be unique and wonderful.
**Printed Hardcover - $12.99 - 978-1-5359-4988-0**

*What's So Wonderful About Webster?* (Children's picture book)
A fully illustrated picture book, this story about Webster's field-day adventures
helps young readers discover that they too are wonderfully made by God.
**Hardcover Picture Book - $12.99 - 978-1-5359-4986-6**
Release date: November 19, 2019

Affirm Films A Sony Company © 2019 Columbia TriStar Marketing Group, Inc.

# STUDY WITH THE WHOLE FAMILY

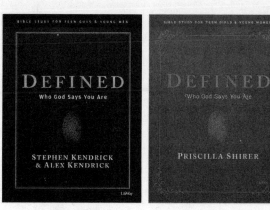

**Guys Bible Study Book**
$13.99 005815893

**Guys Leader Kit**
$59.99 005815899

**Girls Bible Study Book**
$13.99 005815892

**Girls Leader Kit**
$59.99 005815895

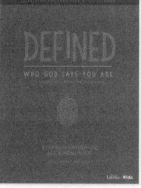

**Kids Leader Guide**
005814776 $14.99

**Younger Kids Activity Book**
005814773 $6.99

**Older Kids Activity Book**
005814775 $6.99

"Who am I?" Someone or something is attempting to answer the question for us. But to accurately answer this question, we must first ask, "Who does God say I am?" The Bible tells us that we are each made in God's image, but that image has become distorted by sin. The only way to restore what was broken is through a relationship with Jesus. These eight-session Bible studies for teen girls, guys, and kids examine spiritual truths found in the Book of Ephesians to address the topic of identity.

# LifeWay®

**OVERCOMERMOVIE.COM/RESOURCES**

FROM THE CREATORS OF WAR ROOM

WHAT DO
YOU ALLOW
TO DEFINE
YOU?

IN THEATERS
AUGUST 23

ALEX
KENDRICK

PRISCILLA
SHIRER

AND INTRODUCING ARYN
WRIGHT-THOMPSON

OVERCOMER

OVERCOMERMOVIE.COM

@OvercomerMovie | #OvercomerMovie

AFFIRM Films A Sony Company © 2019 Columbia TriStar Marketing Group, Inc. All Rights Reserved.

FROM THE CREATORS OF WAR ROOM

# OVERCOMER

A NOVELIZATION BY
**CHRIS FABRY**

BASED ON THE MOTION PICTURE BY
**ALEX KENDRICK & STEPHEN KENDRICK**

Movie Artwork AFFIRM Films A Sony Company
© 2019 Columbia TriStar Marketing Group, Inc.
All Rights Reserved.

Spanish version

## THE *OVERCOMER* NOVELIZATION WILL BE AVAILABLE WHEREVER BOOKS ARE SOLD.

SEE THE MOVIE

OvercomerMovie.com
OvercomerMovie
OvercomerNovel.com

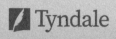 Tyndale

provident FILMS    KENDRICK BROTHERS    SONY    AFFIRM FILMS a Sony Company

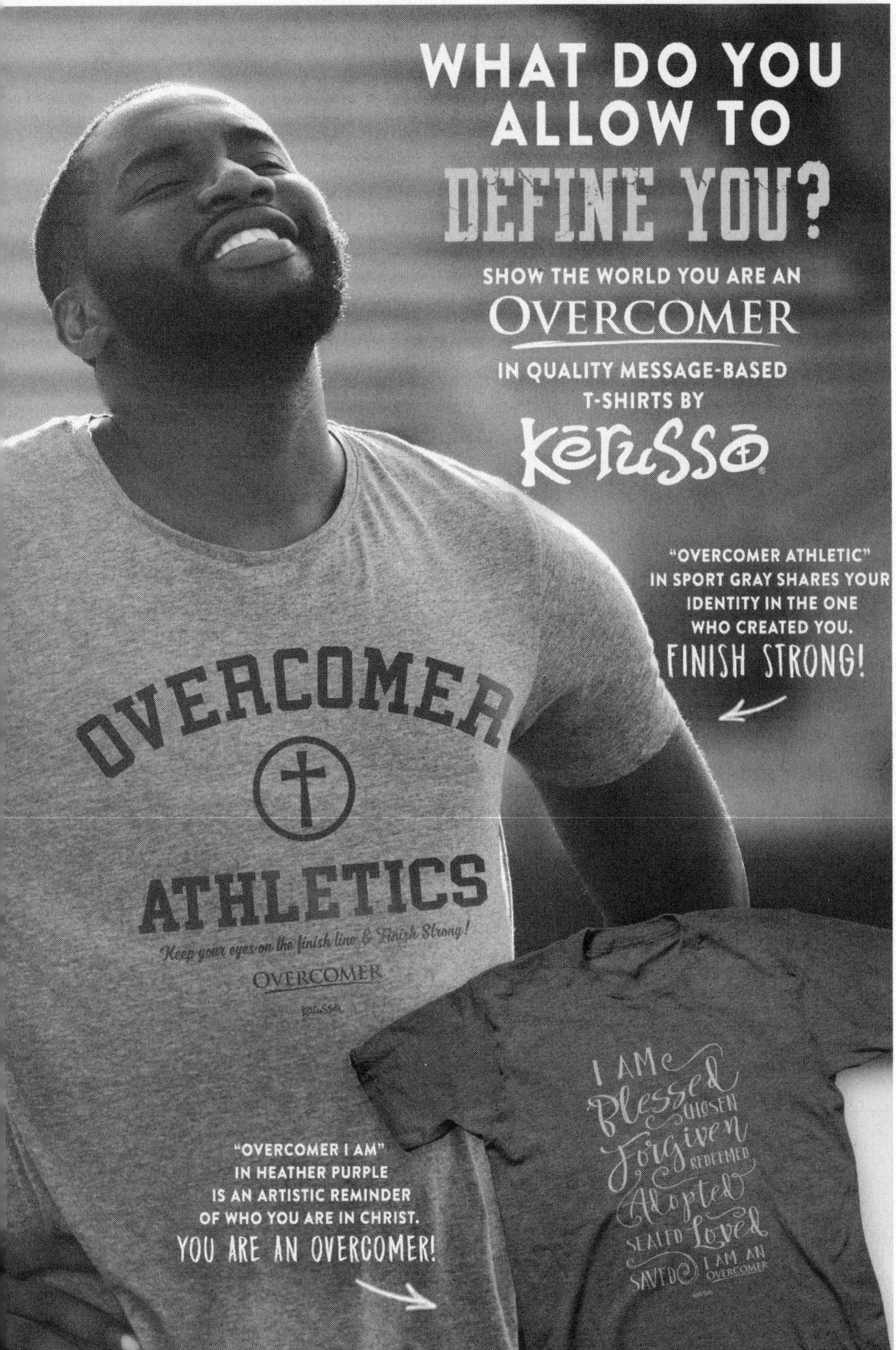

FIND OVERCOMER APPAREL AT A RETAILER NEAR YOU.

FROM THE CREATORS OF WAR ROOM

# OVERCOMER

Affirm Films A Sony Company © 2019
Columbia TriStar Marketing Group, Inc.

## BRING OVERCOMER TO YOUR CHURCH!

### OVERCOMER CHURCH LICENSE

Available Winter 2019 - 2020

For more info:
LifeWayFilms.com